Postcolonial Theory
in the Global Age

I0025083

Postcolonial Theory in the Global Age

Interdisciplinary Essays

Edited by OM PRAKASH DWIVEDI
and MARTIN KICH

Foreword by Rajen Harshé

McFarland & Company, Inc., Publishers
Jefferson, North Carolina, and London

LIBRARY OF CONGRESS CATALOGUING-IN-PUBLICATION DATA

Postcolonial theory in the global age : interdisciplinary
essays / edited by Om Prakash Dwivedi and Martin
Kich ; foreword by Rajen Harshé.
    p.   cm.
Includes bibliographical references and index.

ISBN 978-0-7864-7552-0
softcover : acid free paper ∞

1. Postcolonialism in literature.   2. Literature and
globalization.   3. Literature and transnationalism.
4. Nationalism in literature.   I. Dwivedi, O. P.
(Om Prakash)   II. Kich, Martin.
PN56.P555P677 2013
809'.93358 — dc23   2013020471

BRITISH LIBRARY CATALOGUING DATA ARE AVAILABLE

On the cover: red book (Hemera/Thinkstock); world globe
(iStockphoto/Thinkstock)

Manufactured in the United States of America

McFarland & Company, Inc., Publishers
  Box 611, Jefferson, North Carolina 28640
    www.mcfarlandpub.com

Contents

Foreword

RAJEN HARSHÉ

Postcolonial theory, I am aware, is constantly interacting with the multiple and complex processes that globalization has unleashed in contemporary times. I suppose that before I start dwelling on their interactions and the substance of this edited volume, it will be appropriate if I begin by stating my own understanding of postcolonial theory, on the one hand, and globalization, on the other.

Fanon, Said, Sartre and the Emergence of Postcolonial Theory

Postcolonial theory essentially represents an interdisciplinary mode of inquiry in social and human sciences that sheds light on complex and constantly evolving relationships between erstwhile metropolitan countries and their colonies, primarily between the Metropolitan West and the Orient. However, if one takes a broader view of the field, the erstwhile "Third World" comprising Asia, Africa, Latin America, the Caribbean states, Australia and New Zealand can all fall within the purview of the term "postcolonial." The origins of such inquiry could be traced to Frantz Fanon and his seminal writings, including *Black Skin, White Masks* (1967), *Dying Colonialism* (1965) and The *Wretched of the Earth* (1963). Fanon constantly was reflecting on the interactions between the colonizer and colonized in a context in which the psychological dimensions of colonialism were often overlooked and hence undertheorized. In effect, colonization is also a state of mind, and any colonial power in order to justify its rule tends to construct its subjects as inferior beings. Fanon's *Black Skin, White Masks* is an evocative study that underscores an innate desire of the blacks to emulate the rulers and even equal them

1

in different spheres to surmount their inferiority complex. Psychologically, the entire process of colonization deals effective and even violent blows to the minds of the colonized subjects by burdening them with a sense of inferiority and "otherness." In his *Dying Colonialism*, Fanon ventured to explicate, like a sensitive psychoanalyst, the links between physical and mental processes that are at work under colonization. He has also underscored how in the Algerian war of independence (1954–1962) people chose to embrace precolonial habits and customs, which were considered primitive, in defiance of French colonial rule. Fanon was even more forthcoming against colonialism in his later and more influential work *The Wretched of the Earth*. He advocated the use of violent revolutionary means to overthrow colonial dominance. *The Wretched of the Earth* attained almost biblical status as it inspired the liberation struggle in Vietnam that ended with the fall of Saigon in 1975, and it continues to inspire civil rights movements, as well as anti-racist/apartheid struggles, in places such as South Africa and Israel. It still stands as a testimony to how the life of any good text can be longer than that of its author and how the messages of such texts are received across time and space in different parts of the world. Nonetheless, more than looking at the overt impact of such an influential work, it may be worth underlining a few useful insights of Fanon on the relationship between the colonizer and the colonized. After analyzing the prevailing inferiority complex among the colonial subjects vis-à-vis the colonial master, he emphasized how the subject began to emulate the master. Obviously, imitation is the best form of flattery.

Fanon also argued that the colonial world is violent because it basically relies on force represented by the police and military to survive. Such violence, of course, can be mute as well because the colonial world constantly constructs realities with Manichean forms within which cause and effect appear synonymous. For instance, in a colonial context, if you are white you must be civilized, bright, and cultured, and if you are cultured, civilized, and bright, you must be white. Consequently, if you are black, you must be barbaric, crude, and not so bright. What is more, Fanon went so far as to argue that the dream of the persecuted individuals is not to suppress the idea of persecution but to replace the persecutor. This deep insight does explain several brutal forms of dictatorships in the postcolonial states. Some of these Fanonian insights did set the pace for academic inquires in postcolonial theories and studies.

Edward W. Said's celebrated study *Orientalism* (1978), too, was a major milestone in building postcolonial theory. Said has underscored how Western scholarship was engaged in a profitable industry of constructing the so-called "Orient" for its own purposes. His was a provocative work that began to set the directions and the pace of theorizing the postcolonial.

At a very basic level, it could be argued that despite the end of colonial rule in a formal sense, the spell of "colonial" in the erstwhile colonies is socially, intellectually, and emotionally alive. In fact, in every postcolonial society, the colonial past mediates with the present and even influences the future course of thoughts and practices. As Fanon had argued, like colonization, decolonization, too, is a long, drawn out historical process. I often feel ill at ease while observing one kind of interaction between the scholars located in the West and the Orient. The former, quite often, with unjustifiable pride, tend to be condescending towards the latter, and the latter still pursue their habit of lionizing even mediocrity just because it is located in the West. What is more, they also are unashamed of working as travel agents of theories and concepts that emanate from the West, without taking a critical look at them. Ironically, they are equally reluctant even to acknowledge good work in their own parts of the world unless it is fashionable and politically correct. I hope that this sharp comment of mine will persuade scholars from the Orient to pause for a while and ponder before they rush to participate in the next schedule of seminar-related networks.

At the same time, it would be imprudent to treat the so-called colonial and colonized in the postcolonial world as monoliths. It might sound equally fallacious if they are placed in an adversarial position by forming yet another crude binary. In fact, the histories of the metropolitan countries and colonies have overlapped, and both have drawn something from each other in their continued interactions, and that is why the question of hybrid identities crops up inevitably in the discourses on the "postcolonial." In this context, the intellectual world requires thinkers who understand people on either side of this divide and can recognize and address their converging moments with empathy and sensitivity.

Among the French intellectuals, Jean-Paul Sartre's penchant for equality and association with the journals such as *Presence Africaine* is a case in point. Sartre made efforts to understand French writers of Tunisian origins such as Albert Memmi. He was equally sensitive to pioneering poets of the Negritude movement such as Aime Cesaire and Leopold Senghor. What is more, he even wrote a brilliantly sensitive introduction to Fanon's *The Wretched of the Earth*. Similarly, Said's remarkably eloquent and thoughtful oeuvre to understand critically the other side of this divide is well reflected in his capacity to explore several complex dimensions of intricately evolving ties between the Metropolitan West and the decolonizing world in his seminal work on culture and imperialism (Said, 1992). In this framework, the realm of postcolonial theory/studies could be appraised critically, lyrically, and even cynically by keeping its diverse dimensions, implicit as well as explicit, even in the current context of globalization.

The Current Phase of Globalization

In the context of developing postcolonial studies, how could connections be perceived in social realities that are conditioned by globalization? In fact, the current phase of globalization was accelerated with the demise of the former Soviet Union in 1991. If the Soviet Union ostensibly represented a utopia to the outside world, an attempt to organize an exploitation-free egalitarian society, its disintegration marked the ascent of capitalism both as a formidable developmental alternative and as a world system. Capitalism essentially rests on private/corporate ownership of the means of production, cooperative and conflictual relations between wage labor and capital, socialization of production and privatization of profits that can stimulate the processes of accumulation of capital on the world scale. The current phase of globalization need not be reduced to capitalism, but the latter has been an agency of the former.

In brief, globalization subsumes varying, complex, and dynamic social processes that are simultaneously at work. Although such processes have stimulated free movements of goods, services, finance, trade, knowledge, information, people, diseases, and even terror, the movement of capital appears smoother and faster compared to movement of labor, for labor has to negotiate with nationality, as well as the state rules related to citizenship. Obtaining citizenship in developed countries is by no means an easy task for the labor from the developing countries. Nevertheless, thanks to revolutions in information communication technologies (ICT), the technical jobs (jobs for technicians?) are contracted out to middle-level technocrats in countries such as India at cheaper rates by the countries such as the United States. The idea that jobs are getting Bangalored does signify the prospects of a two-way street or relationship, albeit an asymmetrical one, between advanced capitalist and developing counties such as India under globalization. To put it crudely, any complex social phenomenon such as globalization has its own capacities to bring about packages of advantages and disadvantages to different social segments, classes, and social groups within and across the countries. Most often, I am struck by facile questions that are posed in seminars on globalization-related themes across the world. For instance, are you pro-globalization or anti-globalization? Implicit in such questions is an assumption that globalization is anti-poor or pro-rich. Placing realities in such binary opposites that refuse to observe gray shades of any social phenomenon and historical conditions under which it is operative can hardly be useful in presenting a detached analysis of the ongoing developments under globalization. More often populist discourses on globalization are replete with avoidable simplistic and binary formulations.

I would rather venture to view globalization as a phase inextricably inter-twined with the development of capitalism. Consequently, the logic of the development of capitalism has had its impact on globalization. Capitalism often is characterized by uneven development between the sectors, regions, nations, peoples/classes, and even continents. Uneven development can fuel social and economic inequalities. Moreover, imperialism as a phenomenon signifying asymmetrical relationship of interdependence between materially advanced and backward societies has also been integral to the development of capitalism (Harshé, 1997). In fact, since the sixteenth century, capitalism has proved to be a resilient system because it has adapted to the changing social conditions all along. Thus, capitalism has witnessed transitions from laissez faire to welfare capitalism. On the one hand, in countries such as France when François Mitterand's socialist regime was in power (1981–88), there were four communist ministers in the cabinet that, in effect, ran French capitalism. Capitalism can co-opt its radical opponents. On the other hand, some of the leading financial magnates such as George Soros have been critics of capitalism. For instance, after the fall of Soviet Union, Soros had argued that there is unbridled exploitation of labor under post–Cold War capitalism and that capitalism needs to be regulated in the interests of its own survival (Soros, 1997). Obviously, the *modus operandi* of capitalism is complex and subtle. It has survived and flourished as a world system because it does appeal to gut human instincts. Keeping the possibilities of triangular relationship between postcolonial studies, globalization, and capitalism in sight, I shall proceed to take a look at and reflect on some of the themes in this volume.

Heterogeneities in the Postcolonial Theory

Postcolonial studies as an area of inquiry appears like an omnibus carrying with it multiple histories of the former colonies on different continents. Actu-ally, each location has had a specific history. Is it possible to merge such his-tories into one and build an academic inquiry? What could happen to the heterogeneous evolution of different parts of the world that experienced colo-nial domination from different countries such as Britain, France, or Portugal under these circumstances? At the same time, is it possible to locate a few major, salient features that can bind such diverse histories and heterogeneities? In that case, what could be the point of convergences? I suppose the entire realm of postcolonial studies, at one level, is engaged in identifying or even carving out commonalities and yet a worthwhile postcolonial theory has to capture a differentiated view of diverse histories. Factors including racism, anti-colonial nationalism, human rights, formation of multiple or even hybrid social identities, and the urge to build counterculture against hegemonic forces unleashed by the dominant capitalist countries can act as cementing bonds among postcolonial societies.

While taking such cementing bonds into account, the postcolonial theorists have to be sensitive to diversities in the processes of social, political, and literary theorizing. This is what seems to be a challenge for contemporary postcolonial theory. Postcolonial theory, by definition, has to avoid any form of monolithic conceptions and refrain from getting trapped into simplistic binaries. The editors have alluded to how President George W. Bush, as the United States waged a war against terror, tempted the U.S. allies to accept his formulations, i.e., "You're either against us or with us." In fact, 9/11 unleashed a weird process in which the Muslims began to be projected as the "other." Mahmood Mamdani in his celebrated work has assailed the United States and Bush's tendency to characterize Muslims as either "good Muslims" or "bad Muslims" (Mamdani, 2005). In addition, the editors rightly seem concerned about the response from postcolonial theory to the post–Soviet world. David Huddart's concern for the marginalized "Other" does become more acute in the context of the forms of new "Empire" that are proliferating after the Cold War under globalization. Hardt and Negri have done perceptive work on imperialism. If the new Empire has started demarcating the world into the center and the periphery, can the postcolonial theorist build theories of counter-hegemony in a Gramscian sense? Hegemony essentially involves a queer combination of consent and coercion. Is it possible to build theories that question excesses of capitalist globalization? Will it be possible to build counter-hegemonies in the context of heterogeneities as represented by the postcolonial world? I suppose like many emerging fields, in this case, postcolonial theory is still grappling with such realities and is in search of further elaboration with the changing times.

Fluidity of the Postcolonial

Such elaboration certainly is within the realm of possibilities because of the fluidity in the very being of what is termed postcolonial. Actually, S.V. Gallagher, as pointed out by the editors, has argued that postcolonial is never a specific moment but an ongoing struggle and continued emergence. More often, it deals with the former subjects of the colonizers or more broadly the marginalized and the subalterns. However, the nature of subalterns is fluid and dynamic in the context of social and cultural changes under globalization. For instance, in addition to peasantry, excluded migrants, refugees, contract workers, casual workers, unsettled diasporas, and exiles would also add to the number of subalterns as globalization keeps unfolding itself. Actually, under globalization, the new marginalized or subalterns can open up fresh areas for theorization. That is why this volume also includes essays which deal with the "included" and "excluded" in terms of the prosperity created by globalization. Moreover, during colonial and postcolonial times, mental and geographical displacements experienced by the migrants and diasporas would always demand greater attention owing to the sheer magnitude of the movements of the population as immigrants under globalization. In fact, in the metropolitan places, in addition to the white population, there are sizable numbers of people of the black, brown and yellow races. The existence of multicultural ambience in such places has also given impetus to new forms of identity politics. It would be useful to work out how the immigrant communities perceive their roots in a context that is being mediated through colonial and postcolonial prisms. The linkages between postcolonialism and globalization could also be further explored by keeping the contemporary nation state at the center stage, for, globalization, like capitalism, is capable of stimulating self-contradictory processes simultaneously. For instance, it does facilitate the emergence of a transnational and multicultural world, and at the same time, ethno-nationalist movements or local grassroots movements can also keep surfacing as the processes of globalization are underway.

The editors also have made a reference to an article by Huddart and Ashcroft that deals with Derrida's method of deconstruction. In the 1980s, the idea of deconstructing and perhaps reconstructing texts or unveiling words pregnant with multiple meanings was in vogue in critical inquiries in the human sciences. However, whether the method of deconstruction has the potential to move beyond expectations of sameness and difference has yet to be tested convincingly, and yet it appears to be an imaginative way of looking at Derrida's work. In addition to the themes on which I have already commented, there are interesting set of essays on literatures from Australia and New Zealand that take a closer look at the formation of social identities or hybrid identities in the domain of culture. Identities are built around sameness and continuity and they are relational. Hence they tend to aggravate differences between the "Self" and the "Other."

I have carefully gone through the synoptic overview presented, in the Introduction, of the innovative efforts of scholars in this volume. Their exercise towards understanding the social processes that begin to constitute identities and tying the existence of such identities to language, culture, history, literature, and cinema especially humbled me. In fact, the complexities, heterogeneities, and fluidities that are embedded in the very theme of interrelationship between the postcolonial theory and globalization appeared quite mind-boggling and yet eminently readable to me. I would like to congratulate the editors for their admirable efforts in bringing together essays on such diverse themes in this work. The critical insights that it offers can provide essential guidelines towards further inquiries dealing with postcolonialism and its interrelationship with globalization. I am sure this book will be very useful for students and scholars in humanities and social sciences.

WORKS CITED

Fanon, Frantz. 1952/1967. *Black Skin, White Masks*. Trans. Charles Lam Markmann. New York: Grove.
_____. 1959/1965. *A Dying Colonialism*. Trans. Haakon Chavalier. New York: Grove.
_____. 1961/1963.*The Wretched of the Earth*. Trans. Constance Farrington: New York: Grove.
Harshé, Rajen. 1997. *Twentieth Century Imperialism: Shifting Contours and Changing Conceptions*. New Delhi: Sage.
Mamdani, Mahmood. 2005. *Good Muslims, Bad Muslims, America, the Cold War and the Roots of Terror*. New Delhi: Permanent Black; New York: Crown.
Said, Edward W. 1992. *Culture and Imperialism*. New York: Vintage.
_____. 1978/2003. *Orientalism*. New Delhi: Penguin.
Soros, George. 1997. "The Capitalist Threat." *Atlantic Monthly* (Feb.): 45–58.

Rajen Harshé is a visiting professor in the Department of International Relations at South Asian University, New Delhi, and is a former vice chancellor at the University of Allahabad.

Introduction: Postcolonial Studies in the Age of Globalization

OM PRAKASH DWIVEDI *and*
MARTIN KICH

Posctolonial theory began as an intellectual project to address and over-come the vexing issues of the once-colonized nations. Ever since the publi-cation of Frantz Fanon's *The Wretched of the Earth* which provided a foundation for this theory, much has been written over the decades. The warm reception given to this theory, especially in the Western countries, as a way to approach the study of formerly colonized cultures and societies can be seen as one of the reasons for the sustained interest in this field of study. Indeed, it is not an exaggeration to assert that postcolonial theory has been institu-tionalized in the Western academia.

Nevertheless, over the passage of time, the very nature of this theory has changed, and, in fact, it has now become increasingly defined by interdisci-plinary studies. Scholars and critics seem ever ready to align this theory with fresh political, socio-economic, cultural, and aesthetic perspectives — and, more provocatively, with new syntheses of such perspectives — emerging across an increasingly globalized world. For example, after the Iraq war, postcolonial studies was given a new direction in a special issue of *New Formations*, "After Iraq: Reframing Postcolonial Studies."

Despite, or perhaps because of, all of the attention to postcolonial studies as a new discipline, the relevance of postcolonial studies has been a highly polemical issue ever since its inception. Postcolonial studies, according to the cultural critic Stuart Hall, is the "the bearer of such powerful unconscious investments — a sign of desire for some, and equally for others, a signifier of danger"(242). The 2006 MLA roundtable discussion "The End of Postcolonial Theory" noted that there was a potential exhaustion of postcolonialism as a paradigm. There is substantial merit in viewing postcolonial studies as exhausted because such studies convincingly position and magnify the dominant stature of the West and its solipsistic discourse against the "Orients." In setting out to map a revolutionary change in the erstwhile colonized countries as its visceral mission through postcolonial discourse, postcolonial studies has ended up in distancing the East from the West, as issues of racism, human rights, homelessness, nationalism among many others, are yet to be diminished or effaced. In a similar vein, Timothy Brenan registers his concerns about the relevance of postcolonial studies when he writes, "As the world is being redrawn after 1989, postcolonial studies has done little to keep pace with the changing forms of imperialism as an actual set of strategies and developments" (107). One needs to rethink assumptions about the nature of postcolonial theory because it has been shaped by the institutionalization of postcolonial studies. Initially, the term "postcolonial" was applied by Ashcroft, Griffith and Tiffin to "all the cultures affected by the imperial process from the moment of colonization to the present day" (2). Such an expansive and structuralist view was always going to be polemical. Indeed, it spawned a number of pertinent questions, the most central of which may be whether different cultures sharing different histories can even be thought of converging and being examined under a single term. And the intuitive answer would seem to be, of course not. And yet that is essentially what has occurred.

Another problematic issue that clouds postcolonial theory is its unprecedented reliance on multiple or hybrid identities and multicultural nations. Such a celebratory notion is appreciative provided the intentions are not complicit. But by engendering and sedimenting these practices of multiculturalism or transnationalism through their conceptual alignment with capitalist-based globalization (which is a newer term for colonialism), the very notions that were central to decolonization — such as identity, culture, and most importantly history — are (un)willingly obfuscated and dismantled. We are all cognizant of the fact that postcolonial theorists, especially those from the "Third World" who have settled in Europe and the United States, resolutely and cavalierly promote such capitalist-based thoughts to sustain and justify the sacrosanctity of globalization, because once compellingly demonstrated that globalizing tendencies are beneficial, it will inevitably foster the positionality of capitalist-based globalization and concomitantly warrant unethical moves in the name of its development. Ostensibly, postcolonial theory exacerbates and dismantles any sort of binarism in the supposed celebration of multiculturalism. But one must wonder at the general silence of postcolonial theorists and commentators at critical moments such as when American president

George W. Bush reduced the world to a binary opposition between supporting an ever-expanding "war on terrorism" or being a terrorist. In effect, any Muslim who did not accede to devastating invasions of Muslim nations was choosing to be categorized as the "Other." But the commitment to the marginalized has, at critical times, been witheringly dismissive. As San Juan contemptuously comments on this decisive deafness of these elite critics:

> Where were the postcolonial gurus during the Gulf War? What is their stand on political prisoners like Mumia Abu Jamal, Elizam Escobar, Leonard Peltier, and many others languishing in the US jails? ... How does postcolonial theory ... explain the plight of millions of "overseas contract workers"— women domestics, "hospitality girls," and mail-order brides comprise this large, horizontally mobile cohort — all over the world [13].

This disturbing silence by the critics who have often projected themselves as apostles of revolution and reforms is something that needs to be examined.

Some of the issues raised in the above-mentioned paragraph are brilliantly argued in this collection by David Huddart, who interrogates the ethical approach of postcolonial theory at the present moment and decisively demands a responsible stance towards the marginalized Other. In the same vein, Shaobo Xie grapples with the pressing recent debates about the exploitative nature of capitalist-based globalization that is operating as a newer version of colonialism, or "neoimperialism"—a process which consonantly churns out a new neglected and underprivileged Other and has enveloped the world with severe crises. Xie advocates saying "no" to capitalist modernity and choosing, instead, alternatives that are non-capitalist based.

Quite clearly, postcolonial theory in the twenty-first century, instead of resisting and challenging structures of exploitation, has instead, interestingly, aligned itself with the capitalist model of globalization, which Hardt and Negri identify as the new "Empire" because its emergence once again demarcates the world into a center-periphery model. By doing so, postcolonial theory has become almost an extension of globalization, and hence postcolonial theorists do not seize opportunities for proving themselves as agents of counter-globalization. It is this positionality that makes it untenable to label them as "postcolonial critics," because many of them act as compradors turning their backs on the real victims of racism and capitalism. The political activism and consistent struggle that were supposedly quintessential in this theory, in order to become decolonized, is now absurdly missing. One needs to look at the incisive suggestions by Robert J. C. Young wherein he calls for a revision and reconsideration of the roles of academicians, by urging them "to make academic work accountable and to foreground that accountability by forging links with the lived politics of the social world, recovering histories, and creating possibilities for new dynamics of cultural and political practice" (29).

It was in this context that S.V. Gallagher pointed out a long time back that "postcolonial is never a specific moment but an ongoing struggle, a continual emergence" (377), and it is this "ongoing struggle" which Bill Ashcroft, in this collection, rightly terms "post-colonization."

At the moment, we are facing a strange impasse in postcolonial theory, as incisively argued in this collection by Roderick McGillis, who dismantles any utopian hope by sarcastically remarking that colonialism has become a condition of life. Ostensibly, postcolonial theory constitutes an irony, for all it does is to position the "Third World" in an asymmetrical power relation with the West due to its failure to represent evocatively the history of struggle and exploitation of the once-colonized. Maneuvered skillfully by capitalist-based globalization, postcolonialism has come to work against its origins, the very reasons for its being, as the concepts of national and cultural identity continue to get obfuscated and exacerbated. The failure in encountering the oppressive and exploitative power of globalization can be reversed only by demarcating and identifying the marginalizing tendencies of this form of neo-colonialism. It requires a truly transnational and democratic openness in post-colonial studies, which prioritizes and restores the so-far-ignored rights of the subalterns. Françoise Lionnet and Shu-mei Shih argue that there is a great urgency to reroute the specificities of transnationalism by adopting a more focused approach on the hitherto ignored "minor perspective" because the present discourse "troubles the prevalent notions of transnationalism as a homogenizing force" (5).

In a recent brilliant article titled "What the Postcolonial Theory Doesn't Say," Neil Lazarus ferociously attacks the giddy tendencies of the unmoored postcolonial critics by targeting the core problem that lies in the very heart of postcolonial theory. Lazarus is contemptuous of the fact that postcolonial critics have been resolutely blind in their remarkable failure to situate colonialism within the wider context of "capitalist development." This is an effectual complaint, and Lazarus himself goes on to expose this drawback very pertinently. We quote him at length as this passage very pointedly locates the great divide within postcolonial theory, a divide that scholars must confront if postcolonial theory is to be authoritatively rerouted:

> Colonialism as an historical process involved the forced integration of hith-
> erto uncapitalised societies, or societies in which the capitalist mode of pro-
> duction was not hegemonic, into a capitalist world system. Over the course
> of a couple of centuries in some territories, mere decades in other, gener-
> alised commodity production was imposed: production for exchange rather
> than use; monetisation; private ownership; the development of specifically
> capitalist markets.... Along the way, existing social relations and modes of
> existence were undermined, destroyed, reconfigured; new social relations

and modes of existence were brought into being.... Peasantries were destroyed, along with subsistence, tributary and market economies (some of them vast and elaborate) to be replaced by capitalized agriculture in one location, proletarianisation in another, with waves of migratory labor (more or less regulated, sometimes not at all) in between. Ruling elites were made, unmade and remade, the basis of their power thoroughly transformed [11].

One cannot but agree with Lazarus's incisive analysis of the character of colonialism. The appropriation of social relations based on capitalism in its heightened form has inevitably turned out to be a disastrous phenomenon, destroying rather than preserving the very human world. Capital *was*, and *continues* to be, the main cause of separatism and the concomitant construction of oppositional binarism such as the West and the rest, north and south, we and them, master and servant, developed and underdeveloped. In this regard, Lazarus's views are vital because they point to the *real* enemy against whom postcolonial theorists need to take a stand.

If postcolonial studies must persuasively ameliorate its discourses, it must do away with its present strictures. It must include the excluded migrants, exiles, and refugees who have become a characteristic feature of this increasingly globalized world — a world that emphatically claims to be multicultural or transnational, but is only nominally so. The superficiality of the adoption of a multicultural or transnational perspective has manifested itself in the continued demarcation of victims and victimizers, exploiters and exploited. Benita Parry argues very rightly that

the time has come for postcolonial studies to promote empirical investigations of these unsettled diasporas, and undertake the dissemination of the experiences spoken by scattered, impoverished, and despised populations stranded in temporary and exploited employment as contract workers, casual laborers, or domestic servants in Europe, North America, and the Gulf States [72].

These suggestions are highly valid and applicable, especially if one meticulously examines the magnitude of the problem of this mobilized world. Parry's urgency in advocating the cause of "unsettled diaspora" demands a coherent development of a new vocabulary within postcolonial studies for investigating these unheard and marginalized voices that increasingly go unheard in a world that ostensibly celebrates plurivocality but, in actuality, permits only a singular voice of gargantuan power to operate, further dislocating the experience of émigrés and refugees. Some of the issues surrounding migratory communities have been adequately examined by David Punter, Janet Wilson, and Grant Farred in this collection. Farred's essay brilliantly argues about the issues of homelessness and dwelling that have not been given proper attention in relation to the postcolonial demand for the refusal of binaries — the Self and the Other — and therefore, he rightly pleads for rethinking matters of dwelling.

It is against the backdrop of these highly sensitive and ignored issues that Crystal Bartolovich eloquently poses a series of thought-provoking questions, which need to be given serious thought. Bartolovich asks:

> What about diaspora? When "national" populations are dispersed, what "form" does struggle take? Can there be "transnational" sites of resistance? What would they look like? What "form" furthers most effectively "globalization from below" — the formation of transnational alliances among unions and other groups resisting corporate globalization? [148].

Bartolovich recognizes the need to identify some common ground in a reconsideration of diasporic populations, refugees, and their attendant problems. Postcolonial critics need to provide "transnational sites of resistance" from where political actions and political solidarity can be effectuated by engaging the local and the global as active participants. Such solidarity, we can say, would be an affective transnationalism whose entire attention would be against the common enemy of exploitation and that will eventually dismantle the painful strictures of the current socio-economic and political system imposed by globalization.

The essays in this book look at and acknowledge newer forms of colonialism operating in an increasingly globalized world. It sets out to recognize the complexities and culpability of postcolonial politics and then, through a plausible reconsideration and reconceptualization of the issues, intervenes by trying to fill the gaps that exist at theoretical levels in the discourses on postcolonial studies. In so doing, it proposes a number of cogent alternatives underpinned and anchored by an unfailing plea for a demonstration of solidarity among postcolonial nations in, paradoxically, exacerbating any existing binaries or differences. After all, it is difference that is most clearly visible in this world. The book is driven by notions of ethics, an increasingly influential force at the grassroots if not the international level, and, therefore, the authors respond to capitalism and its attendant drawbacks, a strategy to reverse the tendency toward separatism and to effectuate the ignored human rights.

This introduction has already remarked on some of the essays in the collection in terms of how they are connected to and respond to some of the focal issues in current postcolonial studies. But a more thorough and systematic survey of the essays seems in order to provide a sense of the collection's scope and significance.

In "Postcolonialism and Recovery: A Future Evermore About to Be," Roderick McGillis argues that the diasporas that have continued beyond the formal political end of European colonialism constitute, in fact, a continuation of colonialism. The driving force of postcolonialism has been the desire to recover what was lost from indigenous identities under colonialism. But because of the destruction wrought by colonialism on those indigenous cultures and the enduring character of some aspects of colonial culture, the desire to recover has been transformed into a desire to recreate, to make something new of the hybridity that is the most significant consequence of colonialism. McGillis considers novels for young readers written by Canadians about non–Western cultures, and despite their good intentions, he finds a continuation of the colonizer's assumption of superiority over the colonized — in this instance, framed, ironically and paradoxically, in multicultural terms.

In "Going Global: The Future of Post-Colonial Studies," Bill Ashcroft attempts to take stock of the current state of postcolonial studies as a basis for prognosticating about the directions the field might take. He considers the following: the ambiguities related to the origins of "postcolonial studies" — that is, of both the term and the field; the ramifications of the differences in how it has developed in the United States and in the rest of the world; the predominant interest in Anglophone literatures and the implications for literatures in translation — the Francophone, Hispanophone, and Lusophone literatures, as well as those translated from non–Indo-European languages; and the issues of ontology and chronology that are fundamental to postcolonial studies. He suggests that postcolonial literature can be approached most profitably not as an act of writing but as an act of readings and that the reader must choose from among the following strategies: the symptomatic, the comparative, the dialogic, the multivalent, the horizonal, or the constitutive. Two other fundamental considerations are the aspects of the sacred and the natural environment addressed in the text. Ashcroft builds to the argument that postcolonial studies provide a bridge between issues related to globalization and a re-intensified focus on the local. Its emphasis on migration, hybridity, and multiple or alternative modernities insures that postcolonialism will remain a relevant mechanism for addressing increasingly global exchanges, cultural and otherwise.

David Punter's "'Pity the Poor Immigrant': Pity and the Colony" is a free-ranging reflection on the nature of "pity" in shaping historical circumstances, cultural attitudes, and responses to literature. More narrowly, Punter is interested in how notions about the nature and effects of pity relate to notions about the nature and effects of diaspora. Within this fresh and thought-provoking framework, he considers a variety of colonial and postcolonial works, from those of Rudyard Kipling and Paul Scott to those of Derek Walcott, V. S. Naipaul, and Jamaica Kincaid. But the essay builds to a more extended and perceptive discussion of the novels of the Jamaican-British writer Joan Riley, in particular *Waiting in the Twilight*. Ultimately,

Punter delineates a central and critical ambiguity: whether pity is a prerequisite to or an impediment to the sort of political action that mitigates pity as a cultural reflex and as a cultural rationalization of inequality, even if the difficult circumstances of individuals remain pitiable.

Punter's emphasis is on colonial and postcolonial diasporic experiences that involve geographical and cultural displacement, for both the European colonials and the migrants from former colonies to Western nations have inevitably adjusted, albeit in very different ways, to the geographical and cultural displacement that is inherent to the experience emigration. In "From Colonial Outsider to Postcolonial Insider: Screen Adaptations from Australia and New Zealand/Aotearoa," Janet Wilson shifts the focus to former colonies in which the colonial cultural mythos has borrowed from but largely subsumed the precolonial mythos. Wilson examines the ways in which novels drawing on the central motifs of colonial Australian and New Zealand cultural and historical identity have been reshaped by their adaptation to the medium of film. Those motifs include the "Lost Child" in Australia and the "Man Alone" in New Zealand. And the films in which they are transformed — or, to use Wilson's term, "re-imagined" — to resonate postcolonial realities include Peter Weir's *Picnic at Hanging Rock* (1975), Roger Donaldson's *Sleeping Dogs* (1977), and Brad McGann's *In My Father's Den* (2004).

In "Resistance to Responsibility: Interrupting the Postcolonial Paradigm," David Huddart extends Ashcroft's observation that postcolonial literature is defined less by authorial intention than by reader response. But Huddart is much more pointedly concerned with the ethical dimensions of postcolonial texts and the responses that they provoke. He considers several seminal criticisms of Derrida's work by prominent postcolonial theorists, and in a very carefully considered and articulated analysis of Derrida's work, he suggests that deconstruction actually provides a means for "moving beyond expectations of sameness and difference." In one way or another, this effort continues to be the core concern of postcolonial theory, regardless of whether it is framed in primarily political, economic, cultural, or literary terms. Huddart explores the gap between postcolonial literary theory and both postcolonial literature and the mainstream criticism of that literature.

In "Cultural Translation in the Age of Globalization," Shaobo Xie begins by considering all of the paradoxical effects of globalization. In essence, the advancements that it promotes in one area seem inevitably to come at the cost of detrimental developments elsewhere. Xie argues that the sum total of these changes amounts to an unprecedented crisis — largely because the promoters of globalization have overstated its benefits while dismissing many of its costs and, worse, because their understanding of even its supposed benefits is in many ways deficient. Presenting an overview of the work of Slavoj Žižek and

Judith Butler, Xie locates the center of this crisis in the growing gap between those "included" in and those "excluded" from the prosperity created by globalization. The resolution to this crisis is available, however, in "alternative modernities" that are based in some way on "cultural translation," through which a "pluralistic notion of universality" might be realized.

In "Hybridity and Identity in New Zealand Māori Literature: Alan Duff's *Dreamboat Dad*," Alistair Fox narrows the focus to the central issues of cultural identity in colonial and postcolonial New Zealand. Initially, however, Fox provides a theoretic framework for his discussion of Maori literature by delineating the competing — or, perhaps more accurately, evolving — theories of hybridity based on domains of difference, polyculturalism, strategic syncreticity, and bricolage. Within this context, Fox suggests that hybridity in Maori literature can be best approached through the "structure of the double helix," one of the most resonant symbols in Maori culture. His discussion of Duff's *Dreamboat Dad* is enriched by insightful comparison to three other seminal works of contemporary Maori literature: Patricia Grace's *Mutuwhenua*, Witi Ihimaera's *The Rope of Man*, and Keri Hulme's *The Bone People*.

If Fox narrows Wilson's focus by discussing just the literature of New Zealand — and, in particular, the Maori literature of New Zealand — Susan Hosking provides a complementary discussion of postcolonial Australian "texts" but one that reaches both beyond "text" in its conventional sense and beyond Australia itself. In "Slumdogs and Dogs' Breakfasts: Reading Danny Boyle's *Slumdog Millionaire* and Baz Luhrmann's *Australia*," Hoskings presents a multi-leveled consideration of the two films, working from the obvious contrast in the ways in which the two films were produced and received. *Slumdog Millionaire* was produced with a modest budget and seemed an unlikely candidate to garner the sort of international acclaim that it has received. In contrast, *Australia* was conceived as a blockbuster film with an star-loaded cast, but it has been widely criticized for providing spectacle at the expense of a meaningful exploration of themes. Hosking points out, however, that while the international responses to the films reflect the responses to the two films in Australia, the initial Indian responses to *Slumdog Millionaire* were in some ways as mixed as the responses of Australians to the Luhrmann film. Given the tendency to dismiss completely those blockbusters that fall short of inflated expectations, Hosking is interested primarily in why *Australia* fails to resonate with Australians. Ultimately, her discussion of the contrast available in the earlier response to *Rabbit-Proof Fence* may indicate as much about the limitations of Luhrmann's film as the more readily available contrast with *Slumdog Millionaire*.

In "Gender, Hybridity and the Transcultural 'Man Alone' in the Short

Fiction of Frank Sargeson and Doris Lessing," Joel Gwynne returns to the motif treated in Janet Wilson's essay. But Gwynne extends the discussion somewhat thematically and considerably geographically and culturally. In extending Wilson's discussion of the gender-related elements in postcolonial treatments of the motif, Gwynne directly addresses the concept of hybridity, which frames the discussion in the essay by Alistair Fox. Moreover, Gwynne analyzes Sargeson's stories not in comparison to or contrast with other work by New Zealanders in the genre, but against the African stories of Doris Lessing, whose work has been informed as much by pointedly feminist themes as by broader postcolonial concerns.

Gwynne's interest in the ways in which postcolonial and feminist issues intersect is continued within a different frame in Varghese Thekkevallyara's "Postmodernist Postcolonialisms and Feminisms: A Passion for Justice." Thekkevallyara grounds his discussion in theoretical works such as Chandra Talpade Mohanty's "Under Western Eyes Revisited," Marina Ortiga's "New Mestizas: 'World-Travellers' and *Dasein*," Maria Lugones' "Playfulness, 'World-Travelling,' and Loving Perception," and Morny Joy's "Method and Theory in Religious Studies: Retrospect and Prognostication." His interest in the linkages between a grounding in postmodernism and a commitment to social justice leads naturally into a discussion of the complementary aims in the growing movements against globalization and racism.

Just as Wilson and Hosking move outside literature into film studies, Leslie Sklair considers postcolonialism through the ways in which it has been manifested in architecture. In "Postcolonialisms, Globalization and Iconic Architecture," Sklair distinguishes between generic globalization and capitalist globalization, arguing that they are contending forces. Generic globalization has great "emancipatory power" while capitalist globalization oppresses the interests of the great mass of humanity to promote the interests of the very small and ever-shrinking group that controls most of the capital. To delineate the tensions between these contending forces of globalization and the still unrealized emancipatory potential of generic globalization, Sklair focuses on four phenomena: "the electronic revolution, new forms of cosmopolitanism, postcolonialisms, and the creation of transnational social spaces." In architecture, a nearly century-long debate has pitted international modernism against architectural realism. Although architectural regionalism has been receiving increasing notice, international modernism remains pre-eminent, defining even the framework in which architectural regionalism is understood.

Grant Farred's "Radical Homelessness: David Malouf Writing in the *'Blut'* of Martin Heidegger" focuses on the Australian author David Malouf who has long been read as a Heideggerian, a trend that this essay extends by drawing upon Martin Heidegger's notion of "Wohnen"—dwelling and using that notion to argue for the radical homelessness that can be extrapolated from both these thinkers. The specific (Heideggerian-Maloufian) turn here is toward the postcolonial as the articulation of a radical homelessness that has not been thought in relation to the postcolonial. What Malouf's delineation of radical homelessness, which is grounded in the inclination toward dwelling, evinces is an asymmetry that, as is characteristic of Malouf's work, demands the refusal of binaries — the Self and the Other must be thought in their difficult gathering, to use Heidegger's term — while retaining a strong sense of inequity. All desire for dwelling is not the same; all propensities for dwelling cannot be equivalenced; all desires for dwelling, even in death, demand a gathering that recognizes the act of drawing from somewhere else, from something other than the self; every inclination toward and aptitude for dwelling must be thought, as Malouf's short stories in particular make clear, in its history.

The concluding essay is Clara A.B. Joseph's "Global Victorians: Is Colonial Decadence to Blame for Postcolonial Deconstruction?" Joseph finds striking correspondences between British colonial attitudes during the Victorian heyday of the Empire and American neocolonial attitudes during the current era of globalization. Furthermore, she finds the attitudes characteristic of both periods reflected in the mainstream literary criticism of those periods and, ironically, ineffectually challenged the ostensibly cutting-edge literary criticism of the periods — the Aesthetic and Decadent movements and postmodern critical theories. Simply put, Joseph argues that linguistic theories provide an insufficient basis for addressing issues of economic and cultural inequality. So, in a very compelling, if open-ended, way, Joseph is seeking the same sort of "justice" that Thekkevallyara calls for in his essay, but she doubts that the currently available–isms, including postcolonialism, provide the mechanisms for achieving it. In effect, she seems to be suggesting that as long as postcolonial theory accepts its core assumptions from Western theorists, even if they seem radical theorists, it will not truly be postcolonial.

The essays thus try to intervene in this moment of danger at the theoretical and methodological levels, interrogating the present conjuncture through a reconceptualization of problems ranging from issues of modernization and identity to the problem of establishing a political economy of postmodern times that could open up new grounds for imagining alternative worlds. In doing so, it develops a critical postcolonial standpoint that extends the focus and terrain of postcolonial theory, drawing still on the discursive formations with which it has been in solidarity, such as feminism, race studies, cultural and development studies, but equally on positions in the social studies of science and technology and in critical phenomenology in order to interrogate the material cultures and the complex character of the apparatuses that constitute the plural-life-worlds of today.

WORKS CITED

Ashcroft, Bill, Gareth Griffith, and Helen Tiffin. *The Empire Writes Back: Theory and Practice in Post-Colonial Literatures*. London: Routledge, 1989.
Bartolovich, Crystal. "Global Capital and Transnationalism." *A Companion to Postcolonial Studies*. Eds. Henry Schwarz and Sangeeta Ray. Oxford: Blackwell, 2000.
Brennan, Timothy. "The Economic Image-Function of the Periphery." *Postcolonial Theory and Beyond*, eds. Ania Loomba, Suvir Kaul, et al. Durham: Duke University Press, 2007.
Gallagher, S.V. "The Backward Glance: History and the Novel in Post-Apartheid South Africa." *Studies in The Novel*, 29 (Fall 1997): 377–395.
Hall, Stuart. "'When Was the Post-Colonial'? Thinking at the Limit." *The Post-Colonial Question: Common Skies, Divided Horizons*, eds. Ian Chambers and Lidia Curti. London: Routledge, 1996.
Juan, San, Jr. *Beyond Postcolonial Theory*. New York: St. Martin's, 1998.
Lazarus, Neil. "What Postcolonial Theory Doesn't Say." *Race and Class* 53,1 (July 2011): 3–27.
Lionnet, Françoise, and Shu-mei Shih. *Minor Transnationalism*. Durham: Duke University Press, 2005.
Parry, Benita. "Directions and Dead Ends in Postcolonial Studies." *Relocating Postcolonialism*, eds. David Theo Goldberg and Ato Quayson. Oxford: Blackwell, 2002.
Young, Robert, J.C. "Academic Activism and Knowledge Formation in Postcolonial Critique." *Postcolonial Studies* 2,1 (1999): 29–34.

Postcolonialism and Recovery
A Future Evermore About to Be
RODERICK MCGILLIS

"We have no history of colonialism." Stephen Harper, Canadian Prime Minister (October 30, 2009).

"I don't think colonialism is over." Edward Said (1997).

"Why would I bring food back here? I'm not responsible for all these people!"
　"Yes, you are. And so am I. We have two good legs, two good arms, two good eyes, and minds that work properly. We have a responsibility to those who don't have what we have." Deborah Ellis (*Mud City* 130).

On board the *Battlestar Galactica* (TV series 2004–2009), humans and machines, called Cylons, come to an uneasy alliance for mutual benefit. Meanwhile, a separate group of Cylons plots the eventual eradication of humans and of course a number of humans harbor the hope that they can eradicate the Cylons. With the virtually endless room of outer space for these two warring factions to find places to settle, they cannot come to a comfortable accommodation. I begin with this TV series because what the program chronicles strikes me as indicative of the future of postcolonial studies; it must continue to roam the disciplines just as it must continue to foster peace, tolerance and goodwill, knowing full well that the achievement of peace, tolerance and goodwill is devoutly to be wished but elusive and always just an hour before us as we reach for the future. On board *Galactica* are representatives of a number of human races: Anglo-Saxon, Oriental, Hispanic, and African. The last three remain firmly in the minority, although interracial marriage is taken for granted, at least in the case of intermarriage between a human and a Cylon. Hybridity finds itself coded in the mixture of Cylon and Oriental and Cylon and Hispanic. A more profound hybridity is evident in the children produced

21

by miscegenation — human/Cylon offspring. The Cylons appear to mimic human variety in their creations. In other words, *Galactica*, like the world we inhabit, seems to offer us a multicultural world that is somehow after or post the condition of colonial rule. In fact, colonialism has gone up in a nuclear storm with the result that survivors are in a state of near permanent diaspora or dispersion. They are looking not for a return to a wasted home planet, but for another world to colonize. For these weary travelers, recovery from disaster means finding a home, a place to settle. Colonial rule has only ended ostensibly. The point is that colonization is the condition of life.

As the series ends, the near permanent diasporic state appears to come to an end as humans, Cylons, and human/Cylon hybrids come to rest on a planet called Earth. The remnants of the holocaust that took place on their planet of origin, New Caprica, some 350,000 humans and an unspecified number of Cylons, land in a primitive land that is clearly continental Africa. They see primitive people, and their plan is to give these people the gifts of language, culture, and progress. Beware aliens bearing gifts. As the series closes, we fast-forward 150,000 years to see the results of evolution on a social and scientific scale, if not on a biological one. As the series closes, things are about to begin again. The clever twist at the end of this series is that the new-comers to Earth bring the gift of domination, and they begin their gift giving in Africa. Some things resist change precisely because the stories told by the group that dominates cannot understand the stories of the dominated group. Desire is everything. And the desire is for recovery. Recovery means covering things with that which has served as covering for generations; recovery is not so much renewal as it is return. Recovery seeks to return us to the condition we feel most suits us, that is, the condition of supremacy. Recovery in this sense is deeply conservative, and in a colonial sense it perpetuates the hierarchy of colonizer/colonized. Recovery also means recuperation. In this sense, recovery is the process of healing and returning to a condition of health before some alien germ — say, a colonizer — had initiated a period of ill health. In a postcolonial sense, recovery of this sort is the reestablishment of an independent identity, rather than one fashioned by the language and perspective of the colonizer. Recovery of this sort is, however, beyond reach in the sense of returning to the condition prior to the coming of the colonists. Recovery must mean recreation, the fashioning of something new.

The movement we see in the *Battlestar Galactica* series is, however, the movement of the eternal return, the return to a state of colonizer/colonized that will evolve into a clash of binaries that precipitates the whole process over again and again and again. Even the post human cannot bring about a state of tolerance, peace, and good will. As imagined by the human being, the machine is just as desiring of power and dominance as the human has been. What prompts this cycle of power, resistance, and renewal of power is fear, fear of that which appears other than familiar and similar. Otherness breeds distrust, apparently, even as it lures us to its charms. What we see in the television series is the desire to recover: to recover a place that is familiar, to recover from the fear of an overpowering menace, to recover from a tremendous catastrophe, and to recover a familiar sense of what constitutes the human — a home nestled in a natural environment that is tended by a caring and settled people. And the caring and settled people are not the people the newcomers find there, but rather the newcomers themselves. As we look over the African landscape at the end of the *Battlestar Galactica* series, we get a sense of a land sparsely populated, so sparsely populated, in fact, that it can remind us of the *terra nullius*, the virgin land, the land ready for habitation and cultivation. We do not seem able to think beyond the circular master plots of Western narrative tradition. Instead, we seem intent on recovering the old stories, and making other peoples' stories our own.

Much of the work of postcolonialism is the work of recovery, the recovery of texts long forgotten, or the recovery of voices previously silenced or ignored, or the surfacing of abuse in order that recovery can happen. Abuse regularly works to cause trauma, and we must know that trauma results from the kinds of treatment meted out to many colonized people. To lose one's home, one's sense of identity, one's voice, and one's way of life must affect the colonized persons traumatically. We know that those who suffer traumatic experiences as often as not retain "only a fragment of the memory" of those experiences, and that this fragment emerges "as an intrusive symptom" (Herman, 45). To restore a traumatized person to psychic health, a number of things have to happen: the assurance of safety is necessary, the story of trauma requires retelling, and the survivor needs to be reconnected with his or her community (see Herman, 3). Health requires not necessarily eradicating the symptom, but enjoying the symptom so that one learns to live with it. And enjoyment derives from the self; it does not come as the gift of another. What I explore in this essay is the gift proffered by someone other than the self. In my country (Canada), a number of authors have written books that examine conditions in other countries. I am thinking specifically of books for young readers that chronicle conditions in such places as Afghanistan, South Africa, Malawi, and Bolivia. These books are socially and politically well intentioned. They set out to educate young Canadian readers by introducing them to unpleasant conditions in faraway countries. The lesson inherent in these books finds direct statement in my third epigraph, the one from Deborah Ellis's story of an Afghan refugee camp in Pakistan, *Mud City*. In the novel, an Afghan adult speaks to a young person from that same country to encourage her not to think of herself and leave for France, but rather to stay and help those in the refugee camp and those left back in the war zone that is Afghanistan. But the adult's words resonate, and are meant to resonate, with the privileged and secure Canadian or North American reader. Because we are so fortunate as Canadians, we have a responsibility to aid "those who don't have what we have" (130). Inevitably, however, a second lesson lurks here: wretched conditions in other countries exist because people in those other countries cannot get along amicably the way people in the Canadian mosaic get along. In other words, a whiff of superiority squeaks from these stories.

But superiority does not get to the point. What these books present to the North American reader are stories of other peoples voiced by authors who inevitably write from outside, patrons who write from the perspective of a comfort zone, and with concerns that might well be honorable, but that are also limited precisely by the situation of the author outside the culture she or he writes about. I am not suggesting that authors should not write about cultures other than their own, but I am suggesting that such writing works or can work to perpetuate colonial activity. The very existence of these novels indicates that the writers assume they have to speak for Others, and in doing so they inevitably displace Others from telling their own stories, or at least nudge them aside. The situation is awkward because no one, I think, would argue that stories of genocide in Rwanda or elsewhere in the world, of child exploitation in Bolivia, of racist policies in South Africa both prior to 1994 and after, or of the dire effects of war in Afghanistan and other countries should not be told and retold in order that we continue to confront brutality, injustice, bigotry, and hatred as they infect the human community. The difficulty, as Nancy Batty has demonstrated in the context of International Children's Relief programs, is "the Western world's investment" in such stories (Batty, 19). The stories of strife, dislocation, and disorder elsewhere in the world work to congratulate the West for its stewardship of democracy, freedom, and tolerance both at home and throughout the world. In other words, such stories seldom, if ever, examine the complicity of the West, politically and economically and even militarily, in the trouble spots of the world. The world, or at least the Middle East, parts of Eastern Europe, places in South America, and of course Africa, suffers regularly from atrocities and disasters rarely experienced in prosperous Western countries such as Canada.

The kinds of stories I am considering here set out to capture the history of ferment in faraway places. The idea is to recover or bring to light again difficult conditions. Many of these books deal with contemporary conditions throughout the world, and others recover events from the past, for example life under apartheid in pre–1994 South Africa or the Truth and Reconciliation commission that followed the end of apartheid. Perhaps the book that fits most nicely into what I am discussing here is Deborah Ellis's *Jackal in the*

Garden: An Encounter with Bihzad (2006). This book is one in a series of books called the Art Encounters series. Books in this series focus on "great works of art" and on the "lives and creative processes of the world's master artists" (book jacket). *Jackal in the Garden* deals, ostensibly at least, with the Persian artist, Kamal al-Din Bihzad (1460–1535). The plot involves a young girl, Annubis (the eponymous jackal), born to a mother who is one of several wives of a powerful man. The man wants a male, not a female child and orders the death of the girl. Coincidentally, the young girl Annubis also happens to be extremely unpleasant looking; the book refers to her as "ugly," although just what ugly means (except for a hump back) remains vague. She is supposedly monstrous in appearance. Anyhow, her mother does not have her killed. Instead, Annubis lives, sees her mother brutalized by her father, kills her father with his own sword, and finds herself at about the age of puberty wandering in the desert. There she comes across other men who brutalize and murder a woman; she kills these men as they sleep, or at least she kills all but one of them. She becomes a legend, the monstrous jackal of the desert. After some time in which she struggles to survive in a forbidding landscape, she makes her way to Herat, a bustling city. The man she left alive in the desert recognizes her and she has to flee for her life. She hides in a garden that happens to be the place of artists, two of whom (Bihzad and Haji) protect her.

The second half of the book takes place in this artist's compound, but we do not learn a great deal about Bihzad, other than that he works as a miniaturist. Like the Breadwinner books or Ellis's other books about Malawi (*The Heaven Shop*) or Bolivia (*I Am a Taxi*), this book is more interested in conventional adventure for young readers with a female protagonist who proves that females are capable and resourceful and that men (or many of them) are violent and uncivilized at best. Violence is swift and intense; it is also okay when perpetrated by a female upon violent men. This book tells us little or nothing about creation, about art in a social or historical context, about a specific kind of painting (the miniature), or about the artist himself. The note at the end about Bihzad's life and work informs us that "not much is known for sure about Bihzad, the man" (173). Consequently, the story does not feature Bihzad as a major player. He appears as a contemplative, modest, kind, but passive figure. The book is not really interested in him; it is interested in the young female protagonist and in the ugly male world that she inhabits. Violence is the watchword for this world. We learn little or nothing about life in fifteenth and sixteenth century Persia. As a historical novel, this novel contains little history. It reads like a cautionary tale for females, warning them that the world is a harsh place for females and that they had best hone their survival skills. The history here is less history than the ever-present tropes of certain folk tales, especially "Little Red Riding Hood" in both its Perreault and Brothers Grimm versions. What we have in *Jackal in the Garden* is a Europeanized cautionary tale focused on the dangers females face under patriarchy.

I want to be clear. Stories that set out the dangers females encounter in a male dominated world are all well and good — even, unfortunately, necessary. The problem appears when these stories purport to tell readers something accurate and balanced about another culture and its history. As far as I can tell, *Jackal in the Garden* gives us as much accurate information about ancient Persia as does George Meredith's nineteenth-century comic romp, *The Shaving of Shagpat* (1856). Meredith's book has the virtues of not taking itself seriously; it is a parody rather than an attempt to capture a culture or its history. In short, both *The Shaving of Shagpat* and *Jackal in the Garden* are fictions through and through. Perhaps it is here that we stumble: fiction does not pretend to accuracy — or so it might seem. But fictions that take situations and places that are discernibly part of our living history as their subject function as purveyors of truths about their subject. To be precise, when a book takes for its setting, say, Afghanistan since the coming to power of the Taliban, it inevitably presents itself as authoritative in its presentation of that country. Perhaps such a book coming from an Afghan writer or even from a writer who has long and deep personal experience of life in that part of the world might claim authority. The same cannot be said, I think, for such a book coming from a writer whose long and deep personal experience is with another part of the world, a long distance from Afghanistan. The intention of such a writer might be laudable, but laudable in the way a well-meaning friend might intervene in order to help a troubled friend recover. The possibility exists for the person recovering to come to depend upon the well-meaning friend. Dependency may lead to the loss of self-understanding and self-sufficiency.

I focus on books by authors from one culture who write about another culture, but what I have to say applies to postcolonial criticism as well. Here's the situation: I am an academic from a Canadian university, trained to read the canonical works of Western culture. Inevitably, I bring the critical as well as the social and political biases I have accumulated over the years to my readings of books that either emanate from other cultures or depict a western perspective on other cultures. Many postcolonial critics are much closer to the societies and cultures they write about than I am, but many others are not. My concern is that both postcolonial critics and creative writers may write from inside a myth of concern rather than from a myth of freedom. I adapt these terms, myth of concern and myth of freedom, from my teacher, Northrop Frye. In *The Critical Path*, Frye identifies the myth of concern as the "fully developed" story of a particular society; the myth of concern "exists to hold society together" (36). In other words, concern addresses a society's desire for cohesion, for order and stability, for a clear sense of the authority of the state. Concern, ultimately, focuses on the social order rather than on the individual. Concern manifests a society's ideological commitment to a set of values and beliefs. We hold certain truths to be self-evident and these are the truths that concern promotes and promises.

The myth of freedom, on the other hand, turns to what Frye calls "self-validating criteria, such as logicality of argument." The myth of freedom fosters "suspension of judgment, tolerance, and respect for the individual" (44). As Frye points out, "the myth of freedom is part of the myth of concern," but it is that part that is not the creation of social forces, but rather the part that stems from "nature." Just what nature means for Frye is not obvious. Nor is the relationship between the myths of concern and freedom to literature. I suspect one might argue either that novels express a society's myth of concern or that they express an author's myth of freedom. Or perhaps a better way of explaining how concern and freedom manifest in works of fiction is for me to say that we read our fictions from the perspective of concern or of freedom. Deborah Ellis's fiction, for example, might strike us as an expression of either the myth of concern or the myth of freedom, depending upon whether we see these books as fostering a genuine concern for universal values or whether we see them as universalizing in the sense of presenting western values as universal values. In this essay, I am choosing to read Ellis's work as expressing the myth of concern.

Because the myth of freedom is part of the myth of concern, we have a difficult time establishing when a book participates in the conservative practice of maintaining a society's sense of concern, its ideological underpinning, and when it succeeds in breaking free of practiced orthodoxies. What I have said up to now will, I think, suggest that recovery is largely a facet of the myth of concern. Critical practice, whether this is a postcolonial critical practice or some other theoretical approach, pursues the literature it is after for the myths that literature contains. I mean, critical practice seeks to validate concern or activate freedom. Recovery is, more often than not, an exercise in validation.

Because recovery's method involves delving into the past, into history, the re-exploring of history often forms part of the work of postcolonialism and of critical race theory and other forms of critical discourse that, ostensibly at least, focus on human rights (e.g., feminist theory or queer theory). We can see just how impure theoretical approaches more often than not are. We might have new historical methods combined with postcolonialism in the effort to affect a recovery of native voices or minority voices. Both new historicism and postcolonialism may share a political agenda with gender studies and disability theory in that all are concerned with the rights of individuals and groups, with "righting" past failures or past injustices, and with recognizing the subjectivity of others. Postcolonialism, like feminism and queer theory and disability studies, finds its beginnings in various events in the late 1960s and early 1970s: Kent State, May '68 in Paris, the Stonewall riots in 1969, the occupation of five buildings at Columbia University in May 1968, resistance to the Vietnam War and so on. The sense of outrage at injustices of various kinds moved into textbooks and into theories of resistance. Postcolonialism takes its place in this history of resistance, but as others have noted, it began its academic life in Anglo-American universities, especially in departments of Literature and Language (see Young 63). As it has evolved, it has moved outward to other disciplines, and it has maintained a pluralistic approach to history and the cultural products history has produced. But pluralism is no defense against the insistence of recovery. Even as postcolonialism endeavors to resist hegemonic enterprises, to resist the master plots of a Eurocentric ideology, it reproduces them.

Let me take for my first example of such recovery at work a few recent books for the young published in Canada. I'll begin with Deborah Ellis's "Breadwinner" trilogy: *The Breadwinner* (2000), *Parvana's Journey* (2002), and *Mud City* (2003). These books examine life in war-torn Afghanistan by focusing on a young girl named Parvana who has to cope with the worst consequences of war in her city and in her country. The action in the first book takes place when Parvana is 11 years old. She lives in Kabul, but this does not mean that she is shielded from difficulty because the story takes place when the Taliban formed the government. The book deals with life for women under the Taliban rule, but Ellis provides no background to the story's events or to the situation in Afghanistan. We learn nothing about the beliefs of the Taliban and the context for these beliefs. Ellis provides no explanation as to why women are to remain hidden in their homes, or why they need men to accompany them outside, or why they wear the *burqa*. The story is clear in its condemnation of the Taliban. They are harsh and cruel rulers who carry out the public cutting off of the hands of thieves, the brutal beating of men and women, the incarceration of citizens for no apparent reason, and book burning. We learn about lack of food, dislocation from homes, and the ravages of war. What we do not learn is the history of the country, its religion(s), its customs, or its difference from any other place under conditions of war. In other words, the story levels and universalizes. The story involves the young girl disguising herself as a boy so that she can earn money in the market place, a plot device as old, at least, as Shakespeare. Parvana, disguised as a boy, earns money by reading letters for illiterate people, and selling various items in the market place. Later she works digging human bones that will be used for soap and animal food, and then selling cigarettes and gum from trays. On the periphery of the story is the women's resistance with its magazine printed in Pakistan. The women's resistance is a small part of this book, but it continues to be a thread through all three books, effectively reminding us that these books are actually about the condition of women under oppression. These books articulate concern, the concern for just and equitable acceptance of females into the social fabric.

Parvana's Journey moves the story along. This time Parvana and her father are on the road to look for the rest of the family; the family has been dispersed by the vagaries of war. While they travel the countryside, Parana's father dies and Parvana finds herself on her own. In a plot that reminds me of the Clint Eastwood western movie, *The Outlaw Josie Wales*, the story recounts Parvana's encounter with the baby Hassan, the one-legged boy Asif, and the young girl Leila. This motley crew of youngsters travels together. They also stay for a while at Leila's home before they are forced to flee from explosions and threats from gunfire. For the short time they remain at Leila's place, Parvana fantasizes that she has found her "Green Valley," her place of final refuge. However, a bomb flattens the place killing Leila's grandmother and sending the youngsters on the road again. Parvana and her companions negotiate land mines, confront death, suffer from malnutrition, encounter refugees and their camp, escape from bombings, experience worm-infested sores, filth, and the ugliness of war. Once again, however, the story takes place in a fantasy Afghanistan, where Parvana remembers the fairy stories she experienced as a child, obviously derived from the Brothers Grimm and the Arabian Nights (see pp. 80–82). The book the children, in desperation and starving, eat near the end of the story is *To Kill a Mockingbird*. We get no real sense of a specific place, with its own traditions of storytelling. Oh, we have the sprinkling of Afghan words, whether Dari or Pashtu we are not informed, and reminders of the cultural marginalization of women, but the story could take place in any war-torn country that has little or no infrastructure. We learn little or nothing about the religion of the area, the various cultures, the history or customs of the people. We have a mention of Ramadan, but no explanation of what this is. The story reminds me of *Lost in the Barrens*, a well-known Canadian survival story by Farley Mowat, published in 1956. Survival, courage, family, and coming of age, these are the themes. Implicit is the sense that this story of struggle, survival, and coming of age is universal. Part of the problem is that this is a story that tries to engage young readers who are safe and secure in a story of people who are not safe and secure, and literature has a way of transposing history into convention. The conventions of quest and heroism work their way out in familiar western fashion in this book. In other words, the story here neatly fits the myth of concern as expressed in a distinctly Canadian (or at least Western) manner.

Mud City, the final book in the Breadwinner trilogy, turns from the adventures of Parvana in order to explore the story of her friend, Shauzia. Shauzia has managed to escape across the border into Pakistan. Here she makes her way to a refugee camp where she sees hunger, violence, dirt, ill health, over-crowding, and loss. Shauzia is an independent young girl, who just wants to get to the sea and from there to France where she has planned to meet her friend Parvana. In an online review, Joan Marshal provides a summary of the plot:

> Shauzia has left her grasping, cold family to strike out in the world on her own, dressed as a boy. While working with some Afghani shepherds, she befriends a dog, Jasper, and the two of them end up in "Mud City," a refugee camp just inside Pakistan, near the city of Peshawar, where she works with Mrs. Weera to run the Widows Compound, a section of the camp for women and children. Irritated by what she sees as inertia, Shauzia leaves for the city of Peshawar… In Peshawar, Shauzia does odd jobs but finally resorts to picking through garbage for items to sell. Finally, she ends up begging and is falsely imprisoned. Shauzia is rescued by a rich American, Tom, who bribes the police to release Shauzia from prison, but Tom and his wife, Barbara, return Shauzia to the refugee camp when she invites other needy people into their opulent home in their absence. After Shauzia's leg is broken in a food riot, she has a lot of time to think about her position, and she finally follows Mrs. Weera back to Afghanistan to nurse the refugees there, leaving the faithful Jasper with another young girl who needs him.

As this summary indicates, Shauzia's adventures constitute a coming of age. She comes to accept her responsibility to others. Before she accepts this responsibility, she lives the life of a picaro, and her story fits neatly into the European picaresque.

Marshall describes Tom and Barbara, the two American characters, as "compassionate," and she also notes that they "represent Western countries that will help the impoverished as long as it doesn't threaten their own lifestyle" (Marshall). Americans (and Canadians too, we can assume) are a compassionate people as long as their compassion does not threaten to discomfort them. Such a reading is not only possible, but probable too given Deborah Ellis's willingness to participate in activist programs beyond her writing profession. The difficulty is that the intricate connection between government policy (American government in this case) and the chaos in Afghanistan and elsewhere remains in the background and easy for a reader to miss because the book reads like a standard adventure story with a female protagonist. Once again, we learn little about Pakistan or the intricacies of life in the refugee camps. What we get is standard hardship and squalor. In the end, as Marshall says, *"Mud City* could have been a horrifying book, far too frightening for children, as the situation in Afghanistan and Pakistan is indeed appalling." Marshall goes on to praise the book for its tact: "Ellis is careful to tell only enough to keep students glued to the story and not so much that children would be terrified. This careful writing ends optimistically as Shauzia takes off with Mrs. Weera for another adventure — this time with a more adult attitude" (Marshall).

Marshall's review offers praise for both the book and its writer, noting that "the author has set an example for students by donating the royalties for this book to Street Kids International, an organization which supports children living on the street around the world" (Marshall). Marshall also singles out the "Author's Note" at the end of the book that explains "the political situation in these countries" (Afghanistan and Pakistan), and that provides the address of "a web site students can access to offer help" (Marshall). Nothing in this review is incorrect or misleading. Like the book itself, the review accepts as authoritative a story that glosses the history and culture of countries far different from those of the author or most of her readers. By implication, the Breadwinner books are praiseworthy precisely because they introduce young readers to conditions in Afghanistan and Pakistan without delving into a thorough depiction or explanation of their history and culture. In other words, they provide children with just the information they require to understand that terrible things are happening elsewhere and that they ought to join in efforts to relieve the suffering in these faraway places. The books are not so much a plea for understanding as they are a call to arms in the assumption that Western values are universal values. Western values may be universal values, but if they are, then we need to point out that this universalism is not a given one. The issues that divide and connect cultures are complex and young readers deserve our confidence that they are capable of engaging with these complex issues.

Another of Ellis's books, *The Heaven Shop*, deals with the problem of AIDS in Africa, specifically in Malawi. The story follows young Binti Phiri, a child star in a popular radio program, as she loses her parents to AIDS and slides from popularity to poverty. As in Ellis's other books, we have a journey to maturity and to acceptance and responsibility. Once again, we have a book that sets out not only to inform readers about conditions elsewhere in the world, but also to promote activism. The Author's Note at the end concludes that even though we do not have a cure for AIDS and HIV, "we can take action to prevent war and alleviate poverty" (181). The idea is that both war and poverty create conditions in which the spread of AIDS and HIV is inevitable. Eradicate war and poverty and we go some distance to eradicating AIDS. No one, I hope, would decry such an ambitious and humanitarian goal. And tucked quietly in the story of Binti and her problems is the brief exchange between Binti and two of her young cousins. One cousin, Machozi, whom Binti thinks is six or seven years old, notes that "we used to get water from a pond that made everybody sick, but some people from Canada built us a pump" (121). The other young cousin, Gracie, asks if Binti knows where Canada is: "Is Canada in Malawi?" This passing reference to International Relief Efforts maintains the myth of concern. Concern here is the universal acceptance of the responsibility of the well-off to assist the less well-off to recover their dignity by providing them with the necessities of life — the bare necessities.

We can see the same acceptance of the myth of concern in Joan Marshall's review of *The Heaven Shop*:

> Present-day Malawi comes alive for the reader as children sell candy out of cardboard boxes on the side of the road, second hand clothing from America is sold from stalls, and Binti sweeps wood chips into a corner of their yard where someone who needs fuel will come to get them in the night. The public hospital is a harrowing warren of patients packed into every available bed and even lying on the floor between beds. In Lilongwe, people are washing clothes in the river and evening light is provided by oil lanterns. In the country near Mulanje, people live in clay huts with grass roofs. Binti constructs coffins of reed grasses before she has access to lumber. The hungry orphans of the Orphan Club eat from huge pots of nsumi and beans and squat over a hole for a toilet. There is no soap for hand or clothes washing. The world of Africa jumps off the page and into the reader's heart.

The theme of looking after each other is stressed throughout the novel. Mr. Taska, a business rival of Binti's father, and Mr. Wajiru, the radio play director, do everything they can to help Binti and her siblings. The stressed aunts and uncles see disobedience everywhere and don't have the strength or education to be compassionate. Consequently, they can't gain Binti's love or confidence. Jeremiah and Gogo welcome Binti unconditionally, expect her co-operation, and address her anxiety over her brother and sister. The community at Mulanje works together to feed the orphans. Ellis is dedicated to reducing the suffering of the world's children, and she believes that young readers of her books will not tolerate in the future the social conditions that swamp Africa today.

The force of Marshall's review demonstrates her acceptance of the concern the book shows for "Africa today." The language of the review — "harrowing," "warren," "washing clothes in the river," "oil lantern," "clay huts with grass roots," "hungry orphans," "squat over a hole," "anxiety," "swamp" — accepts as fact that the country Ellis presents in her book is primitive, undeveloped, even uncivilized. "Harrowing" is a word that reminds us of Hell, and "warren" is the habitation of rabbits. "Swamp" suggests a morass of pestilence. My point is that neither Ellis in her novel nor Marshall in her review take care to notice the irony inherent in a country that shows signs of change in business practices (I am thinking of the changes Mr. Taska brings to the funeral business), that has a culture of celebrity evident in the radio station that Binti works for early in the novel, and that has abject poverty. The mention of "second hand clothing from America" is a delicate reminder of global economic forces that are working to homogenize the world. Perhaps the strongest and most dubious expression of the myth of concern rests in this passing reminder of American power and influence in a book that directs its attention to examining just how a country such as Malawi suffers because it is not like America, but rather has to look to America (and its allies) for cast-off clothing and for the wherewithal to find clean water.

Perhaps I can bring this contemplation of concern to a close on the subject of water. Global concern for fresh water increases in these days of climate change, global warming, drought, pollution of the world's oceans, and population increase. In *The Heaven Shop*, we read about the lack of fresh surface water in Malawi, and the assistance of Canada in building a pump to access water fit for drinking and washing. The pump is significant for two reasons: it indicates the difficulty humans face and will increasingly face in accessing fresh water, and it indicates that water is power. This second reason — that water is power — is the more ominous of the two reasons. As fresh water becomes increasingly scarce and difficult to access, those with power will hold the key to water sources. To put this clearly, I note that the Canadian intervention in Malawi to assist the people to recover fresh water demonstrates the working of a power structure that shows no signs of changing. I might also include those second-hand American clothes in this summation. Forces of global intervention are often well-meaning, just as the books I explore in this essay are well-meaning, but they also put their mark on people. In another of Ellis's books, *I Am a Taxi*, set in Bolivia, a passing reference to a movie theater "where *Batman* was playing" (33) is a reminder of the pervasive influence of colonial activity.

We might remember the newcomers to earth at the end of the *Battlestar Galactica* series. They may come from away, but they take over the new land they "discover." They may consist of a mixture of peoples and machines; they may represent hybridity incarnate. Nevertheless, they are intent on perpetuating a way of life they have lived for aeons. They are not prepared to shift ground, as it were, by listening and learning from others. Hybridity may offer hope for breaking down divisions of race, but the complete breakdown of division based on race or ethnicity or economics or language remains an ideal devoutly to be hoped for.

I began with an epigraph that cites the Canadian Prime Minister's assertion that Canada does not have a history of colonialism. Of course, the reaction of our First Nations people has been quick. Not only does Canada have a history of colonization reminiscent of other settler societies, but its colonial activity has not ceased. We all know this. If colonization can mean the spreading of the influence of one people over another people and the appropriating of stories and histories by one people at the expense of another people, then colonial activity is as vigorous as it has always been. Books participate in this activity, as we know. Even books that have a humanitarian purpose can express myths of concern, in that they perpetuate the ideology of the powerful rather than attempt to understand the ideology of the other. What is valuable in postcolonialism is the effort to transcend judgment and instead approach the history and mores of otherness with reason and impartiality. The myth of freedom seeks to value the individuality of otherness and in doing so to promote justice, peace, good will, and equality. The myth of freedom will only make itself heard if we stop talking ourselves and listen to what others have to say.

WORKS CITED

Batty, Nancy Ellen. "'We Are the World, We Are the Children': The Semiotics of Seduction in International Children's Relief Efforts." In *Voices of the Other: Children's Literature and the Postcolonial Context*, Ed. Roderick McGillis. New York: Garland, 2000. 17–38.

Ellis, Deborah. *The Breadwinner*. Toronto: Groundwood, 2000.

_____. *The Heaven Shop*. Markham, ON: Fitzhenry and Whiteside, 2004.

_____. *I Am a Taxi*. Toronto: Groundwood, 2006.

_____. *Jackal in the Garden: An Encounter with Bihzad*. New York: Watson-Guptill, 2006.

_____. *Mud City*. Toronto: Groundwood, 2003.

_____. *Parvana's Journey*. Toronto: Groundwood, 2002.

Frye, Northrop. *The Critical Path: An Essay on the Social Context of Literary Criticism*. 1971. Bloomington: Indiana University Press, 1973.

Herman, Judith. *Trauma and Recovery: The Aftermath of Violence — From Domestic Abuse to Political Terror*. 1992. New York: Basic, 1997.

Marshall, Joan. "The Heaven Shop." *CM Magazine* (*Canadian Review of Materials*) 11,1 (3 September 2004). Accessed 20 October 2009. *http://www.google.com/gwt/n?u=http%3A%2F%2Fumanitoba.ca%2Foutreach%2Fcm%2Fvol11%2Fno1%2Ftheheavenshop.html.*

_____. *Mud City. CM Magazine* (*Canadian Review of Materials*) X,6 (14 November 2003). Accessed 20 October 2009. *http://www.umanitoba.ca/outreach/cm/vol10/no6/mudcity.html.*

Young, Robert J.C. *Postcolonialism: An Historical Introduction*. Oxford: Blackwell, 2001.

Going Global

The Future of Post-Colonial Studies

BILL ASHCROFT

It is difficult to imagine a more fraught or argumentative field of literary study than post-colonial studies became after the publication of *The Empire Writes Back*. For the last twenty-two years, the future of the field has been prophesied with various degrees of doom and optimism. This, no doubt, has something to do with the nature of "post-colonial studies": such a variety of post-colonialisms emerged over the last two decades, such heated criticism of the field itself and such controversy over the prefix "post-," that it always seemed a tenuous planting in the theoretical landscape. But on the twenty-second anniversary of *The Empire Writes Back*, it seems a fitting time to talk about where post-colonial studies may be headed and suggest directions the field will be taking into the next millennium. How, we might ask, can this discourse approach the increasingly complex questions of cultural movement and contact, the increasingly embattled issue of local identity in a "postmodern" age? Indeed, what directions offer themselves as the best channels for the energies of this growing field? Some of these directions are already being engaged in various forms and are characteristic of a maturing field of literary study. But the major question about the future involves the ways in which the theory of the "post-colonial" may equip us to engage the nature and complexity of global relations.

To begin this task, we need to understand something about the complex history of the field. Post-colonial studies developed as a way of addressing the cultural production of those societies affected by the historical phenomenon of colonialism. In this respect, it was not conceived as a grand theory but as a methodology: first, for analyzing the complex strategies by which colonized societies have engaged imperial discourse; and second, for studying the ways in which many of those strategies are shared by colonized societies, re-emerging in very different political and cultural circumstances. But the historical provenance and material grounding, the *location* of post-colonial discourse, has often been blurred by the use of this theory to address issues which have very little to do with the historical phenomenon of colonialism.

A number of curious features quickly developed in the field. First, there seem to be as many explanations of the origin and history of post-colonialism as there are people writing: everybody has a theory of beginnings. The usual story is that Edward Said initiated the discourse. Yet *The Empire Writes Back* emerged not from the analysis of orientalist discourse that we find in *Orientalism*[1] but from the work of those African, Caribbean, and Indian writers, artists and social theorists who were actually engaging the power of imperial discourse — who were "writing back." Post-colonial studies emerged as a synergy of the deconstructive leanings of colonial discourse theory and the textual analyses of Commonwealth scholars. In fact, neither Edward Said nor Gayatri Spivak used the term until the nineties. Said and Spivak both developed a complicated and uncertain relationship with post-colonial studies. Both, for different reasons, came to reject the post-colonial: Said from an aversion to any systematic theory (all of which he regards as "theological"), and Spivak in favor of what she regards as the more inclusive term "subaltern." The history of the troubled relationship between "post-colonial" theorists and "post-colonialism" reinforces the point that post-colonial studies might best be regarded now as a term for a body of diverse and often contesting formulations of the cultural production of colonized people rather than a discipline or methodology *per se*.

Second, and more broadly, there seems to be two planets in its cosmos, planet America and the rest of the world. This comes as no surprise to many because planet America has been in its own orbit for a long time, but in post-colonial studies it is partly due, I think, to the different understanding of the historical role of Commonwealth literary studies and the actual range of post-colonial writing. This writing had a particular place and accessibility in the British Empire and became a source of energetic, if untheoretical, criticism before the emergence of post-colonial studies. The term "post-colonial" has broadened to include "internal colonization" in the case of Chicano experience in the United States. It has been deployed in approaches to the black diaspora scattered by centuries of slavery, expanding to overlap African American studies. But one obvious omission from the early development of post-colonial theory was the study of the oldest, second largest, and most complex modern European empire — that of Spain. Yet the antiquity and character of its colonization, the longstanding reality of its hybridized cultures, the "continental" sense of difference which stems from a shared colonial language, the intermittent emergence of contestatory movements in cultural production — all radically widen the scope of post-colonial theory.

This raises a third issue in the field: the status of non–English literatures and of translation. Needless to say, a recurrent controversy concerns what some have referred to as the "Empire" of Anglophone post-colonialism, as though post-colonial studies were an institution with strict criteria for entry. But, in fact, there are no limits to the study of Francophone, Hispanophone and Lusophone post-colonial literatures — *if* critics in these languages are interested. Indeed, this is one area in which post-colonial studies has begun to expand radically, along with analyses of the Dutch Caribbean. Despite the longstanding preference for the term "postmodern" in Latin America, strategies of post-colonial analysis have begun to prove their value in these literatures. Because of the historical importance of Francophone African writers in the development of Négritude and the presence of a vibrant Francophone Caribbean literature, French language post-colonial studies is much more advanced.

We can't broach the issue of non–English literatures without addressing what has become and will continue to be one of the most pressing issues in post-colonial studies — translation. The most vigorous region of translation studies has been South Asia, the site of a longstanding (if somewhat wrong-headed) complaint that post-colonial criticism pays no attention to the rich tradition of precolonial vernacular literatures. But in Africa, where oral traditions led to writing in local languages during and after the colonial period, the focus of attention on English texts has been seen as a problem, taking the attention away from a precious, vast, and untapped cultural resource. Nevertheless, it is arguable that the translation of a large number of indigenous novels into English opens up a potentially huge readership both in the post-colonial countries themselves and the world. Such a cultural resource becomes, through translation, a vehicle of cultural communication, and perhaps a mode of cultural survival.

A fourth significant feature of post-colonial studies is that the term very quickly came to be misused as both an "ontology" and a "chronology." The idea of a post-colonial ontology leads to the question: Who is post-colonial? In the fractious battle to define the field, there have been innumerable attempts to draw boundaries around the term. But the search for these boundaries and the idea of cultural fixity which they promote contradict the nature of the post-colonial enterprise. Claims that some societies are "truly colonized" or truly "post-colonial" and others aren't make a very simple mistake: that is, to assume that the Canadian or Caribbean experience of colonialism, for instance, each represents some kind of epistemologically unified phenomenon. The Canadian and the Caribbean subject can only *be post-colonial* according to the different material and discursive ways in which we see colonialism operating in their cultures and histories. "Culture" and "history" are themselves texts, or at least only accessible through texts of various kinds, which are themselves accessible through language. Despite the very obvious material effects of colonialism on the Caribbean — demographically, geographically, economically — the cultural hegemony of colonialism lies in its textual dominance, a process that must be engaged textually. The institutions of imperial (and global) power seem unassailable in their control, but they themselves are fundamentally the constructions of discursive networks that *can* be assailed. Colonialism is not only placed *upon* societies but runs *through* them.

Perhaps the more common error — that the term is chronological — has been an inevitable consequence of the prefix "post," which has, of course, generated controversy out of the assumption that post-colonial means "after colonialism." I have always been amazed at the longevity and recalcitrance of this misapprehension. Yet, from the beginning, the term was defined to refer to all the culture from the moment of colonization to the present day. The "post" meant post-*colonization* and as a strategy of cultural production was the engagement by colonized and formerly colonized peoples with the assumptions, discourses, and technologies of imperial power. But — and here's the rub — it is a creative strategy that is *read* as such. Ultimately "post-colonial" must be understood as a way of reading. Writers do not sit down to write a post-colonial novel; rather, they write a novel, and its post-colonial character emerges as a function of post-colonial reading.

So what kind of reading might post-colonial reading become, how might it develop, particularly in an increasingly globalized world? The first thing we can say is that the post-colonial text does not exist apart from the structures of culture and society, which "run through" the text as constitutive horizons; so the importance of the text's cultural affiliations is paramount, as is a view of culture which includes all of its discursive formations, rather than just the aesthetic. A post-colonial reading will continue to expand beyond a focus on what might be called a "post-colonial" text, and neither will it adhere to any formulaic process.

Strategies of post-colonial reading will include those that are:

Symptomatic: The post-colonial text can be read as symptomatic of the operation of imperial power and the resistances this power generates in post-colonial discourse.

Comparative: Individual texts may be read "through" a comparison of the specific material conditions of colonialism, or with other national literatures.

Dialogic: A post-colonial reading will continue to emphasize the dialogic operation of texts as it dismantles the illusion of cultural and national authenticity.

Multivalent: Such a reading implicitly or explicitly acknowledges the intersecting discourses of oppression and resistance operating in any society, such as race and ethnicity, gender and sexual choice, class and regionalism.

Horizontal: The overlapping and multivalent energies of resistance operating in the text may be located in terms of various "horizons" which articulate them.

Constitutive: The text is not simply a unidirectional discourse, but a transformative space, a field in which the reader and writer functions constitutively produce the text.

Two other foci of post-colonial reading will grow in importance as they have in general discourse: the issue of the sacred and the problem of the environment. During the 1990s debates concerning the traditional and sacred beliefs of colonized, indigenous, and marginalized peoples increased greatly in importance to post-colonial studies. This amounted to something of a paradigm shift in western thinking because, since the Enlightenment, any mention of the sacred had been considered a sign of the worst kind of intellectual bad taste. Secularity, economic rationalism, and progressivism have dominated in Modernity, while "the sacred" has so often been relegated to primitivism and the archaic (Chakrabarty; Scott & Simpson-Housley).[2] Consequently the export of secularism has been an inevitable accompaniment of colonialism. The sacred has followed the trajectory of other "denied knowledges," as Bhabha puts it, entering the dominant discourse and estranging "the basis of its authority — its rules of recognition" (Bhabha, 114). At the end of the twentieth century, this situation began to change. Debates about the sacred became more urgent as issues such as land rights and rights to sacred beliefs and practices began to intensify.

A misleading direction was given by Edward Said's preference for "secular criticism" over what he called the "theological" bent of contemporary theory (Said, 1–30). Said's promulgation of secular humanism seemed to suggest that the theological and the sacred were not the province of enlightened post-colonial analysis. Such an assumption reminds us of the gap that often exists between the theoretical agenda of the Western academy and the interests of post-colonial societies themselves. The sacred has been an empowering feature of post-colonial experience in two ways: on the one hand, indigenous concepts of the sacred have been able to interpolate dominant conceptions of cultural identity, and on the other hand, Western forms of the sacred have often been appropriated and transformed as a means of local empowerment. Analyses of the sacred have been one of the most neglected and may be one of the most rapidly expanding areas of post-colonial study.

The sacred has frequently entered post-colonial debates in relation to environmental issues. Place has always been of great importance to post-colonial theory, but the more material, and global issue of environmentalism is an important and growing aspect of this concept. The destruction of the environment has been one of the most damaging aspects of Western industrialization. The fact that the scramble for modernization has enticed developing countries into the destruction of their own environments, now under the disapproving gaze of a hypocritical West, is further evidence of the continuing importance of a post-colonial analysis of global crises. Post-colonial societies have taken up the "civilizing" benefits of modernity, only to find themselves the "barbaric" instigators of environmental damage. In such ways, the dynamic of imperial moral power is maintained globally.

While the roots of contemporary environmentalism may lie in colonial damage in both settler colonies and colonies of occupation, neo-colonialism, often in association with the colonial past, continues to produce clashes of interests between "the West and the Rest" in, for instance, areas of land and food scarcity, where the well-being of humans and endangered animal species may be at odds (Wolch and Emmel). The death of Ken Saro-wiwa, who was attempting to prevent oil company destruction of Nigeria's Delta region, is a notorious example of the consequences of multinational damage.[3] His death offers a clear reminder that (neo)colonial depredations, sometimes in collusion with local individuals or cadres, continue.

Globalization and Post-Colonial Theory

Post-colonial futures are therefore bound to extend or revise many of the developments dominating its formation: the concern with beginnings, the controversial prominence of Anglophone literatures, the confirmation of the post-colonial as a way of reading, and the emergence of new directions in that reading. But how do we explain the most baffling development of all? How and why did a quite specific theory, developed to address the cultural production of those societies affected by the historical phenomenon of colonialism, become so quickly appointed to the role of the Grand Theory of Global Cultural Diversity? Why was post-colonial theory, developed initially by literary critics, apparently doomed from the start to become a protean term? The reason is, quite simply, that by the late 1980s the world was hungry for a language to describe the diversity of cultures and the intersecting global range of cultural production. Post-colonial theory provided that language, a way of talking about the engagement of the global by the local, particularly local cultures, and, most importantly, provided a greatly nuanced view of globalization that developed from its understanding of the complexities of imperial relationships.

A post-colonial-inspired language became the language of globalization studies in the 1990s. Varied as the discourses of post-colonialism and globalization might be, according to Simon Gikandi,

> they have at least two important things in common: they are concerned with explaining forms of social and cultural organization whose ambition is to transcend the boundaries of the nation-state, and they seek to provide new vistas for understanding cultural flows that can no longer be explained by a homogenous Eurocentric narrative of development and social change [Gikandi, 627].

What made post-colonial theory so useful was its ability to comprehend the postmodern movement of culture beyond the nation-state at the same time as it addresses the particularity of the (largely non–Western) local. This represented not just an appropriation of the language of the post-colonial but also an unprecedented dominance of the Humanities in the descriptions of global culture.

This amazing development can be explained in three ways. First, the systematization of post-colonial theory occurred at about the same time as the rise to prominence of globalization studies in the late 1980s. Second, it was around this time that literary and cultural theorists became convinced that the debates on globalization that had dominated disciplines such as sociology and anthropology had become hopelessly mired in the classical narrative of modernity, in dependency theory, and in center-periphery models. Third, it became clear, particularly after Appadurai, that there were many globalizations, and that far from the homogenizing downward pressure of economic globalization and the Washington Consensus, a circulation of local alternatives could be seen to affect the nature of the global. It was through *cultural* practices that difference and hybridity, diffusion and the imaginary, concepts that undermined the Eurocentric narrative of modernity, were most evident. Not surprisingly, the interpolation of post-colonial theory in the analysis of globalization and the mainstreaming of cultural discourse has meant the reappearance of the local, though characteristically, now a local culture much more ambivalent and much more globally inflected than that rural backwater dismissed by modernity. But it is nevertheless the local that compels a re-thinking of the present proliferation of modernities.

Clearly the "cultural turn" in globalization studies and the influence of a post-colonial inspired language in that "turn" meant that "post-colonial" could now be used to refer to all forms of cultural diversity, often rendering the term so diffuse and endlessly employable as to be virtually useless. This process might be hard to reverse in practice, at least until some other language of global cultural diversity has been adapted. Curiously we anticipated this diffusion, and it is precisely why we continued to use the hyphenated form of the term. This is a battle that has been long lost and retaining the hyphen seems to be an act of gross recalcitrance since newcomers continue to believe it to be a chronological marker. But the hyphen continues to remind me at least of the dangers of Grand Theory and of the grounding of post-colonial theory in the historical fact of colonialism.

At this point we may be able to see the ways in which a distinctive, focused post-colonial theory may provide strategies to address globalization. While the post-colonial is not synonymous with cultural globalization, and while we must insist on its grounding in the historical phenomenon of colonialism, there are specific analytical tools developed within post-colonial theory to help us understand the present global dispersal of modernity. A major feature of post-colonial studies has been its ability to analyze historical developments of culture: expressions of anti-colonial nationalism; the paradoxical dissolution of the idea of nation along with the continuous persistence of national concerns; the question of language and appropriation; the question of the transformation of literary genres; and the question of ethnicity and its relation to the state.

But the question we need to ask ourselves is: "How is post-colonial theory positioned to approach the continuing issues of global power, global interaction, and cultural difference in the coming century?" Already one answer to this has been a growing, and now well-established, interest in cultural and ethnic mobility of diaspora, of transnational and cosmopolitan interactions. This rise in global mobility at the same time as state borders have become ever more hysterically protected, has interested post-colonial cultural critics for some time. Global mobility promises to be a major feature of post-colonial study because this mobility is a consequence, either directly or indirectly, of the re-structuring of the world by Western imperialism. There is an inherently porous boundary around the phenomenon of colonialism, its experience and its effects. It is probably impossible to say absolutely where these effects begin or end. If we take the example of slavery, we can see that it was clearly a major incentive for imperial expansion and a major catalyst in the theory of race, although it existed before, and arguably after, the period of European imperialism. Can we really say that slavery and its effects (the black diaspora) are not a legitimate element of the colonial and should not be part of what we study to try and understand how colonialism worked? These and similar issues have been argued for a decade or more and seem as little likely to be resolved in the next decade as they have been so far.

Globalization and Multiple Modernities

The way in which post-colonial theory seems compelled to develop lies in the area of globalization studies. We have seen how the language of postcolonial theory became the language of cultural globalization in the 1990s and how this was allied to an egregious casting of post-colonial theory as a master discourse. So the intervention I am suggesting is one that hinges on the strategies developed from literary study, and one way in which this theory might best "go global" is through an analysis of Modernity itself, or to be more precise, the contemporary phenomenon of *modernities*.

The first principle of the post-colonial view of global modernity is the confirmation of its cultural character. A common assumption, possibly receding after the global financial crisis, is that globalization is not only economic, but *is* U.S. economic imperialism. Indeed, the Marxist view of European modernity is that it is capitalism pure and simple. But a nuanced view of globalization lies not only in understanding the variety of global flows — ethnoscapes, mediascapes, technoscapes financescapes, and ideoscapes — as Appadurai postulates, but in understanding the cultural basis of Modernity itself. It is clear that Western Modernity represents a political and cultural revolution that worked itself out through the intersecting forces of imperialism and capitalism. Globalization may now be characterized by the *multiplicity* of its modernities, and post-colonial theory provides a way to understand why this is so.

A substantial literature has developed on the related concepts of "multiple modernities," "alternative modernities," of modernity "at large," "multiple globalizations," and the principles of fluidity, localization, and hybridization that they imply.[4] But because the term "alternative" has sometimes been confused with the idea of a totally different system, these multiple adaptations are perhaps better referred to as *transformations* of modernity rather than as alternatives. Using the tools of literary analysis, we can see that non–Western modernities don't just emerge out of thin air, nor are they simple extension of a Western modernity that has swamped indigenous cultures. They emerge out of a *relation* to other modernities, and the processes of appropriation, adaptation, and transformation have been their characteristic features. Thus, like post-colonial literatures, alternative modernities are transformative — appropriating and transforming global cultural forms, global technologies, and practices to local needs, beliefs, and conditions. This does not make them simple extensions of modernity but, instead, new culturally situated forms of modernization, instances of transculturation. Modernity is not so much adopted, as adapted and re-created, and increasingly, modernities may adapt other alternative modernities. They are versions that may well contest the perceived hegemonic nature of Westernization.

How then did we get to the present condition of multiple modernities? Did modernity simply travel from the West? Was it brought with colonial conquest? Was it a gift of the civilizing mission? Can we talk about modernity without invoking Western modernity? What does the concept of multiple modernities mean to the structure of global relations? These questions remain recalcitrant and to many insoluble. From one point of view, modernity is like a wave "flowing over and engulfing one traditional culture after another." In terms of "the emergence of a market-industrial economy, of a bureaucratically organized state, of modes of popular rule — then its progress is, indeed, wave-like" (Taylor, 182). But the metaphor of a wave is typically acultural. A cultural theory, in contrast, holds that modernity is not simply a function of historical development but of cultural difference. It always unfolds within a specific cultural or civilizational context, and different starting points for the transition to modernity lead to different outcomes (17). Cultures are not necessarily engulfed by modernity, but creatively adapt it to local needs. As we see in the model of post-colonial literatures, transformation is the way "people 'make' themselves modern, as opposed to being 'made' modern by 'alien and impersonal forces'" (Gaonkar, "On Alternative Modernities," 18).

To accept that modernity is not synonymous with Westernization is not to abandon the fact that modernity as an epoch; thus, a privileging of the present over the past and a triumphal teleology oriented to the future emerged in the West. But it does remind us that modernity is plural, and that the historical trajectory of Western modernity was not simply a movement of temporal progress, despite that assumption being embodied in the very idea of "the modern." Modernity is a *culturally* situated phenomenon, even in its economic manifestation of capitalism, and to accept this fact radically changes the way we understand it. Western modernity clearly emerges from a particular cultural milieu, but it is invariably seen in acultural terms as the inevitable (and universal) march of progress towards reason and enlightenment. A purely acultural theory, says Charles Taylor, not only impoverishes our understanding of the West but imposes a falsely uniform pattern on the multiple encounters of non–Western cultures with the exigencies of science, technology, and industrialization. If we don't examine Western modernity, "we will fail to see how other cultures differ and how this difference crucially conditions the way in which they integrate the truly universal features of modernity" (180).

The closer we look at Western, or European, modernity, the more we see its cultural features. As an epoch, modernity is generally regarded as referring to modes of social organization that emerged in Europe from about the sixteenth century, broadly represented by the discovery of the "New World," the Renaissance, and the Reformation (Habermas, "Modernity," 5). Although these upheavals involve a radical break with cultural traditions, "that break was *rationally motivated* by the patterns of meaning in the West's cultural heritage" (Kirkland, 138). In this way, modernity came to be seen as a distinctive and superior period in the history of humanity, a notion that became habitual as successive generations saw their own "present" time enjoying a prominent position. As European power expanded, this sense of the superiority of the present over the past became translated into a sense of superiority over those pre-modern societies and cultures which were "locked" in the past — primitive and uncivilized peoples whose subjugation and "introduction" into modernity became the right and obligation of European powers. Europe constructed itself as "modern" and constructed the non–European as "traditional," "static," and "pre-historical" and thus justified its expansionism. The imposition of European models of historical change became the tool by which these societies were misconceived as lacking any internal dynamic or capacity for development. The prominence of reason as a philosophical mode (see Habermas, *The Philosophical Discourse of Modernity*), and the radical restructuring of time and space became the most powerful discursive tools in the European construction of a modern world reality. Perhaps predictably, a universalist view of modernity as historical progress and development went hand in hand with Western cultural dominance.

Western modernity, then, may be usefully understood as coterminous with both imperialism and capitalism. Wallerstein's persuasive claim that the world system has been capitalism since the sixteenth century leads to the conclusion that capitalism is the economic discourse of modernity, the natural concomitant of European imperialism. Indeed the link between globalism and the imperial dominance of subject nations is clearly articulated by Adam Smith, perhaps the first globalist, whose view of the role of commodities in distinguishing the civilized from the barbarous is deeply embedded in the ideology of empire. Having an abundance of "objects of comfort" is the litmus test that distinguishes "civilized and thriving nations" from "savage" ones, "so miserably poor" they are reduced to "mere want" (lx).

As compelling as Wallerstein's world system theory may be, its center-periphery model is far too structurally static to explain the multi-directional flow of global exchanges, a flow that was most noticeable in cultural exchange. It also fails to explain the present polycentric state of world capitalism. The world system theorist might reply that the system of inequality exists within countries as well as between them, but if that is the case, we need something a little more satisfactory than the geometric model of centers and peripheries to explain it. Post-colonial societies are not necessarily pre-industrial, nor necessarily peripheral according to Wallerstein's view of the world system. They may represent feudal, industrial, or global capital modes of production at the same time. Most obvious is India, a growing and gigantic player in global capitalism where a large proportion of the population has not even encountered modernity.

We need a concept of the world system that is much more polyvalent, and Appadurai's description of globalization as "a complex overlapping, disjunctive order that cannot any longer be understood in terms of existing centre-periphery models" is convincing (Appadurai 32). He makes a crucial distinction between older forms of modernity, whose goal was the rationalization of the world in Weberian terms, to the symbolic economy of a new global culture based on reciprocal rather than hierarchical relationships:

> The master narrative of the Enlightenment (and its many variants in Britain, France, and the United States) was constructed with a certain internal logic and presupposed a certain relationship between reading, representation, and the public sphere... . But the diaspora of these terms and images across the world, especially since the nineteenth century, has loosened the internal coherence that held them together in a Euro-American master narrative and provided instead a loosely structured synopticon of politics, in which different nation-states, as part of their evolution, have organized their political cultures around different keywords [Appadurai 36].

While Appadurai talks about the "symbolic economy of the new global culture," there is no doubt that "part of the attraction of post-colonial theory to questions of globalization lies precisely in its claim that culture, as a social and conceptual category, has escaped 'the bounded nation state society' and has become the common property of the world" (Featherstone, 2). Clearly, the cultural character of contemporary modernities is constantly inflected with this global symbolic economy. But this neither erases nor blurs the cultural specificity of various modernities that characterize the global.

But if globalization is more complex than a geometric model of capitalism, it is also much more than a simple continuation or reformulation of imperialism. A common misconception is that globalization is nothing more than U.S. economic imperialism, an extension or re-configuration of the British empire, a view which underplays the very complex relationship between capitalism, culture, and imperial power. The apparent "homogenization," "contamination," or neo-imperialism of globalization — terms that are commonly used to describe the phenomenon — may more fruitfully be described in post-colonial terms as a transcultural process, a process of interaction, appropriation, and transformation that resembles the colonial transformation of imperial cultures. Neither imperialism nor globalization can be described simply as programs of homogenization because their operations are characterized by multidirectional and transcultural interactions — operating rhizomatically, rather than hierarchically or centrifugally.

Post-colonial theory is so useful because it shows that this transcultural process begins at the level of subjectivity. Post-colonial cultures break the clear distinction between the identity of the colonizer and the identity of the colonized. And thus, as Bonaventure Santos puts it, in the case of Brazil:

post-colonial identity must be constructed in the margins of representation, and by a movement that goes from the margins to the center. This is the privileged space of culture and the post-colonial critic, a liminal, in-between or borderland space. Cultural enunciation creates its own temporality. This specific temporality is what renders possible the emergence of alternative modernities to western modernity, precisely by means of "post-colonial translation." The anti-colonial liberation struggle itself is hybrid and based on translation. It does not sustain itself either in precolonial ancestrality or in pure and simple mimicry of western liberal ideals [Santos, 14].

This "translation" process, which I call "transformation," describes various transcultural interactions between imperial powers and colonial cultures, and these have a correlation in one of the most interesting features of the present globalized world — the degree to which "local" modernities have come to characterize the global, in their adaptation of the principles and technologies of modernity to local cultural conditions.

Transformation is nowhere better demonstrated than in the appropriation and adaptation of colonial languages by post-colonial writers. The key revelation here is that individuals or local communities are not simply passively subjected to the weight of global forces. Achille Mbembe claims that "Like Islam and Christianity, colonization is a universalizing project. Its ultimate aim is to inscribe the colonized in the space of modernity" (Mbembe, 634). But if colonization was a universalizing project, did it succeed? Did it "inscribe" the colonized in the space of modernity, or did the colonized take hold of the pen and inscribe themselves in that space in a curious act of defiance modeled by post-colonial writers? Clearly, not only the post-colonial theory of global flows, but the specific example of post-colonial *literary* production provide a powerful model for the dynamic and productive relationship between the local and the global.

It is here, in the engagement of local communities and subjects with global forces, that post-colonial studies has most to offer. The example of post-colonial writers is a model for global flows and global articulations. But this example, and the future of post-colonial studies in global analysis, hinges on a subtle but critical distinction: post-colonial studies must reject the pressure to become the Grand Theory of Global Cultural Diversity because its distinctiveness lies in its engagement with the historical and material reality of colonialism and its effects. However, the strategies developed from the analysis of post-colonial cultural production can indeed produce models for the analysis of global interactions and for investigating the consequences of global mobility, diaspora, adaptation, and transformation. The analysis of the multiplicity of modernities is one signpost to a path down which post-colonial studies will be increasingly directed.

NOTES

1. In fact, I hadn't read *Orientalism* until *The Empire Writes Back* was published.

2. It is interesting to observe the regularity with which issues surrounding the sacred, religion, morality are relegated to the past. They are either medieval, "Victorian" or even a feature of the conservative 1950s. While Time is a prominent feature of Modernity it is always valued in the context of future change, of further "modernizing."

3. On November 11, 1995, Ken Sarowewa and eight others were executed by the Nigerian government, purportedly for speaking out about damage to the Niger River Delta by the Shell Oil Company. In his address to the tribunal Sarowewa said, "There is no doubt in my mind that the ecological war that the company has waged in the Delta will be called to question sooner than later and the crimes of that war be duly punished."

4. See for instance, a special issue of *Daedalus* 129, 1 on Multiple Modernities; see Feenberg; Appadurai; Gaonkar; Berger and Huntington; Cao; Cooper; Eisenstadt. See Gikandi for the post-colonial language of globalization studies.

WORKS CITED

Appadurai, Arjun. *Modernity at Large: Cultural Dimensions of Globalization.* Minneapolis: University of Minnesota Press, 1996.

Berger, Peter L., and Samuel P. Huntington. *Many Globalizations: Cultural Diversity in the Contemporary World.* Oxford: Oxford University Press, 2002.

Bhabha, Homi. *The Location of Culture.* New York: Routledge, 1994.

Chakrabarty, Dipesh. *Provincializing Europe: Post-Colonial Thought and Historical Difference.* Princeton, NJ: Princeton University Press, 2000.

Cooper, Frederick. *Colonialism in Question: Theory, Knowledge, History.* Berkeley: University of California Press, 2005.

Eisenstadt, S.N. *Comparative Civilizations and Multiple Modernities.* Leiden: Brill Academic, 2003.

_____. "Multiple Modernities." *Daedalus* 129,1 (Winter 2000): 1–29.

Featherstone, Mike, ed. *Global Culture, Nationalism, Globalization and Modernity.* London: Sage, 1990.

Featherstone, Mike, Scott Lash, and Roland Rash, eds. *Global Modernities.* London: Sage, 1995.

Feenberg, Andrew. *Alternative Modernity: The Technical Turn in Philosophy and Social Theory.* Berkeley: University of California Press, 1995.

Gaonkar, Dilip Parameshwar, ed. *Alternative Modernities.* Durham: Duke University Press, 2001.

_____. "On Alternative Modernities." In *Alternative Modernities*, 1–16.

Gikandi, Simon. "Globalization and the Claims of Post-Coloniality." *South Atlantic Quarterly* 100,3 (2001): 627–658.

Habermas, Jurgen. "Modernity vs. Postmodernity." *New German Critique* 22 (1981).

_____. *The Philosophical Discourse of Modernity.* Cambridge: Polity, 1987.

Kirkland, Frank, M. "Modernity and Intellectual Life in Black." John Pittman, ed. *African-American Perspectives and Philosophical Traditions.* New York: Routledge, 1997. 136–165.

Mbembe, Achille. "On the Power of the False." *Public Culture* 14 (2002).

Robertson, Roland. "Glocalization: Time-Space and Homogeneity-Heterogeneity." In Featherstone, Lash and Rash, 25–44.

_____. "Mapping the Global Condition: Globalization as the Central Concept." In Featherstone, 15–30.

Said, Edward. *The World, the Text and the Critic.* Cambridge: Harvard University Press, 1983.

Santos, Bonaventura de Sousa. "Between Prospero and Caliban: Colonialism, Post-Colonialism, and Inter-Identity." *Luso-Brazilian Review*, Special Issue on Portuguese Cultural Studies, 39,2 (Winter 2002): 9–43.

Smith, Adam. *An Inquiry into the Nature and Causes of the Wealth of Nations*. 1776. Ed. Edwin Cannan. New York: Modern Library, 1994.

Taylor, Charles. "Two Theories of Modernity." In Gaonkar, 172–96.

Wittrock, Bjorn. "Modernity: One None or Many? European Origins and Modernity as a Global Condition." *Daedelus* 129,1 (Winter 2000): 31–60.

Wolch, Jennifer, and Jody Emel, eds. *Animal Geographies: Place, Politics and Identity in the Nature-Culture Borderlands*. London: Verso, 1998.

"Pity the Poor Immigrant"
Pity and the Colony
DAVID PUNTER

To attempt to speak of pity is to embark on a difficult and problematic emotional and critical terrain. Pity, of course, should be an admirable emotion: it should signify a field of ways in which we sympathize and even empathize with those less fortunate than ourselves, those who are suffering, for example, and those who are displaced, rootless, homeless. Yet the problem with the term is that it inexorably shades off into less respected, even potentially contemptible, states of mind. On the one hand, it is all too easy for pity to become undifferentiable from self-pity: when we appear to pity the other, who is to say that we are not really pitying ourselves, seeing parts of our own personal plight emblematized in the travails of those objectively less fortunate than us. On the other hand, there is a constant danger of pity turning into — or being mistaken for — an attitude of condescension, such that what may begin as an act of compassion may, in the very moment of action, wherever physical or emotional, turn into a consolidation of the gap precisely between rich and poor, settled and rootless, secure and vulnerable which pity seems at first glance determined to overcome.

Put this way, the links with the diasporic are perhaps obvious. There is, for example, the major locus of pity in Wilfred Owen's "war, and the pity of war," for behind — and not far behind — much diaspora lie the stark, often hideous realities of war, although it remains true that diaspora can be driven by many things: not only by war but by persecution, by the realities of economics and relative economic deprivation, by psychological terror. Or it can be driven by the realization of previously unrealized oppression, by the possibility of new openings, or by escape from past or present collapse — of nation-states, of societies, of local communities. What we can say with certainty about diaspora under present conditions is that what has in the past been — or been regarded as — an exception is rapidly becoming the rule. The absolute dominance of U.S.-led commerce has pointed up more sharply than ever the disparity between wealth and poverty, while the exigencies of climate change will render it increasingly imperative for those from physically low-lying countries, which include many of the poorest, to make their way as best they can towards what we may call, both geographically and economically, "higher ground." In many ways we can see that what is happening today under conditions of so-called "advanced" global capitalism is precisely as the old scandal-monger Karl Marx had predicted, namely, the increasing development and subjugation of an alienated labor force in the name of the extraction of surplus profit. What Marx did not foresee — and neither did any of his nineteenth-century contemporaries, although H.G. Wells certainly had some inkling of what was to come — was that these developments would take place on a worldwide scale, so that entire countries and regions would find themselves pushed into the position of an industrial or post-industrial proletariat.[1]

There remain many questions to be asked about diaspora. If we think of the diasporic trend in Jewish, Filipino and Chinese communities, to take but three examples, we find radically different patterns, so different, in fact, that we might well find ourselves asking whether the term "diaspora" can be properly used in the singular (if "singular" is the issue) at all. One of the most complex of all diasporic patternings, of course, concerns the Caribbean, and one example among many is the "return" of West Indian inhabitants to Britain. The great poet Derek Walcott obliquely addresses this issue in, for example, the twenty-third poem from his sequence *Midsummer* (1984), which begins with a magnificently challenging equation between rioters in London and past imperial notions of the failings of the "native." Here, Walcott compares rioters to "leaves" that "race to extinction" as "they seethe towards autumn's fire — it is in their nature, /being men as well as leaves, to die for the sun" (Walcott, 483).

Certainly there is pity here for the rioters, who imagine, at whatever level of consciousness, that they are striking a blow for freedom while all the time they are merely being "tunneled," channeled, both physically but also through the gross operations of stereotyping, into a place where death clearly lurks. What renders this particular poem so startling, though, is that the dread realities of racism are expressed through a phrasing which has constant recourse to Shakespeare, and indeed this strange melding of violence and beauty runs right through the poem, as do questions of nationality and belonging. The-all-too common imagining by the immigrant of the beauty and superiority of the "host culture" which s/he is in some sense revisiting yet which has also always figured as an ideal to be achieved, to be striven towards, has been dissolved: the reality of the diasporic experience, when confronted with the mean realities of the policing of the Brixton riots, collapses and with it takes down the entire superstructure of culture on which the immigrant has been relying. "'But the blacks can't do Shakespeare, they have no experience,'" and "This was true. Their thick skulls bled with rancor/when the riot police and the skinheads exchanged quips" (*Ibid.*, 483).

And so there is experience and there is experience: on the one hand, triumphal experience sanctioned by the machinery of the State, on the other the pitiful experience of being at the receiving end of State violence. Was this addressed by Shakespeare? The poem leaves the question open as to whether even Shakespeare's powers to invoke pity (and where could pity be more startlingly evoked than, for instance, for another poor immigrant in *The Merchant of Venice*), or other feats of British culture including Turner's paintings, can adequately represent the bitter options — of rejection or assimilation — facing diasporic subjects in their continuing engagement with the host culture.

There is pity everywhere in Walcott: a pity which threatens to unman, to reduce one's individuality as a human and, in this case, as a male, to force one to return alone to the swamp. In that swamp, which Walcott so frequently depicts in his poem, "The Swamp," there are all sorts of relics of diaspora, pre-eminently among them those which remind us of the slave trade, that enforced diaspora which forms the model for so many diasporas, and imaginings of diaspora, since.

The St. Lucian Walcott's touch, however, upon these problems is often deceptively light and ironic, at least as compared with the Antiguan Jamaica Kincaid. In *A Small Place* (1988), Kincaid provides one of the most powerful and damning indictments of colonization ever written; yet in terms of diaspora, it necessarily raises definitional questions. Should the ceaseless attempts of European powers to subjugate in order to exploit poorer areas of the world be regarded as a diaspora of European citizens in its own right, or is the term best attached only to those who are forced from their locality by the incursion of a higher power? The answer is perhaps not as simple as it might at first appear, if only because the movement towards empire resulted in many people being sent out to wholly inhospitable and unsuitable environments in complete despite their own wishes; but Kincaid's concern, all too naturally, is with pity for those who have suffered, and continue to suffer, from these incursions.

This concern emerges in a particular way in Kincaid's 2002 book, *Mr. Potter*— a book which one hesitates to call a novel because at the end (although most readers will have suspected this all along) it emerges that Mr. Potter is in some (perhaps incompletely specified) way the narrator's father, which complicates the (auto)biographical levels of the text. However, this "revelation" simply intensifies the pity we feel for Mr. Potter, a character who, like so many similar ones in the work of postcolonial writers such as V.S. Naipaul, is unable to emerge from the anonymity in which he is sunk — paradoxically, of course, in light of the book which bears his name — and whose life is oddly summarized in the moment and circumstances of his death and burial:

> Hear Mr. Potter wending himself through the maze of his life in complete innocence, without ever knowing how like everyone else he was and without recognizing how ordinary is the uniqueness of life as it appears in each individual. Hear Mr. Potter, who was my father; hear his children and hear the women who bore those children; hear the end of life rushing like a predictable wave in a known ocean to engulf Mr. Potter. Hear Mr. Potter dead and lying on a cold slab of something and then his body placed in a wooden box but the wooden box cannot be placed in its grave, for the grave has filled up with water [Kincaid, 194].

The cry here is for a life to be *heard*; for pity for all those lives which are lived *in absentia*, as it were, lives like driftwood, to use a Walcottian image, which have no fixed location and which are unrecognized. This is one of the true kernels of diaspora: the sense that there is no belonging, there is never any possibility of belonging, there is only death and the pre-imagining of death, an inability to rise above the surface of a river which is always rushing onwards and whose course and flow the immigrant cannot discern or understand.

But then, we might fairly ask, can anybody understand these vast forces of displacement, forces which move whole populations and produce conflicts and misunderstandings which striate the world? One of the questions that the supposed arch-imperialist Rudyard Kipling asked was whether there was in fact anybody in control of these movements, these oppressions, these sufferings, or whether what we were seeing, what we were trying to make sense of in the elaboration and then the critique of empire, was the ceaseless, irrepressible expression of some animal instinct, something territorial and fatal, which affected all within its reach. This, certainly, is his approach in one of his most remarkable poems, "The Hyenas" (1919):

> After the burial-parties leave
> And the baffled kites have fled;
> The wise hyenas come out at eve
> To take account of our dead [Kipling, 328].

This is a far cry from the jingoistic Kipling of popular repute; this is instead a Kipling who is indeed seeing "war, and the pity of war" — if not in a directly diasporic context, then certainly in the context of those who die "in some corner of a foreign field," where they have been sent to fight and die for reasons which, we can only assume, are no more comprehensible to them than to the carrion-eating hyenas. Power, flight and the ubiquity of death are the keynotes here, as they are at the end of the poem when the hyenas: "tug the corpse to light,/And the pitiful face is shown again" (Kipling, 328).

The combination here of pity and shame runs through and through imperial and postcolonial writing, from the fear of shame endemic in Victorian *Boys' Own* books through to Salman Rushdie's *Shame* (1983), signifying the multifarious ways in which pity operates to spread a burden — of course in some sense the self-proclaimed "white man's burden"— which might otherwise be too terrifying to be borne. Pity, we might say, paraphrasing and in the process rather altering Aristotle's reflections on tragedy, is a response to terror; but the question of whether this terror can be truly selfless or remains a reflection of our own all too vivid imaginings of our helplessness, our vulnerability — in the end our fear of being returned to a childhood state of incomprehension and fear — remains open.

After Kipling, Paul Scott, author of *The Jewel in the Crown* (1966–75) and *Staying On* (1977), may now seem the least acceptable of white writers of empire, and there may be good reason for this. He begins the Prologue to *The Day of the Scorpion* (1968), the second in the *Jewel in the Crown* tetralogy, by describing an "encounter" (although it seems merely to have been that they passed each other by) with a Muslim woman in a mainly Hindu town, in a quarter inhabited by moneylenders:

> The feeling he had was that she was coming in search of a loan. She wore the *burkha*, that unhygienic head-to-toe covering that turns a woman into a walking symbol of inefficient civic refuse collection and leaves you without even an impression of her eyes behind the slits she watches the gay world through, tempted but not tempting; a garment in all probability inflaming to her passions but chilling to her expectations of having them satisfied. Pity her for the titillation she must suffer [Scott, 9].

The most remarkable thing about this passage in the context of the "pity" which the narrator claims, somewhat off-handedly, to feel for this passing street apparition with whom he has no actual contact of any kind, is the degree of inversion. He knows, of course, nothing of the reasons why she might be in this street (which, no doubt, might lead to other, quite different streets). The mention of "unhygienic" presumably means that he is already treating this woman as a physical object, considering her in the context of those bodily functions in terms of which she does not want to be considered; he is thus precisely invading the world of the *burkha*, feeling the frustration of a type of imagination which (like, it has to be said, most of the British romantic poets) he considers to be a God-given patriarchal right.

Such feelings among western men are, obviously, not uncommon; indeed, in such countries as France they may soon receive institutional sanction. However, the implicit comparison here between a *burkha*-clad woman and a pile of rubbish is extreme by any standards, and makes one wonder about the exact force of the term "refuse." Perhaps we should re-pronounce it: is it after all more about "refusal," the woman's refusal to accede to the power of the male gaze, than about "refuse"— or is the (occluded) point that they are both the same — that she who "refuses" is consigned to become "refuse," discarded matter? And in what way, one might similarly ask, does the narrator suppose this "garment" to be "inflaming to her passions"? Is this a cheap jibe at the way in which he is imagining that the *burkha* might chafe a woman's body, a kind of sidelong joke at the expense of female native customs, or is it again an inversion? It seems — or should seem even on a moment's reading — perfectly clear to everybody except the narrator that it is in fact the narrator's passions which are thus "inflamed"— inflamed through refusal, through implicit rejection, through the absence of power over that which cannot be approached in the usual terms of gender-based reduction to a scopic object.

Who, we might then ask, is it who is "destined" to "satisfy" these fantasized passions? Why, the narrator himself, we must presume; and thus we could, and surely should, also pass the notion of "titillation" on to him, and we can immediately see how this purported "pity" has turned already into "self-pity": into a sorrow for a desiring self lost in a world whose desires (if they exist at all) cannot be comprehended, a world which holds itself in reserve, a world where one's own quasi-diasporic presence does not receive the valuation it believes it should and where one might find oneself adrift in a sea of absence of meaning, so that in the end one collapses in self-pity, disallowed from providing the "proper' exercise of pity through domination.

Yet Scott, only a few pages later, is capable of seeing some of these issues from a different angle as he writes a diary in the voice of imprisoned ex–Chief Minister Mohammed Ali Kasim. "The English," he writes:

> send Kasim to prison. But it is Kasim who goes to prison. The prisoner in the zenana house is a man. But who is his jailer? The jailer is an idea. But in the prisoner the idea is embodied in a man. From his solitude the man reaches out to others. ... But he cannot reach them as people. They are protected from him by the collective instinct of their race. ... I understand ... why this should be. But to understand does not warm the heart [Scott, 54].

At first glance, this description may seem to resemble a Foucauldian analysis of discipline and punishment, but in fact it is quite differently focused. The issue here is not the need to display sovereignty through the usual historic means of, for example, torture and the display of the body in extreme pain; it is rather on a more insidious requirement of submission, in which the terms are unequal for the different but specific reason that the exercise of power is in the hands of those who have lost, or rather submerged, their individuality within an imperative of racial superiority. Pity, the passage seems to suggest, might be expected from individuals, even though that expectation may be constantly defeated; but can it be expected from a group, race, society, culture? If that were to be a possibility, what then, we might ask (although I have no space to pursue this issue here) would be the relationship between pity and that equally ambiguous term, strung as it is between theology and jurisprudence, "mercy"?

However: to see the connections between diaspora and pity in greater fullness, we can turn above all to the work of Joan Riley, who has documented the fate of Jamaican immigrants into the United Kingdom through a series of novels, including *The Unbelonging* (1985), which relentlessly depict the complex traps which beset diaspora and which place the reader in ever-increasing complications and convolutions of pity. In *Waiting in the Twilight* (1987), for example, the central figure Adella is a cleaner in London. In Jamaica, where she has come from, she had valued skills; but she has attracted a series of chronically unreliable lovers who have fathered her children and then abandoned her. Partially disabled now by a stroke, she is partly reliant on her children, who themselves demonstrate different degrees of assimilation to the England which is all they have known as (a kind of) home, but also bitterly determined to remain independent despite her multiple disabilities.

But our pity is most enjoined by the consequences of Adella's displacement; by the ways in which she is unable to accept the sins, crimes and infidelities of her former partners, particularly Stanton, whose return (impossible as the reader knows it to be) she has been in a sense awaiting all these years. Even on her death bed, she imagines his return:

> Everyone was there. All the children smiling at her. Loyal now. They had never blamed her, kept telling her how great she was, how much she did for them. ... Stanton had come back, just like she knew he would. He had come back and she had kept faith; and now he knew she had waited. The images flickered, faded slowly as her eyes dimmed [Riley, 165].

Stanton, it goes without saying, is not there; neither has he ever fulfilled any of his responsibilities as a father. Yet the ending of the novel leaves the reader with a series of enduring questions: they have to do with diaspora, and they have to do with pity.

The questions to do with diaspora are perhaps the more obvious ones. Adella is profoundly caught between nostalgia for her homeland, a nostalgia continually shown to be utterly without foundation, and a surviving sense that, somehow, her old faith in England as a country which will promise her justice and freedom may yet come through with the results of these promises despite the ever-present realities of injustice, racism, and insult which are all that seem to proffer themselves in practice — even on her deathbed we are made aware, through the more worldly voices of her children, that she is still being treated as, at best, a second-class citizen, and this is set off with the utmost pain against the fantasy world which she comes to inhabit as the terrible realities of her pain, illness, and imminent death overwhelm her — or rather, and perhaps this is the point, they do not overwhelm her; she remains in a strange sense protected from them, while it is we the readers who have to endure the terrible circumstances amid which she is dying.

The treatment meted out to Adella — by her bosses, by her fellow-workers, by her past partners, and even in some cases by her children themselves — makes for almost unbearable reading; one could conclude that she is kept going only by these fantasies in which Stanton, in particular, remains true to the promises he made. Yet the question inevitably arises as to whether pity is the right response to these issues. Adella is determined to the end to remain in some sense independent: although ceaselessly disappointed by the actions of others, she refuses to believe that her adopted homeland can be as cruel and heartless as it indeed appears to be. So she takes refuge in fantasy; but the question remains as to whether we, as readers, are to despise this as a retreat from what is going on around her, as a refusal to see the obvious as she is continually maltreated by the agencies of the State, or on the other hand to see this as the only sane recourse for someone who has been defeated in all her life's objectives, been stripped of her expertise, her hope, and eventually her life by an uncaring society.

The tremendous skill of *Waiting in the Twilight* (and it is true of others of Riley's works as well) is that it leaves us in a zone of response where all is uncertain. We feel the bitterness, certainly; we feel the pang of loneliness, of misunderstanding, of being unable to escape from the trap of stereotype — "you people" (Riley, 3), as her young white supervisor addresses her near the beginning of the story). Yet (some of) her children are impatient with her response to the world around her: they consider that perhaps she has not made sufficient effort to adjust, and so we are back again with the question, posed above by Walcott, whether assimilation or rejection are valid alternatives.

In the end, we might say that what happens to Adella is indeed "pitiless," in the sense that her fate is made to appear an inevitable consequence for the diasporic stranger, and therefore our pity may seem pointless, always already too late. Within the crevices, the haunted nooks and crannies of the host society, stories like Adella's, we suppose, are going on all the time while a kind of willed cultural amnesia (as again Walcott put it) is being practiced, and the danger for the reader is that the sense of pity might mutate into a useless crying over a situation which demands active political intervention rather than compassion for those who are excluded, indeed extruded, from the societal norm. But would this be the end of the story? The question we might ask — or be forced to ask — is whether political change can occur without, as it were, a prior ground of pity; whether we would ever be moved to action were it not for hearing, and sensing, stories like that of Adella. Or is the story of Adella, who in the end compromises with the terror around her by moving into fantasy, an example of how difficult, if not impossible, it is to effect political movement if we continue to reside in the movement of pity, which is, according to some accounts, necessarily ultimately self-absorbed, self-obsessed, self-defeating, fatally lacking in the will to move beyond the isolation of despair and into a more collective arena where pity will itself be rejected in favor of a more strenuous and defiant stance which will prevent us from falling again into the trap of self-loathing which can only play into the hands of the existing self-perpetuating power structures?[2]

NOTES

1. On this and many other issues to do with diaspora, see Sudesh Mishra, *Diaspora Criticism* (Edinburgh: Edinburgh University Press, 2006).

2. See also on some of these matters my *Postcolonial Imaginings: Fictions of a New World Order* (Edinburgh: Edinburgh University Press, 2000), especially pp. 45–60.

WORKS CITED

Kincaid, Jamaica. *Mr. Potter*. London: Farrar Strauss Giroux, 2002.
Kipling, Rudyard. "The Hyenas," in *Collected Poems of Rudyard Kipling*. London: Wordsworth Editions, 1994.
Riley, Joan. *Waiting in the Twilight*. London: Women's, 1987.
Scott, Paul. *The Day of the Scorpion*. London: Heinemann, 1968.
Walcott, Derek. *Midsummer*, XXIII, in *Collected Poems 1948–1984*. London: Faber & Faber, 1992.

From Colonial Outsider to Postcolonial Insider

Screen Adaptations from Australia and New Zealand/Aotearoa

JANET WILSON

Literature, Film and the Nation State

The changing relationship between the nation state and its culture in an era of globalization and transnationalism has come under revised scrutiny during the last two decades. Assumptions such as that the institution of literature is in the service of the nation state or of nationalism were interrogated, for example, by Simon During in 1990, who pointed out that literature works in different social spaces than nationalism, employing different signifying practices, and that the legitimization of nationhood is not a necessary criterion for canonization of a work of literature (During, 138–153). More recently Bill Ashcroft has articulated a position for subjects beyond the boundaries of nationalism and the state in defining the "transnation," a space of potentiality that works within and across the national cultural borders, and the "literary transnation," which has a transformative function because of the utopian function of literature: the imagination's power to envisage a better or different world (Ashcroft, 72–85). The necessary but unstable relationship between the nation and its cultural products is particularly true of cinema, which like literature operates outside as well as within nationalism, being transnational or global in its audience appeal, and inevitably dependent on corporate finances and international co-productions as adjuncts or alternatives to state patronage and funding. National frameworks for the production, reception, and interpretation of cinema persist, nevertheless. In his recent book on New

Zealand cinema, Bruce Babington acknowledges the challenge to the concept of a national cinema in a global era in which boundaries are necessarily more fluid, but he points out that a national cinema is still a force in terms of state policy, because necessary for "registering the lived complexities of... national life" and, in more traditional terms, for offering "coherent images of the nation," "sustaining the nation at an ideological level, exploring what is understood to be the 'indigenous,'" and he argues for a more plural and hybridized concept of the nation than these earlier commentators (Babington, 16).

This essay proposes to draw on such reformulations of the relationship between literature and the nation as During's and Ashcroft's, as well as modified concepts of a national cinema such as Babington's. It claims that screen adaptations of foundational myths and stories, including their recirculation cinematically, intercept with and develop the national imaginary for global and local audiences. Feature films based on written texts and stories provide renewed engagement with the issues and themes of the original narratives. Recurring motifs that are central to the construction of the national imaginary, notably the Lost Child in Australia and the Man Alone in New Zealand/ Aotearoa, are not only reformulated for local consumption by producers and scriptwriters, but also are pushed beyond national boundaries in order to intersect with and interpenetrate other cultural narratives and images. Phil Noyce's feature film, *Rabbit Proof Fence* (2002), which revisits the Lost Child motif, belongs, for example, to the changing cultural climate inaugurated by the national enquiry into the Lost Generation of aboriginal children of mixed race who were taken from their families in order to be assimilated into white Australian culture. Both the enquiry's report, *Bringing Them Home* (1997) and the film had an enormous impact on Australians, and the film's popularity overseas demonstrates the wide appeal on screen of its literary precursor, Doris Pilkington/Nugi Garimara's *Follow the Rabbit Proof Fence* (1996).[1] In challenging received ideas of national identity and belonging through adapting to the screen colonial stories and other non-fictional genres such as reports, historical accounts, diaries and autobiographies, the cinematic medium demarcates the older form of modernity structured through notions of hierarchy from the concept of a symbolic economy of a new global culture, rooted through reciprocity (Krishnaswamy, 8–9).

Literature and film have always operated to some degree outside nationalism (as the global dissemination of texts implies), and literary and cinematic texts are valued for reasons other than reinforcing nationhood. Yet art forms that recirculate key images of the nation contribute to the renewal of national identity by appropriating the very global forces of production that are often identified as undermining the nation state, and the texts thereby often encourage a more self-reflexive nationalism and assertion of cultural authority. The success of Peter Jackson's *Lord of the Rings* trilogy (2001–2003), in New Zealand/Aotearoa, for example, which brought together overseas actors with local production skills and technical expertise, encouraged the Clark government to use a policy of cultural renewal in linking nationalism to its agenda of economic transformation (Williams, 183). Screen adaptations also renew national identity by exploiting productively the time lag from the original text, introducing the insights of a new generation, including critiques of gender and class ideologies through a free response to the original script rather than faithful adaptation. This essay examines three feature films that, in adapting key narratives of national belonging, have helped reshape the national imaginary by reflecting back to the nation a slightly altered (because externally addressed and distanced) mirror image of itself, so promoting national self-reassessment: Peter Weir's 1975 film, *Picnic at Hanging Rock*, adapted from the 1968 novel by Joan Lindsay; Roger Donaldson's 1978 film *Sleeping Dogs*, adapted from C.K. Stead's 1971 political thriller inspired by the Vietnam War, *Smith's Dream*; and Brad McGann's 2004 production of *In My Father's Den*, adapted from Maurice Gee's 1972 novel of the same title (Lindsay, 1998; Stead, 1971; Gee, 1977).

The reception of the three films, although thirty years apart, confirms cinema's role in re-evaluating the cultural value of the original texts and in reshaping the national imaginary. Cinema creates new horizons of expectation and alternative audiences for key national narratives. The novels on which each film is based have gained a new lease of life following the cinematic release, with reprints bearing cover designs that feature iconic images from the films. Now redesigned for overseas distribution, the book covers feature blurbs that allude to the impact of the novel-as-film, thus emphasizing the story's increased social relevance. *Sleeping Dogs*, for example, has long been identified with a turning point in local history and politics, a defining moment in the nation's narrative, as reprints of Stead's novel point out. In depicting a modern dystopia — New Zealand as a fascist state under martial law ruled by a dictator and split between special troops, backed up by American special forces, and factions of opposing guerrilla forces — the film (more than the novel) has been seen as prescient of the civil unrest caused by the 1981 Springbok Tour. In particular, that the Special Police were dressed in helmets and boiler-suits and carried batons made them uncannily resemble the Red and Blue Escort Squads of 1981.[2] This episode from the film is imaged on the cover of the 1993 reprint of *Smith's Dream* deliberately recalling the 1981 crisis, a time when, according to the *Sunday Star Times* comment on the cover, "Stead's own dream of police lines dividing the people of New Zealand came true for so many." Recent New Zealand cinema has also played a significant role in promoting the nation as a tourist destination for overseas audiences.

Both the economy and the national image have benefited from the cinematic profiling and reinterpretation of New Zealand's landscape as "middle erd" in the *Lord of the Rings* trilogy, with new tourist ventures featuring the trilogy's landscapes, while Niki Caro's film, *Whale Rider* (2003), adapted from Witi Ihimaera's novella, *The Whale Rider* (1987) drew to international attention the small village of Whangaroa where the filming took place — and where the completed waka (war canoe), a prop for much of the film and central to the ending, is now located (Wood, 17). The original preoccupations of the novels are renewed, expanded, and ideologically reinflected in the screen adaptations, and the film versions vastly exceed the reach and impact of the prior print medium.

The Lost Child: *Picnic at Hanging Rock*

One of the best-known examples of national cinema's extending literature's role in signifying national history, identity, and heritage is Peter Weir's production of *Picnic at Hanging Rock*, which on its release in 1975 became the break-through film of the Australian film renaissance. Joan Lindsay's novel *Picnic at Hanging Rock* (1968), on which the film is based, draws on a central topos in the Australian psyche, the Lost Child, a motif which epitomizes a central trauma of the white settler experience of the desert.[3] Circulating in both oral and literary narratives since colonization, the trope recurs in numerous real-life stories, some of which have been adapted to the screen: for example, Doris Pilkington's semi-autobiographical story of her aboriginal mother's journey in *Rabbit Proof Fence* was adapted to the film with the same title; the story of Azaria Chamberlain, adapted from the novel by John Bryson, has the cinematic title of *Evil Angels* (1988); and Nicholas Roeg's classic feature film, *Walkabout* (1971) is partly based on a novel, *The Children* (1959), by James Vance Marshall. The Lost Child motif emerged originally out of a nexus of pre-existing Australian anxieties: the perennial struggle between nurture and nature that draws on negative concepts of Australia as the inhospitable mother country and a culture that excludes women.[4] These tensions between the white settler and the hostile environment are played out in a series of archetypal contrasts in *Picnic at Hanging Rock*: images of the outback, symbolized by the brooding, anthropomorphic presence of rock with its teeming wildlife, are presented in sharp contrast to the monolithic, rectangular shape of Mrs. Appleyard's College. Weir follows Lindsay in shifting the focus from the male outback pioneers of the late nineteenth century to women who are little more than constructions of the patriarchal social order, "pawns in the Australian social landscape," and "objects of male adoration."[5] In this and in other ways,

Weir's film, like the two New Zealand films under discussion, illustrates the preoccupations and limitations of the 1970s, the era in which the Australian film revival began. All reflect the male monopoly of screen production and the prevailing monocultural, masculine, white-settler definitions of national identity (Simpson *et al.*, 22; Campbell, 211).

Under Weir's direction, the Lost Child narrative is represented partly allegorically as a form of primitive seduction of three nubile teenage girls and one of their teachers, whose elaborate but incongruous Victorian attire suggests their vulnerability to nature, symbolized by the preternaturally ancient Hanging Rock. Their disappearance, significantly on Saint Valentine's Day, 14 February 1900, as if sacrificial victims to the God of Love, by being devoured or seduced, is marked by the Rock's brooding, menacing appearance, suggestively evoked in Gheorge Zamfir's "Flute de Pan," the film's signature music.[6] Weir also expands Lindsay's contrasts of class and nationality: the English aristocrat, Michael Fitzhubert (played by Dominic Guard), who falls in love with Miranda (the "Botticelli angel" who leads the others into the rock) and returns to search for her, and Albert (played by John Jarrett), the orphaned Australian coachman (who Weir, in his visual economy, casts as the dark "other" to the Aryan, golden-headed Michael), who rescues Michael after he falls unconscious on the rock, thereby ensuring the recovery and survival of Irma, one of the three lost girls.[7] Both young men exist outside the nature-nurture loop in which the women are trapped, and Albert, the true survivor, is associated with "indigenous" Australia in his physical resourcefulness and instinctive awareness of outback dangers. Weir reinforces Australian cultural nationalism in relation to the defining trope of the Australian bush, imaged as both mysterious and threatening, a space that succeeds in disorienting the European subject. Upper-class British colonial life, epitomized in the genteel ambience of Appleyard College, the stifling close fitting outfits of the young women, and the increasingly deranged figure of Mrs. Appleyard, the headmistress, is depicted as out of place, alienated from the pre–European, primeval forces residing in the Australian outback. *Picnic at Hanging Rock* expands on the symbolic innuendo of the Lost Child, and as Alison Rudd points out, shows "the chasm opening up between Britain's imperial assumptions and the new society's emergent myth of belonging based on the need to adapt to the landscape" (Rudd, 117).

Man Alone: *Sleeping Dogs*

A similar foundational motif appears in New Zealand colonial culture in the early twentieth century: the Man Alone trope was formative to the cultural nationalism associated with the masculine literary tradition that dominated in the 1930s and 1940s, and like the American Adam, a symbol of the innocent solitary in nineteenth-century American literature, the Man Alone trope was so ubiquitous as to resemble a Jungian archetype representing an unconscious collective self-identification.[8] A paradoxical figure of both existential alienation and self-sufficiency, the Man Alone resists commitment to marriage, domesticity, or a political cause, and he reacts against the prevailing social structures, often exploding under their pressure. Less a hero than the victim of a puritanical, philistine, and materialistic society, he also displays attributes of the rebel (Jones, 213). The Lost Child, the Man Alone, and the American Adam are all frontier myths stemming from the experiences of isolation in rural settler societies and the encounter with the harsh, unyielding environment. But the behavior pattern of the Man Alone also points to the uncertain identity structures that existed after New Zealand's break from Britain, reflecting what Mark Williams sees as the fundamental weakness of Pakeha nationalism, because New Zealand, unlike Australia, defined itself less by "acts of filial rebellion" against the imperial center than by "maintaining muted links with the parent culture" (Williams, 183–184). Cultural displacement is particularly evident in the ur-text, *Man Alone* (1939) by John Mulgan, whose hero, Johnson, survives a testing ordeal in an encounter with the New Zealand wilderness, while in psychological terms he displays the reduced subjectivity and limited identity structures of the deracinated migrant Englishman who does not belong fully to either culture (D'Cruz and Ross, 32, 34; Fox, 265).

Maurice Gee's early novel, *In My Father's Den* (1972), is another classic portrait of the Man Alone, one which stresses his psychological imprisonment due to his literal and metaphorical withdrawal, emotional retardedness, and non-conformity. Unlike Mulgan's Johnson, Gee's protagonists are associated with the repressive codes of secular Puritanism, a deeply entrenched force in the national psyche in the early twentieth century. This was manifested as a powerful work ethos, a fear of sentimentality, a concern with respectability, a hatred of extravagance, and, in the younger generation, a tendency to swing to the extreme of over-indulgence in reaction against the strict moral code of the parents.[9] *In My Father's Den* demonstrates both aspects in the characters of its *bon vivant*, and sexually free-wheeling narrator, Paul Prior, and Paul's driven, sexually repressed brother, Andrew, both of whom suffer from maternal deprivation, and their mother's joylessness and lack of love (Fox 38, 50). The isolation into which Puritanism thrusts its characters, the self-sufficiency and dislike of commitment, is also a feature of Stead's political thriller, *Smith's Dream* (1971). But, as Lawrence Jones points out, the Man Alone figure is demythologized with successive rehandlings and becomes more complex; sympathy for the figure diminishes after the 1950s, and by the 1970s, when the two novels were written, his loner, rebel personality becomes either more inward-looking and guilt-ridden or, instead, the subject of satire (Jones, 214). Stead's novel shows the extreme threat to the Man Alone's individual self-sufficiency stemming from civil conflict promoted by fascist forces, while Gee's exposes the negative effects of puritanical rectitude on his psyche. The cinematic adaptations take these perceptions into new directions while retaining some links with the trope's original literary articulations.

Roger Donaldson's *Sleeping Dogs*, the first 35 mm, color, feature-length fictional film made in New Zealand, not only marks the beginning of the nation's new wave cinema, but is also rated as the first significant literary adaptation for film (Martin and Edwards, 64; Donnell, 101–107). For most of the movie, apart from the ending, the narrative follows that of *Smith's Dream*. The "Man Alone" is Smith (played by Sam Neill), who leaves his family because his wife is having an affair with his best friend, Bullen (played by Ian Mune), and chooses to live in solitude on an island off the Coromandel. This enigmatic behavior points to an underlying sensitivity and vulnerability that is associated with Maurice Gee's characters, who classically use withdrawal as a form of self-protection, rather than relying on the tough-guy, macho indifference which is characteristic of the pioneering colonial Man Alone figure. According to Russell Campbell, the film has achieved its iconic status by redefining the male Kiwi stereotype in New Zealand cinema, although such a transition had already occurred in the literature (Campbell, 211). Like Stead's novel and Mulgan's *Man Alone*, the Smith of *Sleeping Dogs* resists political involvement. He is the little man who is pulled into big events and forced to take sides, as he reluctantly finds himself joining the guerrillas, the Vietnam-style partisans living in the Coromandel, who are led by Bullen and oppose the martial law imposed by the country's dictator. In this dystopian drama about a society threatened by a brutally repressive government in which ordinary apolitical people like Bullen and Smith's wife, Gloria, are driven into opposition, Smith's lack of commitment and ambivalence about violence cannot last long.

Film critic Brian Donnell has noted that the most crucial change to Stead's story is in the characterization of Smith, who in the novel lives up to the ambivalent "Man Alone" image by abandoning the rebels and striking out on his own, but who returns in the film to the rebels' camp to rescue Bullen, who has been wounded (Donnell, 105). Stead describes Smith's journey through the bush and forest in ways that recall Johnson's marathon crossing of the Kaimanawa ranges in *Man Alone*. His Smith also shows existential angst in questioning the need to surrender his freedom to join any party. But Donaldson and his script-writer, Ian Mune, change these familiar tropes by heightening the action and introducing a completely new theme — that of renewed mateship when the odds are stacked against the pair. The two men, wounded by gunfire and helicopter strafing from the Special Forces, stumble across the range through a hail of bullets and bombs from air force fighter planes, meeting their death on the other side. The movie has been criticized mainly by overseas reviewers for its narrative flaws such as its over-lengthy ending, the lack of explanation for Smith's actions, the clichéd outcome as "a routine psychological drama about the forced reconciliation between rivals in love" (Cagin). Donnell points out that Donaldson may have turned to the genres of Hollywood cinema, namely the buddy movie, because Smith's last defiant minutes are strongly reminiscent of the endings of such movies as *Butch Cassidy and the Sundance Kid*, *Midnight Cowboy*, and *Easy Rider* that were popular in the 1970s (Donnell, 106).

Certainly, in presenting Smith as a rebel to the end, as a heroic martyr in death, while also demonstrating good-guy qualities (carrying the badly wounded Bullen and admitting that he had walked out on his family prematurely), *Sleeping Dogs* flattens the psychological complexity of his literary counterpart in *Smith's Dream*. But Donaldson's formulaic use of the codes of the action thriller genre to show the impact of political events on the lives of ordinary New Zealanders, along with the hints of moral complexity about the need for political commitment, gave the film widespread popularity in New Zealand (Martin and Edwards, 64), and it retains a vital role in the national imaginary because, as Donnell points out, both novel and film experience renewed relevance whenever civic unrest is manifested (Donnell, 102–103). *Sleeping Dogs* is a seminal film. It anticipated the rise of the action thriller, the New Zealand version of the road movie such as *Good-bye Pork Pie* and *Smash Palace*, and the later embodiment of the cultural archetype of the Man Alone who blends macho aggression, a distrust of authority, and a "countercultural rebelliousness" in these and other movies made in the 1980s that star the actor Bruno Lawrence (Spicer, 3).

Man Alone and Puritanism:
In My Father's Den

In contrast to Stead's political thriller, Maurice Gee's crime novel, *In My Father's Den*, explores the psychological consequences of Puritanism (as imaged in the mother's repressive moral righteousness and hostility to any overt physicality, including any form of sexual expression) upon family members. The father retreats to his den, a separate space from the domestic sphere that serves as a shelter. The two sons show pathological dysfunction: Paul Prior, the anti-puritan rebel narrator, is unable to form lasting relationships, and his sexually repressed brother, Andrew, displays archetypal Man-Alone behavior in the irrational act which constitutes the novel's crime — his murder of the school-girl, Celia Inverarity. Brad McGann's film, made 32 years after Gee's novel was written, explores the Man Alone's psychological isolation and social alien-ation in explicitly psychoanalytic terms, through a cinematic investigation of Paul Prior's thoughts and feelings, through his attempts to uncover the mys-teries of the past and to understand himself through the operation of memory. McGann uses flashback in adapting the first-person retrospective narrator who, in the novel, blends showing and telling in piecing together fragments of the past with its silences and repressions, and those fragments are then jux-taposed with scenes from the present which he is trying to understand (Fox, 38). Amplifying this visual representation of Paul's psychology and emotions is a sound track of international music, both classical and popular, allusions to iconic figures of New Zealand literature, and references to contemporary world affairs in Paul Prior's earlier vocation as a war reporter. All widen the scope of Gee's investigation of provincial dysfunction, identified as peculiar to the New Zealand experience, so enhancing the film's appeal.

McGann's is an emotional response to Gee's novel, an imitation rather than an adaptation. Paul Prior (played by Matthew MacFayden), is now a photographer of war atrocities in war-torn Bosnia who has returned to New Zealand on the occasion of his father's funeral (not a school teacher as in the novel, although later he takes up school teaching); the setting shifts from West Auckland in the novel to Roxburgh in Otago; the murder, the catalyst for the novel's story, is announced only half way through in the film; the mur-derer is not Paul's repressed, God-fearing Puritan brother, Andrew, but Andrew's wife who kills Celia by accident; and finally, the repressive mother who survives in the novel, commits suicide in the film. McGann succeeds in overturning the whole puritan scheme of sexual prohibition, the highly reg-ulated sense of conscience, and the powerful corrective sense of guilt and shame that the mother in the novel imposes (or tries to impose) on her sons, only hinting at this in the finale when Andrew's strange behavior is explained as due to his mother's influence (Fox, 267).

McGann follows Gee's novel in showing Paul as psychologically isolated upon his return to New Zealand: unable to take up again his earlier vocation as a photographer because of his haunted memories of Bosnian war victims, he lacks any real reason for staying. But his meeting and friendship with Celia, a student, catalyzes his attempt to try and understand the troubling events of his earlier life by re-experiencing and hence reconstructing meaning through the movements of his consciousness (and his unconscious) in dream, memory, and reflection. This self-examination takes place in the den, the troubled site of past transgressions. In the film, McGann daringly develops into a new mystery an incident only hinted at in Gee's novel, concerning the paternity of Celia with whose mother, Jackie in the film (Joyce Poole in the novel), he had had a sexual liaison years earlier, before he left New Zealand. The question arises that Celia might be Paul's daughter, but in a revelation which comes to Paul in a reverie, it seems that his deceased father had also had a sexual encounter with Jackie, and so the possibility exists that Paul's father could also be Celia's father! This is the shameful secret that Paul has to confront in his attempts to come to terms with the past, replacing the psychological struggle delineated in the novel, caused by the mother's repressive love and her attachment to his mongoloid brother.

In developing this oedipal plot strand, McGann strikes a blow at the Puritan ethos of the novel in which the father should embody the law of God in imposing a moral order. Paul's father in the novel had stepped outside this role by avoiding his wife and seeking refuge in the den. The film goes further in pointing to the father's violation of the moral law, by conducting illicit sexual relations in the den. Gee's emphasis on psychological dysfunction due to the Puritan loathing of sex and its outcome in a heinous crime is displaced through the film's visual emphasis on the workings of memory as Paul, through the stimulus of Celia, a shadow or ghost of his former love, her mother, tries to come to terms with his father's transgressions, as well as seeking images of his lost mother. Critic Laurence Simmons has identified how memory, dream, and reflection coalesce in the double flashback at the emotional core of the film in which reverie, inspired by a soundtrack from Patti Smith's album *Horses*, enables Paul to recall his liaisons both with Celia (in the den) and at an earlier phase of his life with her mother (in his bedroom in a sequence played by different actors) when the same tracks were played. As he points out, the title of Gee's novel acquires added significance as McGann repositions the den as a locale of psychological change and growth, in which Paul comes out from the shadow of his father through rejection, forgetting, and remembering, in a process which can be read as allegorical — a way of escaping the father-nation with its puritan stranglehold (Simmons, 195–196).

Global symbols reinforce McGann's "refitting" of Gee's early 1970s story for the twenty-first century: an image of Hope (taken from a painting in the Tate Gallery in London), the atlas and globe, the international star, Dame Kiri te Kanawa singing the haunting "Bailero" (from *Songs of the Auvergne*). Travel and the future frame the characters' fears and desires: Paul's anxiety that he will not overturn his father's shameful secret on returning to New Zealand and Celia's longing to travel to Spain, her ambitions to write. The intertexts of Gee's novel — Walt Whitman's *Leaves of Grass*, and James Hogg's *Memories and Confessions of a Justified Sinner*, titles which fuelled the community's suspicion and condemnation of Paul Prior for Celia's murder — are replaced by markers of the national literary culture: James K. Baxter's poem "High Country Weather," which Paul's father recites, and Janet Frame's novel *Owls do Cry*, which Paul retrieves from her backpack after the murder. Most radical in McGann's adaptation of Gee's novel, however, is what he calls his anti-linear narrative: the poetic cinematic sequences are interwoven with the murder narrative to the point where they cross-over and reframe it — thereby making the audience intimate with the processes of psychological reconstruction through showing a mixture of events of lived experience with the signs they bear of the affective capacities of cinema itself (Simmons, 197).

Conclusion: Twenty-first Century Screen Adaptations

New Zealand and Australian screen adaptations in recent feature films have significantly reinterpreted dominant core motifs of their white-settler cultures in response to social and cultural change by engaging with national issues and identity structures in ways that convey a wider relevance. In Australia, the effect of the *Bringing Them Home* national enquiry made many white Australians accept for the first time the burden of guilt, a moral awareness that was ratified in 2008 when the Rudd government issued a formal apology. *Rabbit Proof Fence's* narrative of the Stolen Child revises the Lost Child motif through reference to "white Australia's" national policies on race, providing new moral and social dimensions in contrast to the symbolism that accrued round stories like *Picnic at Hanging Rock*, in which mystery brings with it a sense of disempowerment. It also overturns earlier versions of the motif in narrative terms, although still framed for white audiences; the story is told from an indigenous perspective, actors identifiable as Aboriginal were chosen, and the stolen children find their way home (Wood, 11–12). The emblematic lost child who is abducted and abandoned by white Australian society also mirrors the victimization of poor and working-class children in other cultures whose families could not support them.[10] The social amnesia about these acts of abuse and betrayal has found echoes, for example, in the United Kingdom where groups of institutionalized children were shipped off to Australia in the 1930s.

Although 27 years apart, both Donaldson's *Sleeping Dogs*, and McGann's *In My Father's Den*, as adaptations that depart from the narrative formats associated with Man Alone motif, help reshape the masculinist tradition that monopolized the cultural nationalism of the 1930s to the 1970s. Although many films produced since the late 1970s, in their concern over masculine and collective identity structures, show a cultural force which is traceable to the literature of the 1930s, the final moments of *Sleeping Dogs*, which glorify Smith's death as a defiant stand against injustice and dictatorship, overturn the more ambiguous, inward, insular figure of the earlier era in a new-found social relevance (Murray, 247). Smith's heroism illustrates the individual's potential to make a difference, so anticipating some of the causes of civil unrest in New Zealand of the early 1980s. In 2004, McGann's assault on the Puritanism of Gee's novel reflects the confidence of New Zealand cinema since the new wave of the early 1990s, and his ambitious interpretation of Gee's story revises its core nationalism in keeping with the potentialities of the visual medium. McGann's *In My Father's Den* suggests the power of cinema as part of a wider culture narrative to promote a different experience of storytelling, one associated with the image-making power of cinema. Both productions offer the remnants of their original context in the new cinematic medium, with Donaldson's hinting at what will come in the film-making of the 1980s, and McGann's representing a trace of what has vanished.[11]

Yet McGann's film also shows cinema participating in the globalized cultural economy with its complex transnational cultural flows. Simmons invokes cultural nationalism in acclaiming the way *In My Father's Den* places local audiences in a New Zealand location with which they were intimately familiar, and his testimony of a collective pleasure in viewing McGann's revised national myth recalls Arjun Appadurai's concept of a "community of sentiment," one which is powerful enough to generate a sense of identity and allegiance, in Simmons's view, to transform national identity in relation to a system of cultural representation (Appadurai, 8). In claiming that viewing the film is like occupying a "secret space or 'den' which each of us might recognize, and in which each of us might play," he underlines the shift in perception.[12] Far from being on the outer of society, the Man Alone figure through exploring and reflecting his alienated condition in the visual medium of cinema, gives life "to images that claim us and that form our history," that "confirm our place" by staying with us and forming "an enigmatic centre of ourselves" (Simmons, 197). Simmons's metaphor of the "den" of the cinematic experience also points to the new global order in which people use their imagination in the practice of their everyday lives (Appadurai 5), because the communal sharing of the attractions and secrets of filmic engagement suggests this is a new space for the individual reshaping of national identity.

Notes

1. See Felicity Collins and Therese Davis, *Australian Cinema After Mabo* (Cambridge: Cambridge University Press, 2004), 133, and Adi Wimmer, *Australian Film: Cultures, Identities,*

Texts (Trier: WVT Wissenschaftlicher Verlag, 2007), 50. Wimmer points out that widespread praise from critics, the film was a commercial failure.

2. In a special features discussion in the 2008 reissue of the film, one of the special effects men commented that in dressing the special forces they used rolled-up newspaper painted black for batons, boiler suits and cyclists' crash helmets.

3. On visual representations of this "Ur-angst" in the Australian psyche see Wimmer, *Australian Film: Cultures, Identities, Texts*, 83–88.

4. Pablo Armellino, *Ob-Scene Spaces in Australian Narrative: An Account of the Socio-topographic Construction of Space in Australian Literature* (Stuttgart: Ibidem-Verlag, 2009), 77, citing Kay Schaffer, "Woman and the Bush: Australian National Identity and Representations of the Feminine," *Antipodes* 3,1 (1989): 3–17.

5. Armellino, *Ob-Scene Spaces*, 78, 79. In Armellino's symbolic reading the two girls and their teacher who vanished had "metaphorically overstepped the boundaries of patriarchal society" (86).

6. On Weir's decision to use the techniques of European art-house, see Jonathan Rayner, *The Films of Peter Weir* (London: Continuum, 2003), 61.

7. Class conflict is subordinated to the myth of unity and nostalgia characteristic of the AFC film's nationalist discourses. See Wimmer, *Australian Film*, 36–37.

8. Janet Wilson, "Intertextual Strategies: Reinventing the Myths of Aotearoa in Contemporary New Zealand Fiction," in *Across the Lines: Intertextuality and Transcultural Communication in the New Literatures in English*, ed. Wolfgang Kloos (Amsterdam: Rodopi, 1998), 271–291 (278), citing Roland F. Anderson, "The Rise and Fall of the Man Alone?" *ARIEL: A Review of English Literature* 16.4 (1985): 97.

9. Patrick Evans, "The Provincial Dilemma: After *The God Boy*," *Landfall* 117 (March 1976): 34. Evans points out that the New Zealand novel features "parents who are Puritans and children who are alienated."

10. For a study of these transitions see Peter Pierce, *The Country of Lost Children: An Australian Anxiety* (Cambridge: Cambridge University Press, 1999).

11. Williams, "A Waka on the Wild Side," 184–185. Williams identifies a group of films — *Scarfies* (1999), *Stickmen* (2000) and *The Price of Milk* (2000) — which recode the signs and markers of New Zealand identity rather than wrestle with it. In *The Price of Milk*, Man Alone is domesticated, suggesting the collapse of this figure into comedy and satire.

12. Simmons, "The Story of Our Lives," 193–194.

Works Cited

Anderson, Roland F. "The Rise and Fall of the Man Alone?" *ARIEL: A Review of English Literature* 16, 4 (1985): 97.

Appadurai, Arjun. *Modernity at Large: Dimensions of Globalization*. Minneapolis: University of Minnesota Press, 1996.

Armellino, Pablo. *Ob-Scene Spaces in Australian Narrative: An Account of the Socio-topographic Construction of Space in Australian Literature*. Stuttgart: Ibidem-Verlag, 2009.

Ashcroft, Bill. "The Transnation." *Rerouting the Postcolonial: New Essays for the New Millennium*. Eds. Janet Wilson, Cristina Sandru, and Sarah Lawson Welsh. London: Routledge, 2009. 72–85.

Babington, Bruce. *A History of the New Zealand Fiction Feature Film*. Manchester: Manchester University Press, 2007. 16.

Cagin, Seth. "Film 2." *The Soho News* 9 March 1982.

Campbell, Russell. "The Kiwi Bloke: The Representation of Pakeha Masculinity in New Zealand Film." In *Contemporary New Zealand Cinema*. Eds. Ian Conrich and Stuart Murray. New York: Macmillan, 2008. 211–224.

Collins, Felicity, and Therese Davis. *Australian Cinema After Mabo*. Cambridge: Cambridge University Press, 2004.

Donnell, Brian. "Sleeping Dogs." *The Cinema of Australia and New Zealand*. Eds. Geoff Mayer and Keith Beattie. London: Wallflower, 2007.

During, Simon. "Literature — Nationalism's Other? The Case for Revision." *Nation and Narration*. Ed. Homi K. Bahbha. London: Routledge, 1990. 138–153.

Evans, Patrick. "The Provincial Dilemma: After *The God Boy*." *Landfall* 117 (March 1976).

Fox, Alistair. "Inwardness, Insularity and the Man Alone: Postcolonial Anxiety in the New Zealand Novel." *Postcolonial Masculinitie*s, special issue guest-edited by Stephanie Newell, *Journal of Postcolonial Writing* 45,3 (September 2009): 263–272.

_____. *The Ship of Dreams: Masculinity in Contemporary New Zealand Fiction*. Dunedin: Otago University Press, 2008.

Gee, Maurice. *In My Father's Den*. 1972. Wellington: Oxford University Press, 1977.

Jones, Lawrence. *Barbed Wire and Mirrors: Essays on New Zealand Prose*. Dunedin: University of Otago Press, 1987.

Krishnaswamy, Revathi. "Introduction: At the Crossroads of Postcolonial and Globalization Studies." *The Post-Colonial and the Global*. Eds. Revathi Krishnaswamy and John C. Hawley. Minneapolis: University of Minnesota Press, 2007. 8–9.

Lindsay, Joan. *Picnic at Hanging Rock*. 1968. London: Vintage, 1998.

Martin, Helen, and Sam Edwards. *New Zealand Film 1912–1996*. Auckland: Oxford University Press, 1997.

Murray, Stuart. *Never a Soul at Home: New Zealand Literary Nationalism and the 1930s* Wellington: Victoria University Press, 1998.

Pierce, Peter. *The Country of Lost Children: An Australian Anxiety*. Cambridge: Cambridge University Press, 1999.

Rayner, Jonathan. *The Films of Peter Weir*, 2d ed. London: Continuum, 2003.

Rudd, Alison. *Postcolonial Gothic Fictions from the Caribbean, Canada, Australia, and New Zealand*. Cardiff: University of Wales Press, 2010.

Schaffer, Kay. "Woman and the Bush: Australian National Identity and Representations of the Feminine." *Antipodes* 3,1 (1989): 3–17.

Simmons, Laurence. "The Story of Our Lives." Rev. of *In My Father's Den*. *Landfall* 209 (May 2005): 195–196.

Simpson, Catherine, Renata Murawska, and Anthony Lambert. *Diasporas of Australian Cinema*. Chicago: Intellect, 2009.

Spicer, Andrew. *An Ambivalent Archetype: Masculinity, Performance and the New Zealand Films of Bruno Lawrence*. Nottingham: Kakapo, 2000.

Stead, C. K. *Smith's Dream*. Auckland: Longman Paul, 1971.

Williams, Mark. "A Waka on the Wild Side: Nationalism and Its Discontents in Some Recent New Zealand Films." *Contemporary New Zealand Cinema: From New Wave to Blockbuster*. Eds. Ian Conrich and Stuart Murray. London: I.B. Taurus, 2008. 180–196.

Wilson, Janet. "Intertextual Strategies: Reinventing the Myths of Aotearoa in Contemporary New Zealand Fiction." *Across the Lines: Intertextuality and Transcultural Communication in the New Literatures in English*. Ed. Wolfgang Kloos. Amsterdam: Rodopi, 1998. 271–291.

Wimmer, Adi. *Australian Film: Cultures, Identities, Texts* Trier: WVT Wissenschaftlicher Verlag Trier, 2007.

Wood, Houston. *Native Features: Indigenous Films from Around the World*. London: Continuum, 2008.

Resistance to Responsibility
Interrupting the Postcolonial Paradigm
DAVID HUDDART

"One can vary or deconstruct all the predicates of responsibility in general, yet one cannot completely reduce the *delay*: an event, a law, a call, an other are *already* there; others are there — for whom and before whom one must answer. However 'free' it is supposed to be, the *response* inaugurates nothing if it does not come after." Jacques Derrida, "Désistance," 221.

Introduction: Postcolonial Ethical Criticism

What is postcolonial theory or criticism a response to? What is already there? The question of what comes before, the historical and intellectual pre-conditions, is most complex and has led some to question the both the analytic and political value of "postcolonial" as a term (e.g., McClintock). Clearly, the delay identified by Derrida is a key aspect of postcolonial theory (e.g., Bhabha), but this delay has for many critics introduced a secondariness or "bad supplementarity" to postcolonial theory, which has apparently led to political and intellectual irresponsibility. A particularly significant example of the problems of being responsible to that which comes before is postcolonial literary criticism. Postcolonial theory, drawing its emphasis from French philosophy, appears distant and disconnected from actual postcolonial literatures. To the extent that the reader's relationship with the literary work can be described as ethical, postcolonial theory can be rather unethical in its treatment of postcolonial literature, and it is perhaps unsurprising that postcolonial literary writers appear to have, at best, an ambivalent relationship with theory. This can be said of culture in general, upon which postcolonial theory is all too often imposing a political and philosophical demand for difference. In order to re-think our approach to postcolonial culture, I will consider the ethical orientation of postcolonial theory, which derives from its paradigm of difference. I will then consider various challenges to postcolonial theory in the name of sameness or simultaneity. Such challenges question the idea of cultural politics and put emphasis on the relative autonomy of the literary work. While accepting the desirability of a responsible cultural politics, I would argue that it is important to adapt to this challenge by interrupting the fluent postcolonial paradigm.

But why should we want to interrupt this paradigm? One answer is that postcolonial studies ought to replace concern with representation with emphasis on responsibility. The concern with representation is understandable, to the extent that many instances of Western representation are demonstrably inaccurate and frequently prejudiced. Such representation has been put in the service of political and economic domination, consciously or not: that is a founding claim, if not the founding claim, of postcolonial studies. However, following Edward Said's *Orientalism* (1978), postcolonial studies has, much of the time, refined an argument about the impossibility of representing other cultures without bias or indeed prejudice: historical fact has been converted into philosophical constant. According to Robert Spencer, "we are left with a sort of separatist ideology which bears little resemblance to the goal of universal emancipation that has inspired — and, just as importantly, *continues* to inspire — anti-colonial theory and activism" (72). Spencer focuses on the possibility of accurate representation, even if that representation demands that we step outside the literary text. Such texts are inevitably partial, and indeed frequently play with that partiality through, for example, unreliable narration: of course, unreliability implies a reliability against which it can be judged, and so to read literature is far from being an experience of irreducible perspectivism. Indeed, in putting emphasis on the reader rather than the writer, Spencer encourages us to remember our responsibility as critical interpreters; he wishes to shift the act of representing or rendering from being *prior* to the text to occurring *during* the reading process.

Spencer blames the postcolonial investment in a radical perspectivism, and the consequent political ineffectiveness, on post-structuralist thought. Such thought, he argues, is animated by a relativism unable to comprehend the great achievements of anti-colonialism. It is also, as many have argued, apparently antipathetic to many if not all forms of Marxism, at least insofar as they can be specified and concretized in actual activity. While that may be a caricature of some aspects of post-structuralism or postmodernism, it is understandable that certain confusions have arisen, and it is also understandable that the apparent opposition between Marxism and post-structuralism has become a focus within postcolonial studies. At the very least, post-structuralism appears to supplant Marxism in the conversion of anti-colonial to postcolonial thought. However, it is of course not necessarily the case that the two strands of thought are always or simply opposed, and Jacques Derrida himself published on Marx, albeit controversially. Indeed, it can be argued that some of the time at least such thought is most alive to the responsibility that Spencer implicitly puts at the center of postcolonial scholarship. This is obviously the case with the ethical cultural criticism that has built on the work of Emmanuel Lévinas and Derrida, which offers an increasingly attractive model for postcolonial studies. It is arguable that only in responding to the otherness of the text can we be true to the emancipatory impulse invoked by Spencer.

However, some critics suggest that there is an incompatibility between Lévinasian ethical concern for the other and postcolonial political concern for the other. Due to this superficial incompatibility, there has been only limited development of postcolonial ethical criticism. As one example, Simone Drichel formulates this incompatibility suggestively, when she writes the following:

> [The] postcolonial other appears incompatible with the ethical other insofar as both "others" conceptually pull in conflicting directions. Where the postcolonial other invokes a certain ontological closure of politicized identity categories, the ethical other demands an opening up of such categories and pushes us beyond essence. A Levinasian ethics then perhaps puts postcolonialism's founding premises too radically into question — produces too guilty a conscience — for postcolonialism to be tempted to "turn ethical" any time soon [21–22].

It might then be argued that postcolonial studies wants to specify others, to give them clear identities that can then be defended against misrepresentation. That indeed is Spencer's point: it is necessary to know *who* the other is, to learn about them, and to represent them adequately, accurately, and appropriately. However, the danger is that to specify is also to freeze the subject, to deny process and transformation. Perhaps, then, postcolonial studies resolves itself into forms of identity politics all too quickly, reducing difference to the same, or different sames to opposed identities. One way or another, ethics as conceived by Lévinas would be no basis for a postcolonial politics, on this understanding, and would coexist uneasily with the kinds of universal emancipatory politics to which Spencer is committed. Indeed, one way of understanding this ethical demand to respect the other's singularity is to say that it cancels difference. This cancellation comes precisely from making difference an absolute plane that could be, depending on your theoretical commitments, undifferentiated.

Others have suggested that Derrida's reading of Lévinas offers a way of thinking about *concretization* of responsibility. It is here that certain kinds of post-structuralism can begin to contribute to the emancipatory thought desired by Spencer. Despite the ongoing criticism of "deconstruction" frequently found in postcolonial studies, it can be argued that Derrida's work is actually a worthwhile resource that allows us to re-cast the postcolonial paradigm. Specifically, it can be argued that Derrida helps us formulate a kind of criticism that bridges the two forms of otherness Drichel outlines. That is because Derrida, as should be well-known, demands that we think the singular and the general together. Derek Attridge expresses the Derridean idea of responsibility in the following passage:

> Responsibility to the other is not just a question of the obligation or demand that I feel most intensely because it addresses me with the greatest imperiousness. If this were the case, the existing system of power relations would determine the exercise of responsibility, and would thereby reproduce itself endlessly. The subordination of female to male, of black to white, of poor to rich would continue unabated. The future would come not as the other, but as the same. Responsibility has an *active* dimension; it is not merely a passive response. I am obligated to *seek out* the other, to *learn* to hear its voice and see its face [22].

This thought brings together our responsibility to literature, to other peoples, and to the other in general, in a most suggestive way, and helps us to see the ways in which poststructuralism can be a complement rather than an obstacle to the kinds of emancipatory thought to which Spencer is committed. The way in which Attridge reformulates Derrida also draws attention to the way in which there can be no absolute otherness, insofar as something is recognizable to us at all. Therefore, the different and the same come together, necessarily, and responsibility lies in thinking them together: for Attridge, this comes about through the *activity* necessary to particularize the universal in a given context. That activity, I would suggest, is a general way of describing the kind of response Spencer is imagining when he puts his focus on the reader of the postcolonial literary text. Reading, then, must be understood in a general sense — not that we can read or interpret everything as a cultural text, but that we are called upon to respond to each poem, novel, or other text through a particularization of the universal. Furthermore, this way of understanding responsibility gives us a way of responding to recent criticisms directed at postcolonial studies in terms of the same. Again, that is because Derrida enjoins us to think the different and the same at the same time. Attridge continues: "the generalized responsibility of ethics that Derrida talks of can become, at any moment, particularized and imperative — and to act responsibly (though this is now not clearly distinguishable from acting ethically) is to do the *work* necessary to produce such particularizations" (22). And that work is critical interpretation — reading.

Ethics and the Postcolonial Paradigm

It is necessary, however, to make postcolonial studies respond to possibilities that are beyond its current structure of thinking, in order to sharpen the sense in which postcolonial criticism should be responsible. Like other fields, postcolonial studies is often unable to think responsibly about other paradigms, as Spencer suggests with regard to Marxist criticism. It is necessary, we might argue, to interrupt the postcolonial paradigm, although that does not mean that we need to replace it. One way to do this is to put postcolonial studies in the context of other forms of cultural studies, many of which have pursued in their recent guises a kind of deconstructive turn. At its most Derridean, deconstructive cultural studies refuses the production of a Derridean paradigm, or indeed any other paradigm (at least, for any length of time). Indeed, it is arguable that deconstructive cultural studies implies a multitude of paradigms. If, as Paul Bowman has recently argued, "there is clearly nothing outside of the paradigm" (7), cultural studies at least holds out the hope of both other paradigms and *othering* paradigms. This emphasis does not refer to a plurality of paradigms as such, but instead implies a self-differing drive at the heart of each paradigm, which accordingly strives to mutate. Cultural studies want to interrupt itself, to disrupt the fluency of its own theoretical language about culture, and to be interruptive rather than all too fluent. It might appear that postcolonial studies produces a radically *predictable* knowledge, one that is irresponsible to the extent that it confirms what its paradigm already sets up as worth knowing or worth thinking. "Intervention" is a key goal of cultural studies, and by extension of postcolonial studies. However, any "realist" paradigm would fall short of making a difference, *intervening*, and would merely be the repetition of the same, lacking consciousness of its repetitive and somewhat tedious predictability. Despite Stuart Hall's reservations (248–249) about the place of deconstruction in Robert Young's *White Mythologies*, this does not imply that Derrida trumps all other theoretical perspectives, because the danger of repetition is present for any paradigm. Accordingly, in reading Derrida we do *not* find a perspective that comprehends all other foolishly naïve orientations: it is *not* arguable, for example, that Derrida comprehends all other writers with a superior deconstructive paradigm. Instead, one recommendation we can draw from his work is that we should practice the constant interruption of paradigm; we must constantly interrupt not only those with whom we are impatient because their perspective conflicts with our own, but also ourselves. Indeed, from another perspective, postcolonial studies is not at all predictable, but is instead the kind of *inter-discipline* that might result from this interruption, the kind of work that might trouble other more traditional and stable institutional identities: postcolonial studies must be interdisciplinary, according to many practitioners. And yet, to re-iterate the point, it can also be argued that postcolonial studies have become all too fluent in emphasizing difference.

Postcolonial criticism should then, if it wants to be "fully itself" (in being interdisciplinary, or rather disciplinary *but only up to a point)* return and re-read Derrida's work. However, it appears that Derrida is *already* everywhere in postcolonial studies, and for many detractors this is a central problem with the field. That may well be due to the specific nature of the postcolonial reading of Derrida. In his survey of postcolonial theory, Bart Moore-Gilbert suggests the following: "It seems to me a grave misfortune that the attitude towards Derrida in a lot of postcolonial criticism ... has been so influenced by Said's derivative and misleading account of him ... rather than by engagement with his actual writings" (163). Said's account contrasts Derrida and Foucault, the latter's work being found more palatable to historically and politically engaged criticism — and pressed into service in *Orientalism.* That rather inhospitable reading can be written off rather easily as fitting what Geoffrey Bennington (1994) calls an early phase of "moralist" condemnation of Derrida's work. Another version of this reading is put forward by Benita Parry, reading Bhabha and Derrida: "'difference' has been diverted by a post-modernist criticism as a theoretical ruse to establish a neutral, ideology-free zone from which the social dissension and political contest inscribed in the antagonist pairing of coloniser/colonised, have been expelled" (15). For Parry, the emphasis on difference that postcolonial theory derives from Derrida remains at a purely theoretical level, removed from the realities of historical anti-colonialism, and actually-existing neo-colonialism. Accordingly, this difference is a fundamental flaw in postcolonial studies, which assumes too much too soon. Although such a caricature of this account of Derrida is unfair, it is no more unfair than the account it gives of Derrida's work.

Nonetheless, even the derivative account cannot be isolated by more sophisticated postcolonial readings of Derrida. Although there are two principal readings of Derrida in postcolonial studies, they are in fact rather closely related. In the first, Derrida's work is found to be wholly inadequate: this reading can be seen in Aijaz Ahmad's response to *Specters of Marx.* In the second, Derrida is taken as self-evident, with minor qualification: this reading is exemplified by Bhabha. These two readings quite often co-exist, perhaps most obviously in the work of Spivak: usually, the familiar gesture in the situation of co-existence is to say that a theory of difference only gets us so far, before reality kicks in, and brings us to some more intractable examples of difference *on the ground.* In one way, then, the apparently negative postcolonial reading of Derrida is not *really* negative. Instead it simply says that Derrida is interesting but (seriously) insufficient in his analysis of difference. McClintock and Nixon, for example, argue about the lack of historical context in Derrida's discussion of Apartheid, but they would not seriously contest the value of a stress on difference. The grounds for this last reading are the extraction of a logic of difference from Derrida's work, which is clearly something intelligible and useful for postcolonial studies. It is understandable that readers demand something in the way of an abstractable logical structure when reading Derrida's work.

Nonetheless, as Derrida reminds us in *A Taste for the Secret*, reading is also a relationship with the *un*intelligible, without which no invention (of reading, but also of culture or politics) is possible: "If something is given to be read that is totally intelligible ... it is not given to the other to be read" (32). Such a situation is, of course, impossible, however fully self-read a text might try to be. Further, as we read in *Politics of Friendship*:

> [We] cannot, and we *must* not, exclude the fact that when someone is speaking, in private or in public, when someone teaches, publishes, preaches, orders, promises, prophesies, informs or communicates, some force in him or her is also striving *not to* be understood, approved, accepted in consensus — not immediately, not fully, and therefore not in the immediacy and plenitude of tomorrow, etc. [218].

For Derrida, of course, being not understood in a present is not being understood *in presence*. In other words, there is a resistance to being understood "fully," once and for all. If for no other reason, postcolonial studies ought to return to what it thinks it knows and accounts for all too well. Indeed, when it has seemed *most* hospitable to Derrida, in its use of difference, postcolonial studies has really been rather inhospitable, through its reduction of Derrida to a paradigm of difference. Simon Gikandi makes that point when he distinguishes the work of Bhabha and Derrida: "[If] there is a certain skepticism towards difference as a social category in Derrida's work, it is not an exaggeration to say that the postcolonial project, as it was mapped out in Bhabha's early work, was built around radical theories of difference" (117). Bhabha, according to Gikandi, extracts a logic of difference and proceeds to apply it to the social field of postcolonialism. Implicitly, it is this application that leads to conceptual and political problems undermine postcolonial studies. However, others have argued that postcolonialism is not a simple and inaccurate application of Derrida's ideas: for example, Syrotinski asserts that it "would be wrong to conceive of the manner in which Bhabha reappropriates Derridean terms as a simple transposition from one context to another, or a kind of methodological application" (31). Further, even if transposition is what happens in Bhabha's work, that is not necessarily a fatal flaw. Indeed, Bhabha makes the results of such necessarily inexact transposition a fundamental theme in his work (for example, on the "English book"). In any case, it can be argued that, viewed positively or negatively, postcolonial criticism has appeared to apply a logic of difference, with Derrida providing a kind of conceptual framework undermining Western ethnocentrism, etc. In such a way, Derrida is seen to license a postcolonial paradigm of difference. Against this paradigm, working as we should to open postcolonial studies to the others of its thought, we ought instead to think through Derrida's logic of the *same*, which draws his work into interesting comparison with other political thinkers relevant to the postcolonial paradigm, such as Antonio Negri and Alain Badiou.

Interruptive Example: The Same

These thinkers oppose the postcolonial paradigm, and much of the poststructuralism that apparently influences that paradigm. Negri and Hardt, and Badiou and Hallward, in their different but comparable ways proceed to undermine this paradigm of difference, which has already decided what is thinkable and what is worth thinking. In other words, instead of taking on board *différance*, they take aim at difference as a third term, i.e., a product of sublation. This difference is something that Hardt and Negri view as an oppositional force proper to previous stages of production, but quite inappropriate to "Empire." In the current global capitalist system, they suggest, difference is what there is: difference is actually *promoted* by power, and therefore constitutes no kind of opposition whatsoever. As they argue in *Empire*, "Empire" agrees with the post-colonialists about the virtue of difference, chanting "Long live difference! Down with essentialist binaries!" (138). This is because, they argue, "Power has evacuated the bastion [of sameness that critics] are attacking and has circled round to their rear to join them in the assault in the name of difference" (138). Indeed, they suggest that technology provides the necessary context for an absolute simultaneity of revolution, of sameness mobilized against difference. Their position accordingly appears quite opposed to the one animating the postcolonial paradigm. The paradigm of difference is inadequate to the current state of globalization, on their view.

Like Hardt and Negri, in writing about contemporary "alteritist" ethics, Alain Badiou develops his argument based on assumptions fundamentally alien to postcolonial theory. For example, in *Ethics* he writes: "Infinite alterity is quite simply *what there is*. Any experience at all is the infinite deployment of infinite differences" (25). In order to think about what there is, we cannot simply affirm this infinity of differences; in this Badiou is close to Derrida. Thinking and truth require more than straightforward description:

> Against these trifling descriptions (of a reality that is both obvious and inconsistent in itself), genuine thought should affirm the following principle: since differences are what there is, and since every truth is the coming-to-be of that which is not yet, so differences are then precisely what truths depose, or render insignificant. No light is shed on any concrete situation by the notion of the "recognition of the other" [27].

Badiou's idea of thought is here explicitly posed against much of contemporary theory: the criticism of "recognition of the other" is directed at Lévinasian ethics. Against this recognition, Badiou poses the active creation of the same: "The Same, in effect, is not what is (i.e., the infinite multiplicity of differences) but what *comes to be*. I have already named that in regard to which only the advent of the Same occurs: it is a *truth*. Only a truth is, as such, *indifferent to differences*" (27). So, differences must be genuinely put to one side: truth cannot be "my truth" or "our truth"; it must simply be truth. The *situatedness* of postcolonial theory, like other forms of theory, operates to undermine truth: "Every invocation of blood and soil, of race, of custom, of community, works directly against truths" (76). For a theory to be genuinely worthwhile, it must leave behind the world of infinite difference.

Badiou's challenge is to contemporary thinking generally but clearly has great relevance to postcolonial theory, perhaps the single most "alteritist" field in literary and cultural theory. This challenge is given most far-reaching expression in the work of Peter Hallward, who makes the following point in *Absolutely Postcolonial*: "To move from the specified to the specific, without yielding to the temptation of the singular: this is perhaps the only general goal that can be ascribed to a critical theory as such" (48). Theories come from times and places, which means they can be specified. Nonetheless, this does not mean that they are *only* in relation to their time and place, or that their time and place can only be explained through reference to them. They do not have singular and privileged explanatory power, nor do they create their own terms of evaluation. Theories must be made to work, made in fact universal through, most likely, coordination rather than laissez-faire respect for difference. The latter respect leads to the production of an *uncritical* theory. This is Hallward's general position; postcolonial theory, however, is his specific example, and he contends that it operates on an entirely singularizing logic, creating its own terms of evaluation and becoming therefore non-relational. Postcolonial theory seems to him mired in singularity and therefore unable to contribute to contemporary political questioning. Indeed, difference in context does not imply that each phenomenon is enclosed or exhausted by that context: "That everything exists as specific to a situation does not mean that its significance and complexity is reducible to a function of (or in) that situation; that every event has its specific occasion does not mean that its significance is exhausted by that occasion" (39). Theories cannot be explained or explained away simply by reference to their location, or their origin, or whatever else we might call their situation. There is a need for *subtraction* of situation from theory, and this process is one that postcolonial theory in particular seems unwilling to carry out. Hallward suggests that "postcolonial theory in general can only obstruct what is arguably the great political task of our time: the articulation of fully inclusive, fully egalitarian political principles which, while *specific* to the particular situation of their declaration, are nevertheless *subtracted* from their cultural environment" (126). Postcolonial theory, in being actively hostile to the same, is inadequate to contemporary political challenges. The specified locales of thought are what lead to this fragmentation, and they are what must be overcome. In summary, Hallward believes that postcolonial criticism needs to make a move from the singular to the specific, part of which requires a subtraction of difference from the structures under consideration or formation. Following Badiou, he sees the necessity of forming universalizable principles. Postcolonial theory, we might say, functions by *adding* difference. Both Bhabha and Spivak seem to confirm Hallward's view of postcolonial theory as producing a singularizing and indiscriminate and abstract philosophy of difference; in this, they fit the august company of Deleuze (in Hallward's reading found in *Out of This World*), but also no doubt Derrida.

It would appear, then, that if postcolonial studies is to interrupt itself, to interrupt its smoothly fluent paradigm, it has a number of competing alternatives that speak of the same, or the universal: Negri and Badiou are two powerful examples of this kind of thought. Here I am suggesting that reading Derrida's work provides a quite different kind of interruption. Geoffrey Bennington in *Interpreting Derrida* encourages us to consider "interrupting" as a kind of name for Derrida: is interruption not just what Derrida engages in, or even *is*? That position can be argued, but for many readers Derrida is merely adding further discussion of difference to an already significant weight of discourse. And yet, it is arguable that one thing that Derrida's writing constantly attempts is the holding off of the moment of difference: of course, difference is simply what there is, and if Derrida's work proceeded immediately to the moment of difference, then it would not have such a powerful claim on our attention. However, this understanding of his work is hardly universal, with deconstruction understood as a theory of or method for uncovering difference. When Derrida is considered at all, it seems that many critics believe that his work merely keeps the conversation about difference smoothly ticking over. Indeed, while citing the above arguments against the philosophy or politics of difference might well fit my aim of interrupting the postcolonial paradigm, it might also appear to be an argument against Derrida's work, despite what I have argued about the overly hospitable nature of postcolonial studies to the idea of difference. For example, Badiou dismissively calls Lévinasian ethics a *pious discourse*, and following him, Hallward is explicit in his rejection of a Derridean ethics of difference in favor of a less tortuous, more straightforward ethics of the same. Postcolonial ethics, if they are to be interrupted, seem to need interrupting in the name of the same. Indeed, it would seem that any interruption I might make of the postcolonial paradigm could only also be a kind of interruption of Derrida, if not a rejection of (some aspects of) his work. However, it only *appears* to be this way.

Conclusion: The Politics of the Same

An appropriate way to outline the structures in question is to consider an example, in this case the politics of language, something central to postcolonial studies. To many, the spread of English has brought with it various dangers, comparable to the dangers of globalization in general. Analyzing an assumption fundamental to these fears, Michael Holquist asserts, "Monolingualism has at its heart a passion for wholeness, a desire for unity, a lust for order in a world in which variety and contingency seem to rule" (24–25). He suggests that monolingualism strives to manage diversity through the elevation of this "wholeness." From Holquist's position, fundamental to postcolonial studies, monolingualism represents a tyranny of the same that must be countered by a philosophy and politics of difference: *let variety and contingency rule*. Yet, in many areas of postcolonial studies, difference inevitably comes into conflict with other priorities — for example, teachability in language acquisition. Espousing a philosophy of difference in the context of language can be dogmatic political pronouncement, not least when at least some of the time the supposed beneficiaries of this philosophy of difference demand some *sameness*. We need to consider the clash between postcolonial theory's political pronouncements in favor of difference and *actually existing* postcolonialism's co-existing demand for sameness.

Derrida's work can help us think about this clash, even when it appears to express sentiments inimical to postcolonial studies. One example of such sentiments is the following, taken from *Monolingualism of the Other*:

> I do not believe that anyone can detect by *reading*, if I do not myself declare it, that I am a "French Algerian." I retain, no doubt, a sort of acquired reflex from the necessity of this vigilant transformation. I am not proud of it, I make no doctrine of it, but so it is: an accent — any French accent, but above all a strong southern accent — seems incompatible to me with the dignity of public speech. (Inadmissable, isn't it? Well, I admit it.) [46].

This kind of admission *has* made Derrida inadmissible, at least for many in postcolonial studies. It appears simultaneously abstract and absurdly local in its expression of a prejudice. It is difficult to imagine how one so committed to difference can defend such affection for sameness, something which in this context appears to expunge any trace of the local or specific, i.e., difference in language. Willy Maley refers to this as an "allergic reaction to accent *per se*" (127) and admits this reaction has ruined his admiration for Derrida. What, Maley wonders, is the relation between this alarming stress on sameness in accent and the more obviously "acceptable" stress on idiom in writing? Maley himself frames his questions in the context of postcolonial studies. We can consider this a test of a nuanced emphasis on *infinite* difference. Clearly, the assumption normally remains that Derrida's thought is amenable to infinite difference. That seems to be how postcolonial theory, for good or ill, has read him. We might propose a different understanding of Derridean difference, which is that infinite difference is finite. If everything is a question of difference, then there is a danger that everything will be flattened, undifferentiated, and accordingly difference will blur into *in*difference. This possibility can be seen very clearly in *Monolingualism of the Other*, when Derrida insists on the misreading of his "concept" of *dissemination*, something he claims to be "between" the universal and the singular, through the *fold*, licensing testimony, and Derrida's logic of exemplarity. This text ought to be important to post-colonial studies, but not because it is, as it were, *about* colonialism; indeed, it is easy to imagine how concerned many in postcolonial studies have been about the argument that *all culture is originarily colonial*, an argument that really does seem to reduce difference to sameness. The text is important for postcolonial studies in the way it thinks sameness and difference together. To return to what Derrida suggests about accent: "[Despite] everything I some-times appear to profess, I concede that I have contracted a shameful but intractable intolerance: at least in French, insofar as the language is concerned, I cannot bear or admire anything other than pure French" (46). He describes his surrender to purity in the act of simultaneously disallowing purity. At least some of this act is outlined in the context of French literature as an insti-tution, entry into which requires "losing one's accent," as we still say (we might say gaining). Derrida himself admits that "having an accent" seems inappropriate for the poetic vocation (no one can hear through reading, *in theory*) and also that he has not quite lost his, and so has not quite made it "within" the institution. He aims to do something with this language which is not quite his: he aims to "speak in good French, in pure French, even at the moment of challenging in a million ways everything that is allied to it" (49). It will be recalled that Derrida refers to the disappearance of idioms, which is perhaps also the disappearance of dialects, or languages. Why is this not extended to the disappearance of accents? It could also be extended to the disappearance of names (principally his own, "becoming Jacques" from Jackie).

The answer is, on one level, to do with the observance of classical protocols of reading. One way to understand what Derrida is arguing is to say that in order to be heard or read in our innovations, our graphics of otherness, we need to be heard speaking in the most "pure" of accents; or, in a less accented, personalized, or psychologized register, we need to observe classical protocols, but only up to a point. The question remains, what is that point? That point is to be determined in each instance. In short, we need to be recognizably masters of what we wish to transform. In an apparently more psychologized register, we can also consider what Simon Glendinning argues about the *straight road* of philosophical idealism in contrast with all the *by-ways* we actually take. Glendinning observes that those by-ways are often deeply undesirable, as they have been in the context of cultural studies generally, and the study of postcolonialism specifically. Nonetheless, those by-ways remain understandably powerful. On one level, this is what Derrida is admitting when he talks about accent. And so, in fact, it can be seen that Derrida does not keep difference sequestered from the extraordinary everyday, so much of which is *the same*. On another level, of course, and against what Glendinning appears to think, Derrida is precisely defending philosophical concepts' capacity for accounting *quasi-transcendentally*. Despite claiming that Derrida's writing maintains a degree of abstraction unacceptable to the messy realities of politically-engaged post-colonialism, in fact it is postcolonial studies that remains fundamentally abstract in not really thinking about the same. This is the challenge laid out by Derrida's interruption of our fluent discourse on difference, and it produces a most difficult task: to articulate ontological universality and the singular — i.e., to think together the economy of sameness and difference. In the context of a new "embodied" postcolonial politics, Sara Ahmed describes this economy in terms of "a different form of political community, one that moves beyond the opposition between common and uncommon, between friends and strangers, or between sameness and difference" (2000: 180). Moving beyond expectations of sameness and difference continues to be the challenge to postcolonial studies, whatever the object of study: we need to elaborate reading according to universal standards, and also do justice to that which eludes those standards.

WORKS CITED

Ahmad, Aijaz. "Reconciling Derrida: 'Specters of Marx' and Deconstructive Politics." In *Ghostly Demarcations: A Symposium on Jacques Derrida's Specters of Marx*. Ed. Michael Sprinker. London: Verso, 1999. 88–109.

Ahmed, Sara. *Strange Encounters: Embodied Others in Post-Coloniality*. London: Routledge, 2000.

Attridge, Derek. "Derrida's Singularity: Literature and Ethics." In *Derrida's Legacies: Literature and Philosophy*. Eds. Simon Glendinning and Robert Eaglestone. London: Routledge, 2008. 13–25.

_____. *The Singularity of Literature*. London: Routledge, 2004.

Badiou, Alain. *Ethics: An Essay on the Understanding of Evil*. Trans. P. Hallward. London: Verso, 2001.

Bennington, Geoffrey. *Interrupting Derrida*. London: Routledge, 2000.

_____. *Legislations: The Politics of Deconstruction*. London: Verso, 1994.

Bhabha, Homi K. *The Location of Culture*. London: Routledge, 1994.

Bowman, Paul. *Post-Marxism Versus Cultural Studies: Theory, Politics and Intervention*. Edinburgh: Edinburgh University Press, 2001.

Derrida, Jacques. "Désistance." In *Psyche: Inventions of the Other*, Volume Two. Eds. P. Kamuf and E. Rottenberg. Palo Alto: Stanford University Press, 2008. 196–230.

_____. *Monolingualism of the Other: or, the Prosthesis of Origin*. Trans. P. Mensah Palo Alto: Stanford University Press, 1998.

_____. *Politics of Friendship*. Trans. G. Collins. London: Verso, 1997.

Derrida, Jacques, and Maurizio Ferraris. *A Taste for the Secret*. Cambridge: Polity, 2001.

Drichel, Simone. "Regarding the Other: Postcolonial Violations and Ethical Resistance in Margaret Atwood's *Bodily Harm*." *Modern Fiction Studies* 54 (Spring 2008): 20–49.

Gikandi, Simon. "Poststructuralism and Postcolonial Discourse." In *The Cambridge Companion to Postcolonial Literary Studies*. Ed. Neil Lazarus. Cambridge: Cambridge University Press, 2004. 97–119.

Glendinning, Simon. "Preface." *Arguing with Derrida*. Ed. Simon Glendinning. Oxford: Blackwell, 2001. 1–33.

Hall, Stuart. "When Was 'the Postcolonial'? Thinking at the Limit." In *The Postcolonial Question: Common Skies, Divided Horizons*. Eds. Iain Chambers and Lidia Curti. London: Routledge, 1991. 242–260.

Hallward, Peter. *Absolutely Postcolonial: Writing between the Singular and the Specific*. Manchester: Manchester University Press, 2001.

_____. *Out of This World: Deleuze and the Philosophy of Creation*. London: Verso, 2006.

Hardt, Michael, and Antonio Negri. *Empire*. Cambridge: Harvard University Press, 2000.

McClintock, Anne. "The Angel of Progress: Pitfalls of the Term 'Post-Colonialism.'" *Social Text* 31/32 (1992): 84–98.

McClintock, Anne, and Rob Nixon. "No Names Apart: The Separation of Word and History in Derrida's 'Le dernier mot du racism.'" *Critical Inquiry* 13 (Autumn 1986): 140–154.

Parry, Benita. "Signs of Our Times." *Third Text* 38/39 (1994): 5–24.

Said, Edward W. *Orientalism: Western Conceptions of the Orient*. 1978. London: Penguin, 1995.

_____. "The Problem of Textuality: Two Exemplary Positions." *Critical Inquiry* 4 (Summer 1978): 673–714.

Spencer, Robert. "'Listening for the Echo': Representation and Resistance in Postcolonial Studies." *Journal of Postcolonial Writing* 45 (March 2009): 71–81.

Syrotinski, Michael. *Deconstruction and the Postcolonial: At the Limits of Theory*. Liverpool: Liverpool University Press, 2007.

Young, Robert J. C. *Postcolonialism: An Historical Introduction*. Oxford: Blackwell, 2001.

_____. *White Mythologies: Writing History and the West*, 2d ed. 1990. London: Routledge, 2004.

Cultural Translation in the Age of Globalization

SHAOBO XIE

Globalization is an ambiguous concept and a contradictory process of happenings. It calls to mind a number of things at the same time: transnational flows of commodities, technology, information, images, narratives, and ideas; an interconnected global telecommunication system brought about by digital technology; the shrinking of space and distance between geographically separated individuals and communities; universal modernization or capitalist globalization; increasing interdependence among nations and areas in the world. Since its inauguration, postmodern globalization has been evolving as a contradictory process: it expedites trade and increases the accumulation of wealth in some areas and among some classes, while at the same time throwing other areas and classes into greater poverty; it creates millions of new jobs in some regions where labor is cheap and raw materials are less costly, and it diminishes job markets in other regions, reducing the working class everywhere to the status of lumpenproletariat and maximizing the profit of capital by way of a differential wage system; it ignites what Hegel calls a universal desire for recognition everywhere, but, at the same time, it creates a transnational population of the excluded or what Žižek and Agamben call *homo sacer*; it promises democracy and freedom only to make them a privilege of the rich; the ideological aura of globalization seduces a euphoric sense of a prosperous and emancipatory future, and yet, at the same time, it is globalizing structural unemployment, drastic social polarizations, and labor-capital confrontation; last but not least, globalization breeds and encourages difference or differentiation at some levels, and erases cultural, ethnic, and local differences at others.

No matter how ambiguous and how contradictory, the term "globalization" in the last analysis names two closely related or reciprocally constitutive processes: capitalist globalization and the westernization of the world. Both processes are united by what is called modernization. This double process of modernization began a few centuries ago, threatening to eradicate local traditions and customs by way of a universal cosmopolitan language and culture. Over the past five hundred years, the world has witnessed what Michael Valdez Moses calls an "irreversible ... homogenizing worldwide process of modernization" (6). Such a West-led and West-dominated process, predicated on free-market economy, western rationalization, and western parliamentary democracy, has, in the name of progress, destroyed or eliminated worldwide social communities and cultural modes of production that stand as "distinct," "legitimate," and "alternative" to modern society, heterogenous possibilities of organizing human society, different ways of gratifying individual desires and ambitions or of "being-in-the-world," and divergent systems of beliefs, mores, and values that are "radically different from those that have come to prevail in the twentieth century" (Moses, xvi–xvii). This process of modernization or Westernization, though justified by Hegelian historicism as progressive, necessary, inevitable, promising universal human freedom, is throwing the world into unprecedented crisis and causing universal doubts about its rationality and legitimacy.

Perhaps no one has described the dire crisis-laden present more succinctly than Slavoj Žižek and Judith Butler, who, from their respective perspectives, perceive the world today in terms of an included/excluded antagonism. While Žižek situates his discussion of the global excluded in the context of capital-labor confrontation, Butler pursues the issue of the excluded from the perspective of the ethnic-racial antagonism. In his latest *New Left Review* article titled "How to Begin from the Beginning," Žižek maps out four major antagonisms: eco-environmental crisis, challenge to the established parameters of intellectual property, the unethical potential of biogenetic technology, and "new forms of social apartheid — new walls and slums" (53). In his view, the fourth antagonism, "the one between the included and the excluded," stands out as the "crucial one," for without it "all the others lose their subversive edge" (54). In focusing on the antagonism between the included and the excluded, Žižek argues that it is this antagonism that generated and justifies the "need for communism." In his view, the global social excluded have no place "in the 'private' order of social hierarchy" and therefore constitute "what Jacques Rancière calls the 'part of no part' of the social body" (54). These four antagonisms, which are threatening to destroy the world as a livable habitat, are all consequences of capitalist globalization or modernization. To corroborate Žižek's thesis on the four antagonisms, one can cite a few blunt facts: the total number of the unemployed today has reached about 200 million.[1]

There are about one billion people across the world harassed by scarcity of food, and "every day, almost 16,000 children die from hunger-related causes — one child every five seconds."[2] One out of seven people in the world today is malnourished, and one fifth of the world's population lives on less than $1 per day.[3] The world's population living below the international poverty line stands at 1.5 billion today.[4] This situation is further exacerbated by global warming, atmospheric pollution, water and air pollution, deforestation, soil erosion, desertification, grassland degeneration, and water shortage. Although our planet's ecological environment had begun to deteriorate in the pre-modern age, capitalist globalization has been the root cause of massive ecological degeneration. As David Harvey notes in *Spaces of Global Capitalism: Towards a Theory of Uneven Geographical Development*, capitalist development appropriates, uses, bends, and reshapes physical, ecological and social material processes to expedite capital accumulation (78). In his view, all the "problematics posed by environmentalism" loom large in any critique of capitalism, and it is a compelling task for social and cultural critics to investigate how "capital accumulation works through the physical, chemical and biological processes that surround us" (89). Harvey's remarks on how capital accumulation alters and violates ecosystems and the centrality of ecological critique of capitalism in cultural studies highlight the connection between capitalism and ecoenvironmental deterioration.

The picture of the racially/ethnically excluded on the global scene as discussed by Butler is just as bleak and disheartening. Millions of people have been excluded from the domain of the human and have suffered the violence of derealization in the West's representations of the non–Western, particularly in the past decade of global terrors. Alongside the global differential distribution of wealth and power, there is a global differential distribution of sympathy and grievability: that is, some ethnic communities or peoples are so insignificant and valueless that they are regarded as totally undeserving of empathy. The problem is not that thousands of Palestinians or Afghans have been killed in the wars of the past decade directed or supported by the United States, but that they have died in such a way as if they were spectral beings, with no "names and faces," no "personal histories," no "family," no "favorite hobbies"; the problem is also that millions of western TV spectators, sitting in front of these televised bloody scenes, "accept deaths caused by military means with a shrug or with self-righteousness or with clear vindictiveness" (Butler, *Precarious Life*, 32). Butler's version of the global excluded speaks of a population of "unlivable lives" deprived of their legal and political status (xv); they have been excluded from the domain of the human "as it has been naturalized in its 'Western' mold by the contemporary workings of humanism" (32). These excluded are brutally subjected to the "violence of derealization"

(32), whose existence as racial or cultural Other is understood as "neither alive nor dead but interminably spectral" (33–34). The numbers of the deprived and dehumanized should in no way be limited to Palestinians and Afghan people though they are the communities specifically named here; instead, they should be regarded as a register of the global present. It is a global reality that enormous numbers of the world's populations are dehumanized in such a way that their rights and their entitlement to sympathy and grieving are generally ignored or cancelled. The continuity between Žižek and Butler in their respective conceptions of the contemporary global reality consists in their shared insightful emphasis on the subversive nature of the included/excluded antagonism. Their depictions of the wretched world recall what Derrida wrote in a different context, "never have violence, inequality, exclusion, famine, and thus economic oppression affected as many human beings in the history of the earth and of humanity" and never before, "in absolute figures, never have so many men, women, and children been subjugated, starved, or exterminated on the earth" (85).

It is such a global reality that is calling upon every one of us to face squarely the challenge of the world's unprecedented crises; it is these unprecedented crises that are urging us to imagine non-capitalist alternatives to the present by way of borrowing from socio-cultural legacies of all nations, especially the non-western. If the world so far has been dominated by Western or West-led capitalistic civilization, then the true radical thinking about new modes of social and cultural life has to come from outside the whale of capitalism. This is the historical moment which urgently calls for cultural translation as a postcolonial mode of global communication, a way of articulating the concept of universality across cultural boundaries, facilitating the working together among different cultures and communities in coping with global problems and crises. The connection between the battle against capitalist globality and cultural translation consists in that to deal with the crises of capitalist globalization, it is of necessity to redefine the concept of modernity by granting different cultures and peoples equal access to the discourse of modernity and by encouraging different ethnic and cultural communities to imagine alternatives to the hegemonic capitalist modernity. In a different context, Partha Chatterjee argues: "Ours is the modernity of the once-colonized. The same historical process that has taught us the value of modernity has also made us the victims of modernity... . [And] we need to have the courage at times to reject the modernities established by others" (20). According to Roberto Unger, society is artifact, for "it is made and imagined"; it is a human construct "rather than the expression of an underlying natural order" (qtd. in Cui, n.p.); the "current Western system of property and contract is less a reflection of deep logic of social and economic necessity than a contingent outcome of political struggles" (Cui, n.p.). If Western modernity is not what every people are willing to accept, if the ongoing process of globalization has brought the world unprecedented crises in many ways, and if the capitalist system is not "a reflection of deep logic of social and economic necessity," then there should be globally concerted efforts to imagine and build alternative modernities. To redefine modernity is to readmit the excluded to the discourse of modernity, which involves redefining progress, happiness, justice, and humanity itself. And all this cannot succeed except through cultural translation. It is in this context that I wish to stage my argument on the prime importance of cultural translation in the age of globalization.

Cultural translation as a counterhegemonic strategy, a strategy of contesting and negotiating with various regimes of power, a strategy of rearticulating the concept of universality in culture-specific terms to admit or include the excluded, comes to us through Walter Benjamin, Homi Bhabha, Gayatri Spivak, and Judith Butler. Bhabha in his 1994 book *The Location of Culture* acknowledges his indebtedness to Benjamin in the following terms: "With the concept of 'foreignness' Benjamin comes closest to describing the performativity of translation as the staging of cultural difference" (227). It means that Benjamin's notion of foreignness already contains the seed of the theory that performative translation foregrounds irreducible cultural difference, for there is much that cannot be translated from one culture to another. When Benjamin argues that a translation issues from the afterlife of the original (71), what he has in view is not the incompetence or impotence of translation, but that there is an irreducible foreignness of or between languages that can never be domesticated, and it is precisely such recalcitrant foreignness of languages that makes translation as a transferring of meaning or value across cultural boundaries impossible. In his estimate, "all translation is only a somewhat provisional way of coming to terms with the foreignness of languages" and "an instant and final rather than a temporary and provisional solution of this foreignness remains out of the reach of mankind" (75). There is an irresolvable foreignness between languages, for different cultures cut up the phenomenal world in different ways and concepts are culture-specific, hence no identical terms or concepts existing between any two languages. The translated text, according to Benjamin, becomes a fragment, a dangling sign without a context, for when a text is translated from one language into another, it is disembedded from its original literal, literary, and cultural context and intertext. The Benjaminian foreignness of languages serves as the grounds for a number of related arguments: translation is impossible though necessary, which as a poststructuralist thesis has been forcefully argued by Derrida and de Man, the foreignness of languages as a locus of overdetermination gives rise to infinite possibilities of rendering the same text in different ways, hence decanonizing the translation and the original text at the same time; translation is and can be deployed as means of consolidating or contesting any hegemonic regime of power; translation as a site of performative agency contributes to a counter-colonial paradigm of global communication.

Bhabha's most discursively and politically consequent discussion of performative translation comes from the following passage:

> the sign of translation continually tells or "tolls" the different times and spaces between cultural authority and its performative practices. The "time" of translation consists in that *movement* of meaning, the principle and practice of a communication that, in the words of de Man "puts the original in motion to decanonise it, giving it the movement of fragmentation, a wandering of errance, a kind of permanent exile" [228].

Cultural or cross-cultural communication always involves performative or transformative translation. Cultural translation as such both discloses and conceals or both cancels and preserves the agonistic temporalities between cultural authority and its performative citation or interpretation. Performative translation is the deconstruction of the authority of the original, hence the ceaseless process of democratic dissemination of meaning or power. This is how the Master's power is defused by the Slave's skilled hands, or how the colonizer's Master Signifier is uncontrollably at the disposal of the colonized. The core concept of the foreignness of languages lends well to Bhabha's innovative theory of mimicry or hybridity. As the foreignness of languages is irresolvable or irreducible, no mimicry can "faithfully" carry meaning or value or intention across cultural boundaries and an act of mimicry can be either a moment of insufficiency or excessiveness. Either way, mimicry as such tends to undermine or subvert the colonizer's authority. That is also why hybridity is a third space, which as an exemplary act of cultural translation alters, expands, and hybridizes self and the Other at the same time, for at the other end of the translation process neither remains the same that has been known and both become displaced, enriched, and revised. It is in this sense that Butler contends that Bhabha's notion of mimicry or hybridity exposes the limits of the dominant discourse.

The Benjaminian foreignness of languages as appropriated or reworked by Spivak emphasizes the authority of the language one translates from. Spivak seems to call for a surrendering of one's own prejudices and will to power in translating the Other's text, hence to avoid the logic of translation as violation, which unfortunately "describes certain tendencies within third-worldist literary pedagogy" (*A Critique of Postcolonial Reason*, 164). In "Translation as Culture," Spivak notes, "Translation is to transfer from one to the other" instead of the other way round (21). As such translation is an "ethical" moment of "being-for," or of being for the Other, a "relating to the other as the source of one's utterance" (21). Spivak's ethical conception of translation recalls what Benjamin has pointed out: "The basic error of the translator is that he preserves the state in which his own language happens to be instead of allowing his language to be powerfully affected by the foreign tongue." For Benjamin, the solution to this problem is "to expand and deepen translator's language by means of the foreign language" (81). What emerges from both Benjamin and Spivak is a shared Levinasian respect for the Other or the Other's text. However, "as the text guards its secret, [translation] is impossible. The ethical task is never quite performed" (Spivak, "Translation as Culture," 21). This failure can be avoided by "listening with care and patience" that is "the founding task of translation" ("Translation as Culture," 22). Cultural translation in Spivak refers not only to translation between different languages, but to translation within the same language as well. She distinguishes between singularity and generality, idiom and semiosis, and subalternity and hegemony. Such a distinction emphasizes the singularity of meaning, value, or experience, of a certain subaltern or indigenous or native community whose idiomaticities have to be listened to and which get annulled or deleted in the standard language or the semiotic system. In Spivak, there is a continuity between the domination of a subaltern community by a hegemonic regime of power on the national terrain and that on the international terrain. In her view, "The toughest problem here is translation from idiom to standard, an unfashionable thing among the elite progressives, without which the abstract structures of democracy cannot be comprehended" (22). Translation from idiom to standard or from particularity to universality has in history been used to serve the interests and axiomatics of imperialism.

What makes Bhabha's and Spivak's theories of cultural translation particularly useful to Butler is that cultural translation makes it possible and necessary to articulate the universal in culture-specific terms. According to Butler, "Bhabha's emphasis on the splitting of the signifier in the colonial context seeks to show that the master — to use Hegelian parlance — loses some of his claim to priority and originality precisely by being taken up by a mimetic double" ("Restaging the Universal," 37). That is why cultural translation has "its counter-colonialist possibility," for it "exposes the limits of what the dominant language can handle" ("Restaging," 37). What Butler most appreciates of Spivak's notion of cultural translation is "a theory and practice of political responsibility" ("Restaging," 36), and in both Butler's and Spivak's assessments, "the task of the postcolonial translator" is to foreground the non-convergence of discourses or cultures so as to unmask "the founding violences of an episteme" through the "ruptures of narrativity" ("Restaging," 37). Butler cites Spivak saying that "it is impossible for the French intellectuals [referring mainly to Deleuze and Foucault] to imagine the power and desire that would inhabit the unnamed subject of the Other of Europe" (qtd. in Butler, 36). In rehearsing Spivak's position on cultural translation, Butler writes,

> The exclusion of the subordinated other of Europe is so central to the pro-duction of Eurocentric epistemic regimes "that the subaltern cannot speak." Spivak does not mean by this claim that the subaltern does not express her desires, form political alliances, or make culturally and politically signifi-cant effects, but that within the dominant conceptualization of agency, her agency remains illegible. The point would not be to extend a violent regime to include the subaltern as one of its members: she is, indeed, already included there, and it is precisely the means of her inclusion that effects the violence of her effacement. There is no other "other" there, at the site of the subaltern, but an array of peoples who cannot be homoge-nized, or whose homogenization is the effect of the epistemic violence itself … Spivak both counsels and enacts a self-limiting practice of cultural trans-lation on the part of First World intellectuals ["Restaging," 36].

What is at stake here is the culture-specific articulation of universality. Any full enacting or articulation of universality "must undergo a set of translations into the various rhetorical and cultural contexts in which the meaning and force of universal claims are made," for "without translation, the only way the assertion of universality can cross a border is through a colonial and expan-sionist logic" ("Restaging," 35). There is no transcultural universality, and claims to universality or its articulations are always culturally varied. Cultural translation is the method and process of articulating culture-specific versions of universality, and as such it exposes the violence of representational or epis-temological imperialism. Over the past few hundred years, "universality has been used to extend certain colonialist and racist understandings of civilized 'man,' to exclude certain populations from the domain of the human" (Butler, "Restaging," 38). The West has dominated the concepts of modernity, democ-racy, rationality, and agency by way of excluding the racial and social Others. The task of cultural translation is to restore or readmit the excluded. Actually any hegemonic monopolization of the concept of universality has been haunted by the return of the excluded. Butler deploys the notion and practice of cul-tural translation as a strategy of "opening towards alternative versions of uni-versality that are wrought from the work of translation itself" ("Competing," 179). Cultural translation as a site and strategy of rearticulating the concept of universality is no doubt pointing out a new task or a new direction in the combined field of postcolonial and globalization studies. This is because the world more than ever needs a pluralistic notion of universality in mobilizing resources and energies in dealing with problems created by capitalist global-ization.

There is no doubt that, over the past few decades, different areas and cultures of the world have been brought into much closer contact with each other and have cultivated unprecedented respect for one another, and speaking on behalf of the marginalized, oppressed, and underrepresented has become a moral obligation and professional integrity for academics. However, such progressive changes do not obfuscate the irony that some so-called progressive intellectuals or academics in the West oftentimes betray a strong tendency to consciously or unconsciously reproduce the West or the First World as the norm or criteria for determining the quality of life, the definition of democracy, and sites or forms of agency in other parts of the world. This is a point which has been persuasively made by Chandra Talpade Mohanty in her much celebrated essay "Under the Western Eyes," in which she confronts Western feminists with their intellectual and discursive imperialism towards third-world women. One of the illustrative examples given by her is their arrogant, reductive interpretations of burka or purdah, which deny any cultural and historical specificity of the institutions of purdah and totally rule out their contradictions and potentially subversive aspects (267). What Mohanty questions is Western feminists' universalizing assertion of the significance of purdah in controlling women. While purdah is a social site of women's oppression where wearing veils is dictated by mandatory Islamic laws, it can also be an indicator of women's resistant agency. During the 1979 revolution, for example, Iranian middle-class women wore veils to demonstrate "solidarity with their veiled, working class sisters" (267). Mohanty asserted context-specific significations of purdah to argue the point that Western feminists often judge non–Western people's practices exclusively in accordance with their own norms and criteria and fail to see the legible sites and forms of agency in other cultures.

Another instance of the exclusionary concept of universality is Anglo-American feminists' failure or inability to recognize women's roles and contributions in North-American Aboriginal society. According to the authors of "American Indian Women," myths of male dominance are Anglo-American feminist constructs imposed on American Aboriginal women, for in traditional native tribes and clans, Aboriginal women were never subjugated to male power. Rather, women were engaged in all kinds of activity including military activity. Before the European invasion, there were female clan heads, clan mothers, the women's council, for "[m]ost pre-contact North American civilizations functioned on the basis of matrilineage and matrilocality" (304). One defining feature of North American Aboriginal society is a sustained balance on everything including gender relations. It is the European invasion and colonization of the indigenous that changed all this, disempowering women and subjecting them to patriarchy established by Euro-Americans. In the native people's continual battling for their lost land and sovereignty, most of the militants were women. In a word, male supremacy is not their most pressing problem; their problems, which have been weighing upon them for several hundreds of years, are white supremacism and colonization.[5]

At a recent panel discussion on the topic "Will China Drive Alberta's Economy?" hosted by Calgary's Glenbow Museum (October 2, 2008), two panelists talked about China's fast-growing economy and urged Alberta, as well as Canada in general, to take the offered chances to enter the China market to boost or enhance its own economy. After their presentations, a couple of people from both the audience and the panel raised serious doubts about the proposal's feasibility by reason of China being an undemocratic society with a poor human rights record. It was not the questions themselves, nor the speakers' distrust of the Chinese government, that shocked me at the moment, but the arrogance implied in their tones or undertones and their unabashed ignorance and inability to recognize what Spivak calls "the power and desire that would inhabit the unnamed subject of the Other of [the West]."[6] Their views of China and the Chinese seemed to have derived from travelogues and books written over decades ago, and all the sea changes that had happened in China over the last few decades meant little to them. Despite the fact that CPC and the totalitarian Chinese government still maintain an ideological control and often an arbitrary censorship over what can be said or written, Chinese society at large is undergoing what can be called decentralization and detotalization. Disillusioned or disenchanted about Maoist modernity and subjected to no committed faith in grand narratives or traditional Confucian values, the Chinese today enjoy more freedom and discursive space than ever for generating criticisms or complaints about national and international politics, government policies, and abuses of human rights. This is particularly true if one visits the virtual China — thousands of Chinese-language websites. Indeed, the digital virtual space has creatively transformed China into a perfect democratic space of contestatory negotiation with state hegemony and various regimes of power.[7] As a people who usually do not risk openly confronting the government with demonstrations and protests unless driven beyond their forbearance, the Chinese detect and explore discursive power enabled by digital technology and the virtual space it offers. In much the same way, the Chinese use cell phones to pass short messages in writing, to exchange updates on new events or situations in their respective fields of work and life, to compose emails, and more importantly, to circulate all kinds of *duanzi*, which is a funny and often ideologically or politically subversive anecdote or joke, hence *huangse duanzi, hongse duanzi, zhengzhi duanzi, geming duanzi* (namely yellow pornographic or erotic duanzi, red duanzi, political duanzi, and revolutionary duanzi) etc. These duanzis or jokes/anecdotes are of unmistakable subversive potential in opposition to CPC's state ideology.

Another site of rebellious agency in China is the embodied space, the human body.[8] In ancient China, the body was heavily clothed by Confucian ritual and ethics; in Maoist China, the body was simply erased along with all other private space when six hundred million bodies shared one heartbeat and were subjected to one mind. Today, the body is being represented as both capital and fetish in China, as in the West. Dazzling fashion designs, hairstyles, body salons, cosmetic surgeries, fancy dresses, tattoos, nose/lip/ear piercings, and jewelries are all used with a vengeance to produce attractive images of the body. This embodied revolution certainly should in the first place be looked upon as a sign of burgeoning consumer capitalism in China, but it nonetheless deserves to be regarded as a self-conscious call for greater freedom and autonomy, a radical break with Maoist and Confucianist ideologies, and above all, a democratic declaration of "my body, my sovereignty" against totalitarianistic attempts to control social space. The covert and overt sites and forms of Gay and lesbian solidarity in China also evidence culture-specific articulations of agency: homosexual activity in China does not assume the socially and politically high-profiled, visible, belligerent forms that it takes in the West; rather, it is more quiet, reserved, unassertive, but it nonetheless carries as subversive agency of resistance to state heterosexual discourse. The above-discussed instances of agency as encountered in China recall what Michel de Certeau theorizes as tactics and strategies of resistance to an overwhelming system of power. In de Certeau's perspective, the weak, the powerless can transform their everyday acts of writing, reading, walking, dwelling, cooking into spaces of heterotopia within the imposed system of social life. In today's China, such acts or spaces of resistance are encountered everywhere. Beneath the totalitarian capito-socialist system in China today, there exist volcanic layers of such Carnivalesque subversive agency. These instances of culture-specific manifestations of agency give the lie to some of the Western human rights discourses whose West-centric attacks on the Chinese government often turn out to be a disguised inability or unwillingness to recognize culturally specific forms of agency performed by ordinary Chinese people.

The above examples are cited to illustrate the point that, locked "within the dominant conceptualization of agency," Western critics or scholars often fail to identify the subversive sites and forms of power and desire in the world of Others. Western feminism and human rights discourse, when judging the behaviors and practices of other peoples in terms of their own norms, often end up falling prey to some universalizing impulses and attitudes. Purdah in Islamic society does not confine itself to univocal signification, and it can be deployed as a form of resistance to the violence against women. That purdah as a means of oppression of Islamic women can be transformed into a means of resistance to such oppression seems unthinkable outside the domain of cultural translation.[9] Anglo-American feminism's inability to recognize and appreciate culture-specific articulations of female agency among North American Aboriginal peoples is actually an inability or reluctance to translate the universal concept of agency in cultural terms or across cultural boundaries. The failure among Westerners to recognize social spaces of insurgency in China betrays an inability to identify culture-specific manifestations of agency. The above discussion emphasizes the urgency of Spivak's call for translation from idiom to standard and for listening to idiomaticities patiently and carefully, without which there would be no genuine democracy and no genuine transcultural communication. Each people or culture has its own idioms of expression and communication, which are embedded in its language and therefore cannot be annulled or superseded by a standard language (Spivak, "Translation as Culture," 22). In the present context, the standard language refers to the hegemonic discursive language prevalent in the metropolitan West whereas idioms can be taken as non–Western languages.

It is well arguable that, in an important sense, cultural translation is a Hegelian dialectic deployed against Hegelian historicism, a historicism that subsumes or subjugates all histories to one History, the West-centered or the West-authorized history. As such cultural translation always uncovers difference or conflicts between different situations in which the concept of universality is encountered. It always emphasizes the context-specific meaning of a concept or practice and always calls attention to the difficulty of transcoding between different languages. The role of cultural translation is to return the excluded to the discourse of universality, and it forces a rethinking or expansion of the "basic premises" (Butler, "Universality in Culture," 11) of whatever is under discussion. It is in this sense that cultural translation opens our eyes to "the various rhetorical, [cultural and socio-political contexts] in which the meaning and force of universal claims are made" ("Restaging," 35). As such, cultural translation performs a double task: it increases our awareness that different peoples share more commonalities than we have known and that there are more irreducible differences among them than we have been willing to admit. In a world increasingly torn apart by ideological and military wars, biases, and various forms of cultural and political fundamentalism and imperialism, in which whole populations and communities as well as individuals have fallen outside of the human, it is urgently necessary to readmit the excluded by way of cultural translation. It is at this historical moment that Butler in her recent book, *Precarious Life: The Powers of Mourning and Violence*, calls upon us to rethink the human, to contest the racist and imperialistic frames of representation, and to "take up the challenges of cultural translation" (90). Butler's call echoes Spivak's and Bhabha's advocating and valorizing of cultural translation as an empowering strategy of contesting and challenging the epistemic regimes of the metropolitan West. It is well arguable that cultural translation as defined and elaborated by Butler, Bhabha, and Spivak can serve to usher in a new paradigm of transnational communication in the age of globalization, a postcolonial mode of representation, which, to borrow terms from Emmanuel Levinas, opens up to and respects the sovereignty of the cultural/ethnic Others. Cultural translation as such recognizes and appreciates the norms of local cultures, non-western forms and sites of agency, and culture-specific articulations of universality, hopefully enabling and mobilizing discursive efforts on both sides of the (neo)colonial divide to imagine towards an authentic international/intercultural democracy.

In a recent article titled "Democracy: A Lyrical Poem or a Construction Drawing," Han Shaogong, one of the leading novelists and critics in the Chinese-speaking world, questions the adequacy of the currently prevalent concept of democracy and proposes expanding its parameters. In Han's view, as a method of managing public affairs, the current version of democracy is not without deficiencies and there are domains where its application always errs, such as in external-related affairs and future-related affairs. His basic argument is that, as a principle of decision-making procedures in modern society, democracy is ethnocentric and present-centric and is always imperialistic towards the Others located beyond the borders of the nation state and in the future. History is a rich documentation of democracy being used/abused in endorsing colonialist territorial expansion and imperialistic foreign policies and in declaring war on neighbors; democracy is deployed and debated to ensure maximum representation of social interest, but it seldom takes into account the interests of those who are not present or yet to be born. The ethnocentric aspect of democracy, as discussed by Han, recalls what Gayatri Chakravorty Spivak terms "feudalism without feudality"; the present-centric aspect of democracy echoes what Derrida writes on justice or responsibility towards those "who are not yet *present* and *living*":

> No justice ... seems possible or thinkable without the principle of some *responsibility*, beyond all living present, within that which disjoins the living present, before the ghosts of those who are not yet born or who are already dead, be they victims of wars, political or other kinds of violence, nationalist, racist, colonialist, sexist, or other kinds of exterminations, victims of the oppressions of capitalist imperialism or any other forms of totalitarianism [xix].

Han's critical reflection on the imperialism of West-championed democracy proceeds to argue that although democracy as a modern form of political government originated in the West, democracy as a principle of decision-making procedures has been existent in other parts of the world as well, such as Africa and China. In what is called pre-modern China, for example, there were *shanrangzhi* (the system of abdication),[10] *jianguanzhi* (the system of imperial admonition),[11] *jietiezhi* (the practice of imperial news release in the form of pamphlets),[12] and *fengboquan* (the office in charge of refuting imperial edicts and sending memoirs to the throne).[13] In Maoist China, there have been *qunzhongluxian* (the mass route), *minzhu shenghuo hui* (democratic life meeting), *zhigong daibiao dahui* (the congress of workers and staff).[14] The above-cited institutions and practices of democracy prevalent in ancient China and Maoist China have to be attended to across cultural boundaries, and a genuine recognition of their use and impact on Chinese society can be achieved only when aided by knowledge of Chinese history and culture. Han's contestatory negotiation with Western democracy challenges the world to redefine the concept of democracy and expand its parameters to admit the excluded, namely the non–Western, by way of cultural translation, which reveals culture-specific articulations of democracy.

Ours is a world besieged with crises on all sides. Capitalist imperialism is wreaking havoc upon the world at different levels and in different aspects of social life in unforeseen ways. Structural unemployment, increasing social polarizations, destructive eco-environmental catastrophes, ethnic-racial confrontations, the lumpenproletarianization of working forces, and derealization or dehumanization of social or cultural Others — all these are driving the humankind to a historical moment which compels us to say "no" to capitalist modernity and to imagine non-capitalist alternatives to capitalist globalization. This epochal project cannot get started if some populations or cultures are excluded, and, more importantly, there must be narratives, imaginations, and theorizings of the future from outside the global system of capital and outside of Western perspectives. In other words, the world has to begin with new beginnings and has to rethink and redefine modernity and its coordinates such as democracy, rationality, equality of being, justice, and human rights. Different cultural pasts and presents have to be turned to for socio-political resources and legacies in thinking towards alternative modernities. This counter-capitalist project is counter-colonialist in nature, not only because it seeks alternatives to capitalist modernity outside western hegemony, but because it is predicated on cultural translation, without which there would be no enabling traffic between universality and particularity, or between abstract and concrete, that is free of imperialism. To translate from idiom to standard is to enhance or foster respect and appreciation for idiom-specific articulations of what is understood in terms of the standard. There are as many differential manifestations of universality as there are languages and cultures. Only when we are able to recognize culture-specific articulations of agency, rationality, and democracy can there be a truly postcolonial world, and only when the world is truly postcolonial can there emerge non-capitalist alternatives to the present. All cultures are translational, for culture always goes with a certain concept of Otherness, and as such it carries infinite sedimented other times and spaces in itself. However, to move from translational culture to cultural translation is self-consciously to deploy translation as a counter-colonialist strategy of battling against capitalist imperialism or against the West-championed homogenizing process of modernization. While describing contemporary capitalism as "one dominant global system structured around the transnational corporations, a transnational capitalist class and the culture-ideology of consumerism," Leslie Sklair envisions a "flowering of alternative non-capitalist forms of globalization" in the beginning decades of twenty-first century (1). It is to be hoped that when non-capitalist forms of globalization are arising on the horizon, cultural translation will be the cultural logic of globalization itself.

NOTES

1. According to Nimrod Raphaeli, "the number of unemployed people worldwide climbed to new heights in 2005; the total number of jobless stood at 191.8 million people at the end of 2005, an increase of 2.2 million since 2004 and 34.4 million since 1995."
2. See "Hunger Facts: International."
3. See "Garden Harvest: Facts about Hunger."
4. "Hunger Facts: International."
5. See Annette Jaimes with Thersa Halsey, "American Indian Women."
6. Similar arrogant, biased attitudes towards China or the Chinese are registered by Henry Zhao's *New Left Review* book review of Gloria Davis's *Worrying About China: The Language of Chinese Critical Inquiry.* As Zhao notes, Davis's basic position is that the "Chinese intellectuals remain positivist, essentialist and foundationalist" (Zhao 155). The unmistakable implications of Davis' criticisms of Chinese intellectuals are that Chinese intellectual discourse is inherently inferior to its Anglophone counterpart. The Chinese intellectuals are characterized by intellectual inferiority and epistemological naïveté, because they are still impassionedly pursuing grand narratives of national rejuvenation, social progress, objective truth, and national allegory. Davis's disparaging remarks on Chinese intellectuals can be boiled down to one central argument: Their writing is devoid of critical agency.
7. It has been reported that by the end of June 2007 there were 500 million cell phone users in China, and by 2008 the number reached 600 million ("Cell Phones Booming in China," n.p.). By the middle of 2008 there were 253 million broadband users and more than 2.6 million websites (Wikipedia). There are today hundreds of virtual forums hosting open debates on China and the world economically and politically.
8. If the rediscovery of the body is a newly emergent event "after a millennial age of Puritanism" in the postmodern West, then the same can be said of its revalorization in China except that the Puritanism that has to be removed for the emergence of the body has endured there for five thousand years. The memory is still fresh of a 1960s and 1970s China to many people in and outside of the country that everyone in the forbidden space of Maoist ideology at that time was dressed and fully covered in black or blue and female and male faces looked the same by reason of banned cosmetics.
9. It means that the concept of resistant agency alternates between two moments of life — the moment of universality and the moment of its culture-specific articulation. The concept of anything, in order to be a concept, as Hegel as well Butler has taught us, has to enrich itself by constantly moving between universality and particularity or by gathering particularity to expand the parameters of universality. However, the concept of resistant agency, when applied in western feminism in judging non-western women's subjectivity, does not walk on two legs, and does

not lead to a recognition of its culture or place-specific manifestation, because many of western feminists, imprisoned in their exclusionary repertoire of forms of agency, are blind to the eligibility of agency performed in forms unknown to them.

10. A peaceful way for the throne to pass from one person to another in ancient China. There were two kinds of *shanrang*, one took place within the imperial family and the other between the incumbent emperor and someone else outside the family, which usually brought about a new dynasty.

11. The role of the imperial admonisher (*jianguan*) in ancient China was to admonish the emperor against making wrong decisions, pointing out or correcting his mistakes. The imperial admonisher was granted exemption from penalty no matter how harsh his opposition was to the emperor's will. The office of imperial admonition was at its height in the Tang Dynasty and began to decline in the Ming Dynasty. See Qian Mu, *Guoshi xinlun* (*New Perspectives on Chinese History*) (Beijing: Sanlian Shudian Press, 2001), pp. 87–92.

12. A protected manner of direct communication between the emperor and his officials. The role of *jietie* was to advise the emperor of the true state of things or of the measures to be adopted or rejected in dealing with a certain situation.

13. *Fengboquan* (the right to refute imperial edicts), as much as *jianyiquan* (imperial admonition), was another official way of voicing opposition to the emperor, preventing the monarch from making mistakes.

14. In Mao's time the masses of the ordinary people were the privileged classes and what is called democratic.

WORKS CITED

Benjamin, Walter. "The Task of the Translator." *Illuminations*. Ed. Hannah Arendt. New York: Schocken, 1969.

Bhabha, Homi. *The Location of Culture*. London: Routledge, 1994.

Butler, Judith. "Competing Universalities." *Contingency, Hegemony, Universality: Contemporary Dialogues on the Left*. Judith Butler, Ernesto Laclau, and Slavoj Žižek. London: Verso, 2000. 136–181.

_____. *Precarious Life: The Powers of Mourning and Violence*. London: Verso, 2006.

_____. "Restaging the Universal." *Contingency, Hegemony, Universality: Contemporary Dialogues on the Left*. 11–43.

_____. "Universality in Culture." *For the Love of Country: Debating the Limits of Patriotism*. Ed. Joshua Cohen. Boston: Beacon, 1996. 45–52.

"Cell Phones Booming in China." 2 December 2008. *http://en.chinagate.cn/news/2007-10/03/content_8998266.htm*.

Chatterjee, Partha. *Our Modernity*. Rotterdam: Sephis and Codesria, 1997.

Cui, Zhiyuan. *Introduction to Politics: The Central Texts*. Roberto Unger. Ed. Zhiyuan Cui. London: Verso, 1997. 16 May 2006. *http://www.robertounger.com/cui.htm*.

Derrida, Jacques. *Specters of Marx: The State of The Debt, the Work of Mourning, and the New International*. Trans. Peggy Kamuf. New York: Routledge, 1994.

"Garden Harvest: Facts about Hunger." 15 November 2009. *http://www.gardenharvest.org/HungerInternational.htm*.

Han, Shaogong. "Democracy: A Lyrical Poem or a Construction Drawing." (*Minzhu:shuqing shi yu shigong tu*). 20 August 2009. *http://www.forum1.cn/show.aspx?id=884&cid=225*.

Harvey, David. *Spaces of Global Capitalism: Towards an Uneven Geographical Development*. London: Verso, 2006.

"Hunger Facts: International." 15 November 2009. *http://www.bread.org/learn/hunger-basics/hunger-facts-international.html*.

Jaimes, Annette, and Theresa Halsey. "American Indian Women." *Dangerous Liaisons: Gender, Nation and Postcolonial Perspectives*. Ed. Anne McClintock, Aamir Rashid Mufti, and Ella Shohat. Minneapolis: University of Minnesota Press, 1997. 295–329.

Mohanty, Chandra Talpade. "Under Western Eyes: Feminist Scholarship and Colonial Discourses." *Dangerous Liaisons: Gender, Nation and Postcolonial Perspectives.* Ed. Anne McClintock, Aamir Rashid Mufti, and Ella Shohat. Minneapolis: University of Minnesota Press, 1997. 255–277.

Moses, Michael Valdez. *The Novel and the Globalization of Culture.* New York: Oxford University Press, 1995.

Qian, Mu. *Guoshi xinlun (New Perspectives on Chinese History).* Beijing: Sanlian Shudian Press, 2001.

Raphaeli, Nimrod. "Unemployment in the Middle East — Causes and Consequences." 12 November 2009. *http://www.memri.org/bin/articles.cgi?Page=archives&Area=ia&ID=IA26506.*

Sklair, Leslie. *Globalization: Capitalism and Its Alternatives.* Oxford: Oxford University Press, 2002.

Spivak, Chakravorty Gayatri. *A Critique of Postcolonial Reason: Toward a History of the Vanishing Present.* Cambridge: Harvard University Press, 1999.

_____. "Translation as Culture." *Parallax* 6,1 (2000): 13–24.

Zhao, Henry. "Caring for the Nation." *New Left Review* 54 (November-December 2008): 153–60.

Žižek, Slavoj. "How to Begin from the Beginning." *New Left Review* 57 (May-June 2009): 43–55.

Hybridity and Identity in New Zealand Māori Literature
Alan Duff's Dreamboat Dad

ALISTAIR FOX

Since Homi K. Bhabha's articulation of a theory of hybridity, in which the postmodern subject is caught up in an endless and uncontrollable process of personal self-recreation within the infinitely variable interstitial space resulting from the overlap and displacement of domains of difference, scholars have identified other models, including ones based on polyculturalism, strategic syncreticity, and bricolage. Through an investigation of representations of hybrid experience by New Zealand Māori writers, focusing on Alan Duff's novel *Dreamboat Dad* (2008), this essay identifies another model of hybridity, analogous to the structure of the double helix — a powerful symbol in Māori culture — that may be distinctive to the mixed race literature of this country.

In Duff's representation, identity is found not in the delusional identifications and projections that his chief character constructs from his relationship with other cultures, but in the recovery of an understanding of how his originary culture has invested him with a core sense of self that can make his engagement with other cultures meaningful and productive. By comparing the paradigm to be found in Duff's novel with those in Patricia Grace's *Mutuwhenua*, Witi Ihimaera's *The Rope of Man*, and Keri Hulme's *The Bone People*, I conclude that Duff's representation of hybridity is not idiosyncratic, but rather typical of Māori writing at large.

The Debate on Hybridity

Since the appearance of Homi K. Bhabha's *The Location of Culture* in 1994, a growing number of scholars have expressed dissatisfaction with the account of cultural hybridity that it propounds. For Bhabha, culture is located in the act of traveling itself, with the postmodern subject being caught up in an endless and uncontrollable process of personal self-recreation within the infinitely variable interstitial space that results from "the overlap and displacement of domains of difference" (2, 4–9). Hybridity, in this articulation, is "a theoretical meta-construction" that not merely characterizes the condition of postmodernity itself, but also renders any fixed or determinate identities impossible (Werbner, 1).

Against this supposition — which has been broadly embraced within postcolonial studies — subsequent scholars have pointed out that in actuality identities often show a marked resistance to hybridization (Werbner, 3) and, further, that an increasing trend towards ethnification allows "little room for the [de-territorialized] hybrid identification discussed and pleaded for by cultural elites" (Friedman, 84). Instead, critics have posited alternative models of hybridity, based on representations that can be found in literature. Jeffrey F. L. Partridge, for example, detects a "polycultural hybridity" in Gish Jen's *Mona in the Promised Land*, in which different lineages are strategically accumulated as a means of activating dialogic interplay without any loss of cultural objectification (112–114). Similarly, Paul Sharrad has argued in a study of Pacific literatures that they display a type of cultural mixing that manifests strategic syncreticity, rather than hybridity as conceived by Bhabha:

> Some indigenous voices — here especially those from Oceania — have been developing strategies all along that allow the continuation of ethnic identity as a partly racial/ised phenomenon while also validating the cultural mixing, both in society and literature, that contemporary postcolonial life entails [106].

Others, like Roger Bromley, have pointed to the deployment in diasporic literatures of a form of calculated "code-switching" that allows migrants to "play with their identities while still valorising them and putting into question the over-ethnification of public social areas" (103, 107).

The identification of these alternative models of hybridity, each of which implies a greater degree of purposeful agency on the part of the subject than is possible within Bhabha's articulation, suggests that we need to look more closely at the specific forms, motives, and outcomes of cultural mixing, rather than to assume automatically that the effect of hybridity is to subvert the possibility of any fixed form of identity because of the deconstruction of categories that is alleged to take place when one inhabits the interstitial liminality of a "third space." As a number of commentators have observed, such a conception of hybridity really applies only to a group of nomadic cosmopolitan intellectuals who are self-identifying and, indeed, in the words of one critic, "selfessentializing" (81). Within academia, this articulation of hybridity has threatened to assume an ideological hegemony of its own that threatens to obscure other possibilities. With respect to this danger, it may be profitable to recall Gramsci's notion of the difference between the traditional *intelligentsia*, who appear to stand apart in the interstices of society, and the "organic intellectual," a spokesperson from a specific class or group who expresses the ideas and aspirations of the group to which he or she organically belongs, because of the experience he or she shares with its members (3–14). In considering the issue of hybridity, I believe, it is incumbent on scholars to listen to the voices of organic intellectuals, rather than just those of a privileged cosmopolitan elite.

To do so, I shall examine representations of hybridity in the work of New Zealand Māori writers. Māori writing is unusually apposite for this purpose — especially since the rise of studies of mixed race literature (see Somerville) — given that almost all Māori in contemporary New Zealand are of mixed race ancestry. Indeed, all of the Māori writers I will discuss have Pākehā blood in their ancestry, with varying degrees of proximity, which invests them with a biological hybridity from the outset that provides a powerful incentive for their investigations of cultural hybridity. For a specific case study, I shall focus on the most recent novel by Alan Duff, *Dreamboat Dad*, published in 2008. Duff is particularly interesting, because, being himself of mixed race, having a Māori mother and Pākehā father, he tackles the issues inherent in hybridity head-on by recurrently inventing heroes who are themselves of mixed race, as in the case of Mark in *Dreamboat Dad*, for whom hybridity is a literal biological reality and whose character incorporates many details drawn from Duff's own experience (Bollard, "Alan Duff").

Mark's Fantasies of Identity

As his vehicle for the exploration of certain issues arising from hybridity, Duff creates a coming-of-age story in which his protagonist, Mark (also known as "Yank") seeks to discover his true identity. Mark was born as the result of a liaison between a Māori woman, Lena, and an American solder stationed in New Zealand during the absence of her Māori husband, Henry Takahe, who is overseas during World War II. Perturbed by his failure to win the affection of Henry after the latter's return, Mark grows up with a desperate urge to know his real father, whom he construes in his imagination as a "dreamboat dad" — an idealized, handsome, white American Marine who alternatively resembles John Wayne and Elvis Presley. In actual fact, Mark's father, Jess, turns out not only to be a "Negro," in the terminology Duff uses, but also a descendant of slaves from a very abject and underprivileged background in the Deep South. Mark's shock at this discovery precipitates a process of self-examination, through which he is faced with the challenge of working out who he really is in the light of this new knowledge.

In his portrayal of Mark's character, Duff reveals how Mark's unhappiness at his circumstances — as an unowned son in his step-father's house and as a Māori in a society in which he perceives whites as dominant and superior — prompts him to construct a succession of identities for himself that turn out to be based on delusional projections. Each of these attempts involves identifications with aspects of other cultures that make it possible for him to disavow or disguise his own Māoriness, as a way of escaping from the disadvantage he believes it imposes on him. Significantly, the elements that he draws upon to construct these identities are never found in present actualities, but are always located elsewhere — in another time, place, or race. Mark's efforts to construct a new, hybridized identity are not constrained within an encounter with the cultures of other ethnicities; he also draws upon a cultural alterity that he detects within Māori culture itself — in the contrast between the values of the traditional past and those of the postcolonial present.

Mark's attempts to reformulate his identity operate simultaneously at a number of different levels. The first level involves his attempt to redefine himself in terms of the values and practices of a vanished Māori past. His motive for doing so arises from his awareness of the contrast between traditional Māori society, in which everyone confidently knew who they were, and Māori in the present, who, like Henry (and indeed himself), are no longer sure of who they are. This contrast of cultures within Māoridom itself is imaged within the novel in the difference between the "muscled warrior from another time" who performs a ritual welcome to the servicemen returning from overseas, representing "a millennium of warriors in the proud past," and the servicemen themselves, who appear "disorientated, unsure of where they are" (14–15, 17–18). Duff provides a spokesperson for the former world in the form of Merita, an aged *kuia* with "tattooed lips and chin etched and chiselled in the old way" who misses "the old times" of the traditional Māori warrior culture, when "[e]veryone knew their place." In contrast, Mark perceives Māori life in the post-war world as abject and dysfunctional, as when Henry savagely beats up his wife, Lena, or when Mark's friend, Chud Kohu, is brutalized by his father, who himself looks "like a male baboon," spending much of his time drunk in the company of "a pack of apes" (42–44).[1]

To escape from this fear of being trapped in an abject present, Mark constructs an identity that is based on the vanished culture of the past, in which, as the old *kuia* tells Mark, "all the great Maori chiefs had slaves, some destined for the cooking ovens" (31).[2] Accepting Merita's consoling reassurance that he is the son of a mother who is "high born," Mark fantasizes that his mistreatment at the hands of his adoptive father, Henry, merely attests to his own superiority:

> The high-born endure pain as a mark of their superior status. This high-born kid endures the pain of living in Henry's house.
>
> One day I'll make you one of my slaves, Henry Takahe. One day my father is going to arrive and then we'll see you tremble in front of a real man. Kneel, slave, my father will say. And you will kneel. Then he will behead you for how you treated his son [31–32].

By investing both himself and his natural father with the superiority and power of the high-born, in accordance with the values of traditional Māori society, Mark, in his fantasy, is seeking to invert the roles of victim and abuser in order to maintain a kind of narcissistic homeostasis in the face of actual conditions in the present that threaten to destroy it. The problem is that the scenario Mark has constructed to sustain this sense of himself, being entirely fanciful, involves a script that can never be enacted in reality. After Mark discovers the true facts of his parentage, he realizes that had he actually been alive in the old days, he would have suffered the abject fate of a slave, being low born, rather than enjoyed the privileges and power of the high-born.

The second level at which Mark seeks to escape from the actuality of his circumstances involves his relation to the world of the Pākehā. To Mark, the things of the white world seem superior to things Māori, which he automatically registers as inferior. The disparity between these two worlds in Mark's imaginary is starkly evident in the contrast he draws between his "real" father, whom he imagines as "[t]all and handsome, muscular, with shining white teeth and of paler complexion than my olive," and his *de facto* father, Henry, whom he registers as never having been "what you would call handsome," as "not of high-born lineage," and as being "quite dark of complexion as if his blood line has not been diluted by white blood that runs in most Maori veins of today" (20–21).

Mark's sense of the relative inequality between the two worlds is reinforced when he and the other "poor naive village Maori boys" enter high school, and find that whereas the Pākehā sons are destined to be prepared for "jobs we'd never heard of. Surveyor. Accountant. Doctor. Lawyer. Banker. Chemist. Landlord. Pilot. Scientist," the Maori sons from Waiwera "feel like dunderheads straight out of the backblocks who can't apply ourselves to anything of the mind. Alien beings of limited ability from planet Waiwera in outer space just a thirty minute bus ride from high school" (62–63). When Mark forms a friendship with a Pākehā boy, Nigel Blake, his sense of these disparities in status and power fills him with a conviction that "his race ruled and my race were the darkies of the country, a minority too. Their right to

issue invite, our privilege to receive" (64). In response to this sense of inferiority, Mark seeks to gain entrance into the "broader" white world by having
a liaison with Isobel Blake, the Pākehā mother of his friend, Nigel, when he
is seduced by the "older woman's sophistication and womanly wiles" (92).

The third level at which Mark attempts to escape from abjection through
contriving a new hybrid identity concerns the contrast in his mind between
America and New Zealand. He imagines the super-country as offering opportunities denied to people like himself in his smaller, insignificant one. For
Mark, the symbols of this enhanced possibility are two American pop-singers:
Little Richard and Elvis Presley, both of whom strike him as having offered
a means of escaping the system. Coming first, Little Richard, "a crazily out-
fitted and behaved Negro ... dressed and acted like an effeminate clown so
white Americans couldn't put a label on him and therefore would let him be"
(66). Elvis was even more influential: "He could have been Jesus Christ he
was so important ... . He came like a letter from America, addressed *Dear
Young World ... I, Elvis Presley, give you permission to be whatever you want*"
(67). Significantly, just as earlier he had construed his father as looking like
John Wayne, when Mark receives a letter from him and learns that his name
is Jess Hines, he images him as being like his idol: "a tall, lean man, very
handsome, thick dark hair like his son's, musical and probably rich. Looks
like Elvis" (70). The letter from his father thus becomes conflated in his imagination with the metaphorical letter sent by Elvis to the world: that is, it
carries the burden of all Mark's fantasized hopes for some kind of magical liberation from the world in which he feels miserable and deprived.

Not surprisingly, Mark combines all the elements of his fantasized attach-
ments — to the Pākehā world, to American culture, and to his imaginary white
father — when he enters into a musical partnership with a Pākehā friend, Nigel
Blake, in preparation for forming a "'unique father and son combo'" that he
imagines he will eventually perform "'to adoring audiences throughout America'" some time in the visionary future (68).

Mark's Dis-Illusionment

Duff's purpose in depicting these various attempts by Mark to formulate
a new culturally hybridized identity is to expose the insubstantial foundations
of the identities so constructed. This exposure takes the form of a number of
ironic revelations. Chief among them is Mark's discovery, when he sees a pho-
tograph of the American father whom he has idealized, that Jess Hines is actually an African American — a realization that exposes the underlying prejudices
he has unwittingly internalized:

> *This can't be.* My father is *white.* With uncanny resemblance to Elvis. Or the ruggedly handsome features of John Wayne. When I was younger my dad was a cowboy — and they're all *white* — with six-shooters blazing, saving my life from Injuns. I've carried this choice of images in my mind for years. This is *not* him.
>   I think of coal, boot polish, the Devil, evil, all the bad and negative moods described as black and dark, even the night is black and the day is glorious light. A virgin doesn't get married in black. Nothing black is pure. No food is black. Black is what is worn at funerals [114].

What Mark is discovering here is the extent to which he has unconsciously internalized the assumptions of an extremely racist discourse that he will eventually realize he has no need to accept, given that it is only his acceptance of the prejudices propagated through this discourse — which merely reflects the values of a hegemonic white majority — that has caused him to feel disadvantaged in the first place.

Following upon this revelation is a further one — that Merita, the old *kuia*, had been lying when she told Mark that his mother was high-born. When Lena, his mother, disabuses him by revealing that her families on both sides "are ordinary," Mark's response is vehement: "Well I'm no child of a descendant of slaves. And I'm sure as hell not a nigger" (114). The reality of the fact that he is both of these things delivers a tremendous shock to the comforting, but delusional, assumptions that have supported the sense of identity Mark has fancifully crafted for himself. This, in turn, prompts him to reconceptualize who he might actually be: "I have urge to rush to a mirror and reconsider my face. Get the alarming thought of my contempt for Maori slaves of the old days: Negroes were slaves" (113). In one fell swoop, his discovery of his real parentage has exposed the fallacious grounds of the racial prejudice upon which his sense of self has depended, while at the same time it exposes the iniquity of the class prejudice that he had enthusiastically endorsed as a meritorious feature of the old Maori culture. Painfully, Mark learns the truth of what his mother says to him: "Remember we're only slaves to ideas and attitudes" (115).

A further shock is delivered to the settled nature of Mark's assumptions when he actually goes to America to visit his father. Whereas Mark had believed that America opened the route to opportunity, he discovers that his father, in reverse, had viewed New Zealand in exactly the same way — at least in comparison with the Deep South. As Jess Hines puts it, when he was stationed in New Zealand he was astonished to discover that

> the native Maoris ... had the same rights as the whites, they played sport together, married one another, had representation at political level, a born right to be whatever they chose. How could Negroes be permitted to drink

in the same bars as whites? Back home that would cause a riot, cops would arrest us, a white judge would throw us in jail [127].

In Jess's view, it is New Zealand's society that is enlightened and utopian as far as race relations and lack of prejudice are concerned, not the other way around. Mark discovers, in fact, that whereas he had believed Māori to be a disadvantaged race, relative to the Negroes of the American South in the 1960s (the period during which most of the action of the novel is set), they are not:

> You see the reality, of every store queue giving priority to whites not blacks. How deferential, even subservient, they've been made. I see how unlike Maoris Negroes are: no Maori would put up with being treated with such contempt for a second. In our country some whites are scared of Maoris. We are the warrior class and let none forget that, no matter the ones with the least money. We have law on our side, do Maoris, and rights [204].

He also comes to realize how privileged his own upbringing has been, compared with that of his Negro father who, as a child, had been traumatized by the sight of a black woman being lynched off a bridge: "Where was I at the same age? Safe in Henry's house, told every day by my mother how special I was" (205). In short, Mark's actual experience of "black life" in the southern United States leads him to understand that he had grown up "worshipping a false idol" (202).

What Mark learns through this process of literal disillusionment is the relativity of perception and the extent to which it depends upon the assumptions of the subject position one occupies. The most brutal demonstration of this relativity occurs when Mark, having swung to the opposite extreme by wholly identifying with his father—"I don't want to be any other race but Negro now. A member of my father's race so I might right some injustices. Do not want to go home. Have become my father's son" (205)—finds that this new identification is also illusory. This final dismantling of his illusions occurs when he visits a black club with his father, only to find himself regarded with hostility as a "pet Klan boy"— someone from a "Planet called White" on account of his relatively pale complexion (223). Ironically, the "niggers" in the club impute to Mark the very identity that he had earlier longed for in fantasy — that of a white man — but regard it as cause for contempt, rather than pride.

Mark's Discovery of an Authentic, Essential Core Sense of Self

Had Duff ended the novel at this point, its exposure of the illusions and projections informing Mark's self-sense might have suggested that Duff shared the view that it is impossible to attain a determinate sense of identity. Mark would have been left in a condition very similar to that of the dis-located postmodern subject as described by Homi Bhabha — that is, of someone who can only ever be "in-between" and for whom identity can only inhere in the act of traveling itself, without the possibility of arriving at any destination. This, however, is precisely what Duff does *not* show, because there is one further stage to be achieved in Mark's education: his discovery that, beyond anything else he may be, at the heart of his being there is indeed an essential self, and that this self is *Māori*.

This final movement in the evolution of Mark's self-sense is triggered by the sight of his father's abject behavior when confronted by two white cops who try to intimidate him out of participating in a Civil Rights protest (212– 215). When Mark sees his father's "fawning, lowered head" as he descends into "slave mode" to appease the cops, he feels an upwelling of "Maori warrior pride" that makes him realize the difference between himself and his father. In turn, Jess's perception of the fact that his son is ashamed of him induces a new found courage that achieves full expression when the two men find themselves being pursued by Negro-hating white rednecks after they have taken part in a Civil Rights march. During the car chase, Mark suddenly begins to understand who he really is: "I get this thought: I am my mother's blood too: Maori. I am *Maori*. I am also *Scots*, a bit of *Irish*. They were warriors too. They knew oppression. Since when did they stop being warriors?" (234). As his father — who has finally decided to throw off the shackle of oppression — seeks Mark's help in preparing an ambush to destroy their pursuers, Mark feels the inculcated responses of the Māori warrior rising up in him: "'I am what I was raised as. I don't have to understand it. I am not Negro, coloured or black. I was raised a Maori.'" Realization of this fact makes it possible for Mark to overcome his fear in order to act effectively by assisting his father: "'If I am not myself first, I can never be of and for my father'" (235). Significantly, this recovered sense of what it is to "be himself" leads to his becoming an accomplice in the killing of the two white racists who are pursuing him and his father. Perhaps, in this action, we can see a symbolic "killing off" of his former desire to identify himself with the white world, which he now registers as persecutory and "self"-destructive. At any rate, the certainty of Mark's new sense of personal identity, in which everything seems "crystal clear," makes the "'hell'" in which he and his father find themselves after the killing feel "like heaven" (236). Through this catalyzing interaction with his newly recovered father, he has at last attained a sense of identity that he finds coherent, and capable of sustaining him.

Proof of this is seen after Mark's return to New Zealand — at the instigation of his father, who is determined his son should avoid the retribution that he is doomed to suffer. Mark's experience with Jess has made him realize "'how your birthplace, your culture, can make you'" (246). Consequently, he feels more respect for and tolerance of his step-father, Henry, whom earlier he had despised, says goodbye to his Pākehā lover, Isobel, and enters into a relationship with Giselle, a mulatto girl from Brazil, which marks a reversal of his original prejudice. Self-acceptance based on an accurate perception of reality leads him to cease attempting to distort it through the fabrication of fanciful identities. As his mother observes, Mark has also become "'strong enough to accept being ordinary'" (247).

The Strategic Construction of Hybridity and Personal Agency

Duff's novel, by implication, offers a number of insights into the functions of cultural hybridity, especially as represented in literature. It shows how the encounter with other cultures can provide an individual with a powerful tool for confronting reality, because of the capacity for symbolic representations to be created from cultural mixing that objectify the subject's hopes and fears with respect to that reality, along with strategies whereby he or she might seek to address them. From Duff's fiction, we can see that these strategies can take several different forms. Representations of hybridity can facilitate the creation of imaginary identifications and projections that serve to elaborate a wish contrary to present fact — as we see in Mark's initial attempts to disavow or downplay his identity as Māori, in order to counter his feeling of being unloved, and to escape from his fear of inferiority. Hybridity can also allow a subject to generate expectations contrary to past experience — as when Lena leaves her abusive Māori husband to move in with a wealthy Pākehā businessman, Ralph, "'not so much [on account of] the higher quality of life money brought as much as the knowledge'" to which she gained access through such a relationship, providing her with "'a degree of happiness she has never known previously'" (238). Finally, as Mark's later experience shows, hybridity can activate a process of triangulation that allows one to attain, or to recover, a sense of originary identity as the precondition for engaging with reality in order to transform it, rather than simply seeking to distort or transcend it. For Duff, this acknowledgment of the formative influence of the culture within which one was raised is the foundation of agency itself, because without it one is forever doomed to be chasing phantoms.

The presence of these various motives for exploiting cultural mixing suggests that Duff's view of hybridity is much more complicated than that articulated by Bhabha. For Duff, hybridity is not experienced simply as an uncontrollable, generalized consequence of the intersection of cultures in the contemporary globalized condition. Rather, it is the product of purposeful symbolic constructions of which the individual subject is the active architect. Nor does Duff accept that the encounter with cultural others of necessity leads to an indeterminacy of identity; to the contrary, in the case of Mark, he shows that such encounters can induce a restored sense of identity by clarifying the extent to which the individual subject has been inescapably conditioned by the regime of subjectification inherent in the culture within which he or she has been raised. In Duff's view, recognition and acceptance of this influence provides the only sound basis for a transformative engagement with the outer world — because in its absence the subject is unlikely to be able to maintain any coherent self-sense that can survive the test of reality.

Duff's emphasis on the continuing importance of the culture of origin as a primary constant given in the encounter with cultural difference means that the model of hybridity he invokes is somewhat different from other models that have been proposed. The sense of identity Mark achieves by the end of the novel is not the result of fusion; nor is it the product of creolization, with the form of one culture being filled with the content of another; nor is it primarily constituted of a syncretic assemblage, or bricolage. Instead, it is an identity that rests upon the coterminous presence in Mark's imaginary of the original Māori culture in which he was raised, along with elements that he draws from other cultures for the sake of constructing images of desire and aspiration, or else of possibilities that are to be feared and repudiated. The coexistence of these twin sources of cultural influence attests to a transformative purpose that motivates the construction of symbolic representations to embody hybridity. In the case of Duff, therefore, hybridity can be seen as instrumental in promoting the attainment of a future goal, rather than being an outcome or consequence in its own right. As such, it serves as a catalyst for the activation of agency.

Hybridity in the Works of Other Māori Writers

A question arises whether Duff's articulation of hybridity is typical of other Māori writers, or idiosyncratic. To address this issue, I shall briefly compare Duff's novel with works by Patricia Grace, Witi Ihimaera, and Keri Hulme. In all cases, these writers share Duff's concern with reaffirming the validity and importance of their identity as, first and foremost, Māori. The heroine of Grace's novel *Mutuwhenua*, for example, replicates the movement of Mark's trajectory, in that initially she wishes to escape the constraints she believes are imposed on her by her Māori identity, by entering the world of the Pākehā: "I decided that if I had the chance I could be someone different, and thought that it would be much better to be a girl in buckled shoes bowing a violin than the girl I was" (24). To accomplish this transformation, she changes her name from Ripeka to Linda, and takes as her partner a Pākehā man, like Lena in *Dreamboat Dad*, and moves to the city. Ripeka/Linda discovers, however, that however much she may love her Pākehā husband and the comforts that life in the Pākehā world may bestow, she cannot cast off the Māori side of herself—the part of her "'that could never be given and that would not change'" (9). Near the end of the novel, this reality presents a supreme challenge to Ripeka's Pākehā husband, Graeme, when she decides to give up their baby to be raised by her mother in accordance with Māori custom, so that "'he would have a place to step from and to return to when the future time came'" (152). Having done so, she is able to return confidently to the Pākehā world and her husband, who, out of love for her, has been able to accept it, but only because she knows the integrity of her commitment to her culture remains intact. The paradigm implicit in this story, then, is virtually identical to that in Duff's *Dreamboat Dad*: a hybridized life is desirable and sought by the Māori subject, but for it to be possible, the originary culture needs to have an existence that is coterminous with one that he or she lives in the Pākehā world — one that does not entail a loss of indigenous identity.

A very similar pattern is found in Witi Ihimaera's mature works, such as *The Rope of Man* (2005). In this novel, Tama, like Ripeka in Grace's *Mutuwhenua*, takes a Pākehā name, forms a relationship with a Pākehā woman, and seeks to succeed in the Pākehā world. Despite his ascent to the pinnacle of success — reflected in his status as a world-famous TV anchorman, his life as an A-lister in London, and his fraternization with the rich and famous — Tama, now renamed Tom, cannot escape his Māori origins. Having been impelled to return by the news his mother is dying, Tama is forced to confront his own guilty conscience concerning the betrayal of filial, tribal, and cultural obligations that have been the price of his success. In the event, Tama discovers that he cannot disavow the Māori part of himself, coming to realize that his connection to Aotearoa, his home, and Māori culture is like an umbilical cord that will ensure that he and other members of his generation will "'never be lost.'" Metaphorically speaking, Tama reaches the same conclusion as Mark in *Dreamboat Dad* and Ripeka in *Mutuwhenua*: that is, despite their attempts to escape it, their Māoriness remains the foundation of their identity. In so far as Māori and Pākehā cultures have, as a result of historical contact between the two races, become blended, their relationship to one another is like that found in the structure of DNA, in which "two helices spiral around each other, connected by molecular bonds, resembling a rope ladder that has been repeatedly twisted along its length'" (276). Once again, then, the Māori element has its own identifiable and distinctive existence, but within a structure in which it is "blended" or "laminated" with the Pākehā element, forming a hybridized unity that does not depend upon fusion, but upon the coterminous existence of its parallel parts.

The final Māori writer I shall discuss, Keri Hulme, also confirms the importance for the mixed race subject to maintain access to the Māori side of himself or herself. In *The Bone People*, Hulme creates a heroine, Kerewin Holmes — "'blue-eyed, brown-haired, and mushroom pale'" — who is clearly a surrogate for herself. As Hulme herself would be able to say, Kerewin in the novel makes the following observation: "'If I was in America, I'd be an octoroon.' Paused. 'It's very strange, but whereas by blood, flesh and inheritance, I am but an eighth Māori, by heart, spirit, and inclination, I feel all Māori. Or,' she looked down into the drink, 'I used to. Now it feels like the best part of me has got lost in the way I live'" (76). The problem for both Kerewin and the male protagonist of *The Bone People*, Joe Gillayley — also Māori, but whose father's father was English — is that they have lost contact with the Māori part of themselves. In Kerewin's case, this is because of estrangement from her family. In Joe's case, who was brought up by his Māori grandmother, it is because his English grandfather was "ashamed, secretly ashamed" of "'Nana and her Maoriness,'" and took it out on his grandson "'for being like her, for being dark, and speaking Maori first, all sorts of things,'" which caused Joe to suppress his own Māoriness (277). As a result, they both suffer from self-imposed isolation, and experience acute psychic pain that is expressed in dysfunction. Kerewin is depressed, frigid, and incapable of experiencing joy or pleasure. Joe is beset with "'evil shadows,'" is prone to explosions of uncontrollable violence, and suffers the torments of guilt from the inescapable conviction that he is a "'fallen boy'" (109, 213). Both drink themselves into a stupor in at attempt to self-soothe.

For this pair, Hulme shows, psychic and physical healing can only begin when they reconnect to the values of the Māoritanga they have respectively lost and disavowed. For Joe, this is symbolized in the *mauri* ("life principle"), which he rediscovers after having been tended to by an aged *kaumatua* (elder). For Kerewin, it occurs after her cancer has been healed by a mysterious old woman, and she hears a *karanga* (call) welcoming her back to her people, following which she reconstructs her tower (which she had earlier burned to the ground in an act of despair) in the shape of a spiral shell — a powerful symbol in Māori culture for growth, development, and life itself. Hulme shows, then, just as the other Māori writers I have considered do, that the experience of hybridity for a subject of mixed race can only be fulfilling or productive if the culture of origin enjoys a coterminous presence in the life of the individual alongside any other culture that may impinge upon his or her experience.

It remains to be seen whether this strong and persistent emphasis in Māori Pākehā writing on the need for a parallel presence of the indigenous culture within the overall structure of a hybridized existence may be specific to New Zealand, or whether it is found in the literature of other societies. That question will only be able to be answered when further case studies involving the literature of other cultures have been conducted. In the meantime, one can only hope that such studies will be forthcoming.

NOTES

1. Chud, like Mark, is a character based on Duff's real-life experience: "Chud was important because there was this happy world, and yet there were these people who were living right there in the heart of it and they were totally blind to it, and they were literally blind; they were blind drunk.... And they were, you know, they were raising their children in a horrendous way, and growing up I saw some of that" (Boland, 3576).

2. In Duff's novel, the words "Maori" and "Pakeha," contrary to regular contemporary practice in New Zealand, are printed without a macron. Duff also uses the plurals "Maoris" and "Pakehas," rather than the more usual "Māori" and "Pākehā." In quoting Duff's text, I retain his practices, although "Māori" and "Pākehā" are spelled with a macron whenever the words are used in my own commentary, and I adopt the standard plural forms "Māori" and "Pākehā."

WORKS CITED

"Alan Duff: Debts, Dads and Dreams, Episode 1." Saturday Morning with Kim Hill, Radio New Zealand National. Aired 15 November 2008. *http://podcast.radionz.co. nz/sat/sat-20081115-0810-Alan_Duff_debt,_dads_and_dreams-048.mp3.* Accessed 12 May 2009.
Bhabha, Homi K. *The Location of Culture.* London: Routledge, 1994.
Bollard, Mary Jane. Interview. *New Zealand Listener* 22–28 November 2008: 3576.
Bromley, Roger. *Narratives for a New Belonging: Diasporic Cultural Fictions.* Edinburgh: Edinburgh University Press, 2000.
Duff, Alan. *Dreamboat Dad.* Auckland: Vintage, 2008.
Friedman, Jonathan. "Global Crises, the Struggle for Cultural Identity and Intellectual Porkbarrelling: Cosmopolitans versus Locals, Ethnics and Nationals in an Era of De-hegemonisation." In Werbner and Modood.
Grace, Patricia. *Mutuwhenua.* Auckland: Penguin, 1986.
Hulme, Keri. *The Bone People.* London: Picador, 2001.
Ihimaera, Witi. *The Rope of Man.* Auckland: Reed, 2005.
Gramsci, Antonio. "The Formation of the Intellectuals." In *Selections from the Prison Notebooks.* Trans. Quintin Hoare and Geoffrey Nowell-Smith. New York: International, 1971. 3–14.
Partridge, Jeffrey F. L. "Re-viewing the Literary Chinatown: Hybridity in Gish Jen's Mona in the Promised Land." In *Complicating Constructions: Race, Ethnicity, and Hybridity in American Texts.* Eds. David S. Goldstein and Audrey B. Thacker. Seattle: University of Washington Press, 2008.
Sharrad, Paul. "Strategic Hybridity: Some Pacific Takes on Postcolonial Theory." In *Reconstructing Hybridity: Post-Colonial Studies in Transition.* Eds. Joel Kuortti and Jopi Nyman. Amsterdam: Rodopi, 2007.
Somerville, Alice Te Punga. "*Waharoa*: Maori Pākehā Writing in Aotearoa/New Zealand."

In *Mixed Race Literature*. Ed. Jonathan Brennan. Palo Alto: Stanford University Press, 2002.

Werbner, Pnina. "Introduction." In Werbner and Modood.

Werbner, Pnina, and Tariq Modood, eds. *Debating Cultural Hybridity, Debating Cultural Hybridity: Multi-Cultural Identities and the Politics of Anti-Racism*. London: Zed, 1997.

Slumdogs and Dogs' Breakfasts

Reading Danny Boyle's
Slumdog Millionaire *and*
Baz Luhrmann's Australia

S U S A N   H O S K I N G

In a globalizing world, any new work entering the fields of textual production can affect the way we read earlier texts. This phenomenon is especially apparent when large sums of money are involved. New texts, especially "blockbuster" films, invite comparison, at the very least in terms of commercial success, with other texts in circulation. Baz Luhrmann's film *Australia* (released November 26, 2008), which makes a feature of its intertextuality, has been both applauded and reviled. It has been criticized particularly in comparison with Danny Boyle's very successful (financially and in terms of awards) *Slumdog Millionaire*, filmed in India, with Indian actors and untrained street children from the slums of Mumbai. Both films were made for the international marketplace. The fact that they were received so differently, both at home and abroad, raises interesting questions in the context of postcolonialism.

Slumdog Millionaire was immediately acclaimed at its première at the Telluride Film Festival on August 31, 2008, and took the People's Choice Award at the Toronto International Film Festival in September 2008. By July 23, 2009, it had climbed to the top of the foreign box office and grossed A$16 million from 34 reported markets for A$96.5 million total takings. In Australia, following the Awards, attendance at the film increased by 53 percent, making it the most commercially successful film both in Australia and India (Bresnan). This essay considers the public and critical reception of *Slumdog Millionaire* and *Australia* as films that represent sensitive aspects of national cultures. It particularly considers the way in which Luhrmann's *Australia* has renewed debate in Australia on the most shameful part of the country's history and how that should be represented, especially when the eyes of the world are upon us. The essay also revisits Phillip Noyce's more modestly successful and less controversial film *Rabbit-Proof Fence* (2002) and questions the effectiveness, in social terms, of consumer response to notionally "true" (hi)stories over an "eccentrically postmodern account of a recent frontier" (Marcia Langton, "Faraway Downs Fantasy," 1).

The release of the film *Australia*, less than three months after the internationally successful *Slumdog Millionaire*, focused attention initially on what many Australians see as the decline of the film industry since the 1970s. In February 2009, Greg Sheridan, in the national newspaper *The Australian*, described *Australia* as a "big budget fiasco." He criticized the film as "not so much ... a failed epic as a ludicrous, camp pantomime" with an air of "contrived unreality," "pretentiousness," and "contrived nods to other films." At the heart of his discontent, however, was what he saw as the (mis)representation of "the most morally troubling aspect of our history" (40).

While much of Sheridan's wrath was prompted by what he saw in the film as clichés, banalities, plot confusions, and a script that he said was thrown together like "a dog's breakfast," it is clear that the sensitive issue raised by the film is the representation of the Stolen Generations: our adoption and enforcement of government policies which for over seventy years insisted upon the removal of mixed-race Aboriginal children from their parents in an attempt to erase the "problems" of race, including, of course, acknowledgement that Australia was occupied prior to colonization.

Some critics responded positively to the fact that Luhrmann's *Australia* actually represents Aboriginal Australians. Brian McCoy, writing for *Eureka Street*, applauded the film's reminders of colonial insensitivity and violence, but was especially approving of the parallel story that, "despite some of its historical errors and exaggerations" (1), humanized the face of Aboriginal Australia through the child narrator Nullah, played by the engaging eleven-year-old boy Brandon Walters, "discovered" by Luhrmann in the Bidyadanga Aboriginal Community in Broome, Western Australia. In McCoy's view, Nullah, the mixed race child, "becomes a bridge" between two cultures, revealing "one to another ... what each can become in risking a new relationship" (1). But one of the concerns raised by the film is that, as if our contact history is not sensitive enough, *Australia* plays with the facts. If Luhrmann is dealing with a huge historical issue in his film, he cannot expect viewers to take it seriously if events are presented "that not only didn't occur, but could not possibly have occurred in the universe we happen to inhabit." The film, Sheridan insisted, "grossly defames our nation" (40).

Germaine Greer, arguing likewise in *The Guardian* (December 16, 2008), described *Australia* as a "fake epic" and focused on the film's lack of credibility. The character Drover, Greer snarled, bears no resemblance to an historical equivalent, Matt Savage, known as "Boss Drover": a white man who married an Aboriginal woman, treated her "rough," but nevertheless stayed with her for forty years and "produced many children who rode with their father" (2). The representation of droving in Australia, according to Greer, is incorrect: drovers are not American cowboys or ranch-hands. The cattle station, Faraway Downs, is "like no other"; it could never have been run by a staff of eight, including "a disloyal manager" and "a drunken accountant." The camera, Greer complained, does not travel to the "verminous and filthy" Aboriginal humpies where the workers would have lived in unsanitary conditions. The territory is hybridized: neither Arnhem Land nor the Kimberley. Luhrmann's Darwin is more "salubrious" than the "real" Darwin of the war years, where "the authorities were running a system of veritable apartheid" (3); in fact Darwin was "rebuilt," for the purposes of the film, in the "pleasant town on Bowen on the north Queensland coast" (3).

The outrage that some reviewers and critics have vented over the historical inaccuracies of Luhrmann's *Australia* indicates the depths of sensitivity to the country's uncomfortable past. While Australian historians are embroiled in their own "history wars,"[1] still arguing about the facts and figures of frontier violence, the task of any film-maker like Luhrmann or novelist like Kate Grenville,[2] who wishes to engage with ideas of reconciliation is fraught with hazards and likely to be thankless. Words like "fantasy," "fake," "pantomime," "fraudulent," "romantic," "sentimental," "theatrical" and "melodramatic" have been directed as criticisms at representations that were never envisaged as "real." Should a film-maker like Baz Luhrmann not attempt to reinvent a past, in order to represent a future? If that conceptualization of a future is a "fantasy" of reconciliation, is that not better, as an expression of desire, than an anticipated war without end, or a continuing system of apartheid or exclusion?

Australia appears to be a "whitefella's dreaming." "Faraway Downs" is certainly located in the land of the story-teller, rather than in the historical archives. It is a "somewhere over the rainbow," in a place of magic. While *Australia* may distort history, to dismiss the film for its historical (and geographical and other) inaccuracies is to deny the story-teller the right to attempt to create hope for a better future. Approaching his subject through "Hollywood Dreaming," inevitably Luhrmann's inclinations are to "stylize, mythologize, and at times trivialize" the social world represented (Quart and Auster, 4). The film most obviously invokes *The Wizard of Oz* (1939) and *Gone with the Wind* (1939), both contemporaneous with the era of Luhrmann's film. But it also revises historical Australian creative representations of contact on the frontier: in particular, Xavier Herbert's epic novels *Capricornia* (1939) and *Poor Fellow My Country* (1975), Charles and Elsa Chauvel's film *Jedda* (1955; released as *Jedda the Uncivilized* in the United States, 1957) and Tracy Moffat's experimental short film *Night Cries: A Rural Tragedy* (1989). *Night Cries* responded (in some respects with a vision not unlike Luhrmann's) to *Jedda*; in a reversal of the mother-daughter tie in *Jedda*, a young Aboriginal woman, played by Marcia Langton,[3] cares for her dying white mother and dreams of faraway places. It was filmed entirely in the studio, with no pretence of realism, the sets are dramatically lit and colored, and the "scenes" almost static.

To dismiss Luhrmann's *Australia* as mere pastiche, or "a dog's breakfast," is to miss the point of its revisions. Perhaps the most significant of these revisions is the way in which Luhrmann reverses Australian colonial anxiety about the power of the primitive and the "lure of the wild," as represented in Chauvel's *Jedda*. *Jedda* is acknowledged as setting "many precedents for Australian feature filmmaking": "[It was the] first Australian feature film [to be] shot in colour, ... to use magnetic sound recording equipment, to star Indigenous Australians [Ngarla Kunoth and Robert Tudawali] in leading roles, and the first Australian feature film to go to the Cannes Film Festival" (National Film and Sound Archive online). Like *Australia*, *Jedda* is set in the Northern Territory and also centers on a mixed race child adopted by the wife of a childless (in *Jedda*, the woman's baby has died) white station owner. As she reaches puberty, Jedda is increasingly disturbed and confused about her heritage and feelings she does not understand. Attracted to a visiting "full-blood" Aboriginal stranger, Marbuck, Jedda succumbs to the "call of the wild" and follows her abductor, through landscape she is unfamiliar with, to his country, where they are both rejected for having broken tribal laws of marriage. Exiled by Marbuck's people and chased by Jedda's adoptive family, the pair finally plunge over a cliff to their deaths, Marbuck holding tightly on to Jedda. This is the film that Chauvel proclaimed "only Australia could make," following a suggestion from a *Time* reporter in a restaurant on Fifth Avenue in Manhattan: "You know, Chauvel, Australia should do something different, something that nobody else has done before. Something that they cannot get the ingredients for outside your country" (Kalina, 1). At the height of the removal of mixed-race children from Indigenous communities, a poster advertising *Jedda* proclaimed, "It was DEATH for him [Marbuck] to look on this Girl!" and on the same poster Jedda was described as "EVE in EBONY!" Although the Chauvels were sympathetic to Aboriginal people, and their film clearly represents its characters with emotional depths, *Jedda* nevertheless reinforced then current policies of separation (of "full-bloods") and assimilation (of "half-castes" through marriage to whites[4]). At the première of the film, only the indigenous stars were permitted to sit with the white folk; "coloreds," as was the custom at the time, were separated from the rest of the audience (Romaine Morton).

Chauvel's *Jedda*, like Luhrmann's *Australia*, was produced with international audiences in mind. If *Jedda* was better received in its own time, arguably that was because, probably unconsciously, it reinforced deeply held values and anxieties about race. Glamor, escape, and thrills are synonymous with blockbuster films, but so is "a sense of emotional security to a mass audience" (Quart and Auster, 4) — something that Luhrmann's *Australia* did not deliver. What could provide "emotional security," in the context of such sensitive subject matter as the Stolen Generations, is a complex question. That question becomes even more complex in light of the success of *Slumdog Millionaire*.

Slumdog Millionaire, which arguably exploits poverty, crime, and corruption in contemporary India, for the entertainment of the West, was well received in Australia. Sheridan described the film as "exquisite." If commentators such as Sheridan censure *Australia* for failing to come to terms with "the most morally troubling aspect of our history," why is he (and why are many others) untroubled by a film, the second most commercially successful film in Australia, that lends itself to criticism of the kind that applies to "poverty tourism" or "poverty porn"?[5]

Christina Patterson, from the comment desk of *The Independent* in London, drew attention to the inherent humiliations of *Slumdog Millionaire*:

> For the 6,999,999 (at a rough guess) human beings who remain in their slums, or their drains, or their streets, it is, you could argue, a little bit humiliating not to have anywhere you can excrete the food you have scavenged in privacy, or anywhere you can wash the dust, and excrement, from your body in privacy. And it's a little bit humiliating to be in a country which is, apparently, undergoing an economic miracle and still be living like this.

Curiously, while there were certainly protests recorded in the media in India about *Slumdog Millionaire*, they related mostly to the title of the film. "Slumdog" is not a familiar term in Indian English, and "dog" is insulting. Komal Nahta, editor and publisher of *Film Information*, India's largest circulated film trade journal, speculated that the title initially affected the film's performance at the Indian box office. Furthermore, the fact that the children from the slums spoke English seemed to perplex general filmgoers. The dubbed Hindi version of the film did much better at local box-offices, suggesting that filmgoers who had viewed the English version were less concerned by the "credibility" of slum children speaking English than frustrated by failures of communication. When the film was first released in India, protesters were televised expressing their concern more in relation to the representation of Ram than to the exploitation of the slums and children who lived there. A blog written in the name of Bollywood's top actor, Amitabh Bachchan (although he later denied that he had written these comments himself[6]), declared: "If SM projects India as third-world, dirty, underbelly developing nation and causes pain and disgust among nationalists and patriots, let it be known that a murky underbelly exists and thrives even in the most developed nations" (reported by Randeep in *The Guardian*, January 14, 2009). But this warning seems to have gone largely unheeded. On *Lazy Lump Revisited*, a popular blog devoted to Indian film, negative criticism of *Slumdog Millionaire* is refuted:

> I don't understand the criticism that is being heaped on the movie about it depicting our country in a negative light. Boyle has presented what our filmmakers have been doing for decades. The film captures the darker shades of Mumbai but hasn't everyone from RGV to Zadhur Bhandarkar done it before. I would honour the director's prerogative to not sugarcoat his subject, even if it means stringing in cliché after cliché.
>
> Some of us have gone ahead and challenged the film for projecting India as a "Third World dirty underbelly developing nation." In fact, I believe it is quite the opposite. Alongside all that is shown as wrong, there is an undercurrent of hope that flows throughout the film. The film manifests the much-talked about "spirit of Mumbai" through the resilience of the protagonist. The ability of the characters to survive against all odds, come what may, forms the fabric of the screenplay [1].

Slumdog Millionaire is not a Bollywood film of the kind defended by Amitabh Bachchan or analyzed by Vijay Mishra, but others have accepted it as "a potboiler that has Bollywood written all over it" (*Lazy Lump*). Certainly the ending is pure Bollywood: a grand song and dance finale inviting everyone in. Criticism of Danny Boyle's film, attributed to Bachchan, appears to be focused as much on the exploitation of Bollywood by the West, as on the representation of India as a "dirty underbelly developing nation." After years of failure in the West to acknowledge "the commercial escapist world of Indian cinema" with its "fantasy and incredulous posturing," suddenly a British film-maker appears on the scene and achieves "globe recognition" (*Lazy Lump*). But the more common response from Indian commentators is applause for recognition of a film that is inspired by what India is proud of: Bollywood, an Indian novel adapted to screen by an Indian scriptwriter, with a soundtrack composed by A. R. Rahman (himself described as "a Bollywood icon" [Snyder, 1]). On the night Rahman was awarded his Golden Globe, he dedicated it to the people of India. "India is a big fan of Hollywood," he said in an interview with S. James Snyder, "but we also love our regional stuff, and it's a great moment for the country when one of their own gets recognized. When I won, I felt from my heart I should say, 'This is for you guys, you've been wanting it'" (Snyder, 2).

While Satyajit Ray's films won critical acclaim and respect in the West in the 1960s and 1970s, the celebrations in relation to *Slumdog Millionaire* are about India making its mark in the global arena with award winning, commercially successful entertainment. This is part of the making of modern India: an India that acknowledges the importance of packaging and marketing "in a way no India-themed movie ... has ever been done before," to put "India ... at the centre of the world" (*Lazy Lump*). The huge success of the film on the world stage has been received, generally, as "good news for Indian cinema," changing the outside perception of Bollywood as a "song and dance factory" into something worthy of global recognition. But more than that, it seems to suggest that "a western audience is becoming willing to hear an Indian story, the Indian way!" (*Lazy Lump*).

Slumdog Millionaire can be "understood" in the context of Indian commercial cinema, where Hindi or Bollywood Cinema is "the largest player" and "the model for popular regional cinema," which as Vijay Mishra points out, makes it "closer to being an all–India cinema" (3). In this respect, "although there is something rather artificial about the culture that [Bollywood] Cinema constructs ... it does give rise to the possibilities of a 'shared experience'"(3). Extending this argument further and drawing upon Etienne Balibar and Immanuel Wallerstein's *Race, Nation, Class* (1991), Mishra suggests that Bollywood Cinema "seems to have transcended class and even linguistic difference" (3) through an emphasis on myths that sustain the social order, regardless of change (Raina, 131). Mishra draws attention to the way in which Bollywood films are "designed to accommodate deep fantasies belonging to an extraordinarily varied group of people, from illiterate workers to sophisticated urbanites" (4).

This raises a question in relation to Luhrmann's *Australia*. Australians certainly attended the film, out of curiosity, patriotic duty, or a fondness for Luhrmann's earlier films — *Strictly Ballroom* (1992), *Romeo and Juliet* (1996) and *Moulin Rouge!* (2001). But despite good box office takings (*Australia* is the second highest grossing "home-grown" film since Peter Faiman's *Crocodile Dundee* [1986][7]), the film failed to win so much as a nomination for best picture at the Australian Film Industry Awards. Whatever *Australia* represents, clearly, it is not what Australians, or the rest of the world, think of as "the Australian way."

To call a film "Australia" (not Luhrmann's first choice) is asking for trouble. The title, as overseas and local critics mostly agree, is too "weighty": not what the world has come to expect of the land "down under." To Australians in the street, it suggests that most un–Australian of behaviors: self-promotion. Indeed, in its making, the film was recognized as a "unique opportunity" (Australian Government News Release) to revive not just Australia's film industry, but the tourism industry as well. Tourism Australia applauds the partnership with Luhrmann, stating the industry's belief that "this movie [*Australia*] will make audiences all over the world fall in love with Australia and help to make our country a highly fashionable tourism destination" (*Tourism Australia's destination campaign*). The "objective" of the campaign was to "ensure Australia reaches its forecast growth rate of 3.2 per cent in international arrivals in 2009 and halt the predicted decline in domestic travel within Australia" (News Release). While the advertising campaign was "conceived by Luhrmann to be completely stand-alone," Tourism Australia "also entered into a promotional partnership with Twentieth Century–Fox to leverage Baz Luhrmann's new epic film *Australia*, starring Nicole Kidman and Hugh Jackman" (News Release). At a cost of A$40 million dollars, 160 integrated programs were delivered to support the launch of the film and the Tourism Australia campaign. The compatibilities, in a single film, of "a new destination brand campaign" and "universal appeal" are questionable, let alone the wedding of tourism and sensitive history with an eye to improving Australia's future economy.

Promotion and marketing are one thing. In India, the marketing team behind *Slumdog Millionaire* received the highest-ever recognition and praise, outshining even the publicists for the critically acclaimed *Lagaan: Once Upon a Time in India* (2001). Richard Corliss, remarking on the success of *Slumdog*, compares its trajectory in the west to "the crazy-wonderful plot twists in a Bollywood musical — both improbable and inevitable." He notes that "Oscar-favored dramas" of the 1980s (Richard Attenborough's *Ghandi* and David Lean's *A Passage to India*) offered "a British view of the subcontinent and its people," while "*Slumdog* has no Western intermediary onscreen to explain the native folkways to the international audience" (*Time*, January 29, 2009). Nor is there any trace of Raj nostalgia. Admitting that "exotic helps," Corliss attributes the success of the film not to its foreignness, but to the fact that it "strikes universal chords about personal fulfillment, romantic obsession and the chance to rise from the bottom of the slag heap," not to mention its "speed and energy" (*Time*, January 29, 2009).

In *Australia*, Luhrmann certainly draws attention to the importance of story telling: through Nullah, the narrator, who finds comfort in songs and stories, and through Drover, who insists that "all you ever own is your story." Peter Conrad sees these gestures as "sanctimonious reverence," asking: "But whose story is Luhrmann telling?" (34). His complaint is that "the stories Luhrman tells about Australia are all second-hand, an ill-fitting and incoherent anthology of American movies": *The African Queen, Gone with the Wind, Pearl Harbor, The Wizard of Oz* (34).

It may well be that Luhrmann's *Australia* is not as "exquisitely" structured as *Slumdog Millionaire* (Sheridan) and that the "committee" approach to scriptwriting (*Australia* had four scriptwriters, including the novelist Richard Flanagan and Luhrmann himself) jeopardized coherence, although collective screenwriting is commonplace in Hollywood. Nevertheless, criticisms couched in terms like "second-hand" seem to misunderstand the heart of Luhrmann's project as a filmmaker. Sumita Chakravarty, in her work on *National Identity in Indian Popular Cinema* (1993), draws upon the work of Chidananda Das Gupta to suggest that a country's epics and myths "present the most widely acceptable base for ... artistic development" (125). If this idea can be applied to *Australia*, then at least Luhrmann should be given credit for seriously approaching his project through literary and filmic representations, including Hollywood films that have been inextricably part of Australian popular culture since at least 1939, although Conrad (like Greer, chastising Australia from Great Britain) would reject such "craven" identification of Australian culture as an adjunct of American culture (35–36).

In Bollywood, the most powerful text that enables "discursivity" (Foucault 1980: 154) is the *Mahābhārata* which, as Mishra points out, "demonstrates a delight in mixed forms, a kind of restless generic permutation ... 'replete with all the poetic sentiments: the humorous, the erotic, the piteous, the wrathful, the heroic, the terrifying, the loathsome, and the rest [1984: sarga 4, sloka 8]'" (5). In the absence of such a longstanding epic tradition in (non–Indigenous) Australian culture, determined by notions of genealogy, dharmik codes (or their equivalent) and spiritual values, any attempt at "generic permutation" is likely to be perceived as "a dog's breakfast." While Luhrmann's mixing of forms, visual puns, and clichés may appear "banal," "pathetic," and excessively arty (Sheridan), the Indigenous scholar Marcia Langton responded immediately to *Australia* as "fabulous[ly] hyperbolic" (*The Age*, November 23, 2008). Baz Lurhmann, she claims, "has leaped over the ruins of the 'history wars' and given Australia a new past — a myth of national origin that is disturbing, thrilling, heartbreaking, hilarious and touching" (November 23, 2008).

Australia, like Bollywood film, which "is itself a genre that is primarily a sentimental melodramatic romance" (Mishra, 13), is not concerned with realism or psychological drama. Defending himself against criticism that his film is cliché ridden, Luhrmann asserted that "to label the film clichéd is to misunderstand the fundamental mechanics of melodrama" which has been "the building block of story-telling in cinema since the form was invented" (*The Australian*, November 3, 2009). Robert Dixon, in his chapter on "Literature and Melodrama" in *The Oxford Literary History of Australia* (1998) notes the transformation of the terms "melodrama" and "melodramatic" from pejorative to worthy of "serious critical attention, particularly within areas of theatre studies" (66). He begins with an observation by Christine Gledhdill, noting that melodrama was "constituted as the anti-value for a critical field in which tragedy and realism became cornerstones of 'high' cultural value, needing protection from mass 'melodramatic' entertainment" (5) and goes on to show how more recent debates, stimulated by Peter Brooks's *The Melodramatic Imagination* (1976), have included revisionist criticism, paying attention to the role of melodrama "as a mediator of social change and in the demarcation of 'high' and 'low' culture" (Dixon, 66). He argues that despite "persistent attempts to read [melodrama] as the expression of a particular social class, it became a central cultural paradigm precisely because it emerged at a meeting point of class interests whose differences it was able to perform and mediate" (67). Clearly then, melodrama has always been able to serve a "Utopian function" (Kelly, 112–113). This is something that Luhrmann is very much aware of, but something that Australian audiences and critics, in relation to his film, are ambivalent about.

If *Australia* is not a film that Australians are proud to identify with, it is worth asking what alternatives exist. Luhrmann's *Australia* invites reconsideration of an earlier Australian film that dealt explicitly with the Stolen Generations. Phillip Noyce's *Follow the Rabbit-Proof Fence* (2002) told the story of three Aboriginal girls, Molly, Gracie and Daisy, who embarked on a 1500 mile (2,400 kilometers) trek home from the Moore River Native Settlement, to which they were forcibly removed from Jigalong, in the north-west of Western Australia. The film, like *Australia*, targeted not just a national audience, but at an international audience as well. A poster, designed for Miramax's promotion of the film in North America, invited viewers to consider: "What if the government kidnapped your daughter?" informing them that that was what happened every week in Australia from 1905 to 1971 (eniar.org, 1). There was considerable unease in Australian political circles about these posters; Liberal MP Peter Slipper told the *Sunrise* program on Channel Seven that promoters were "sensationalising and misleading and grossly distorting what actually happened." They were, he insisted, "wrongly" inferring that "Australians are racist" (eniar.org, 1).

Rabbit-Proof Fence was based on a life story, *Follow the Rabbit-Proof Fence*, written by Aboriginal writer Doris Pilkington (Nugi Garimar). *Follow the Rabbit-Proof Fence* is the story of Pilkington's mother, Molly, the eldest of the girls who found their way back to Jigalong. First published in 1996, the book enjoyed modest success, enough to warrant re-printing in 2000. In 2001, it was re-released and retitled as a film edition, with the shortened title, *Rabbit-Proof Fence*. In Australia, the film *Rabbit-Proof Fence* captured the popular imagination. Director Phillip Noyce described his response to the story in the following terms: "'overwhelmed by the story. Emotionally over-

whelmed. I really strongly identified with the three girls ... massively identifying with them'" (quoted in Hughes-d'aeth, 3). Stories of how affected audiences were, in turn, by the film, have circulated widely and been recorded in
reviews and academic criticism: travelers wept openly on Qantas flights
(Hughes-d'aeth); water and tissues were placed on every seat before a screening
of the film in Camberwell, Victoria (Birch).

The story of how three young Aboriginal girls embarked on such a pun-
ishing trek home is certainly inspirational. But we might speculate on the significance of the generally very positive public response to the film. Clearly,
there is a strong desire on the part of many non–Indigenous Australians to
applaud Indigenous heroes (especially sportspeople) and to wish the mistakes
of history be "put right." Since the release of the film, debate has continued
on whether this positive response to an Indigenous story should be read as a
continuation of the arrogant discourse of assimilation, "sanctioned by the
empathetic imperative of Hollywood film" which enables viewers to "become"
Aboriginal (Hughes D'aeth, 9), or whether the film "exceeds its own boundaries" (Potter and Schaffer, 5), prompting "moments of opening for complex
histories to unsettle the present" (Potter and Schaffer, 7), enabling us to think
in new ways about an uncomfortable past.

In both the book and even more so the film, the emphasis is on the
return home. In the written text, Pilkington certainly uses the word "abduction," and the anguish experienced in the camp when the girls are driven away
is clearly conveyed. But the shock of this scene interpreted by Noyce in his
film is close to unbearable. This is where, as viewers, we are invited to "massively identify" (Noyce) and weep. But the danger of such "sanctioned"
(D'aeth, 9) displays of grief is that they are likely to serve as a substitute for
the genuine discomfort of mourning.[8] Drawing upon their expectations of
Hollywood, viewers are likely to recognize Noyce's film as a "chase movie"
(Birch), as a classic fairy tale of the Hansel and Gretel type (Olsen), or as war
story (Olsen), particularly of the Great Escape genre.

In Pilkington's "true story," *Follow the Rabbit-Proof Fence*, the girls are
taken by car to Marble Bar, by train to Port Hedland, and by boat to Fremantle. While there are moments when they are frightened and worried, as
girls from the Western Desert they respond with interest and curiosity to the
wider world described to them by one of the sailors and to the new sights of
the ocean. As they travel from Fremantle to Perth in an ambulance, with a
crippled Aboriginal woman from the Pilbara, they behave, as Pilkington says,
like "young tourists": "The moment they left the wharf they changed from
shy, confused girls to curious, young tourists, interested and amazed at everything they saw, which was all new and different to them" (58).

The book, as distinct from the film, has a suggestion of travel narrative, with the young girls excited by strangeness, different energies, unfamiliar places, other ways, and the shock of the new. In a different context, such reactions have been observed by anthropologists. Deborah Bird Rose, writing about Aboriginal views of landscape in *Nourishing Terrains*, discusses mobility and the rights to travel that have long been part of Indigenous experience. "Those who travel," she writes, "experience excitement along with the homesickness and fear of being in an unknown place" (43). Furthermore, traditionally, those who traveled beyond familiar country, on negotiated routes, could expect cultural exchange (Rose, 43).

Interestingly, in his film, director Phillip Noyce has not included the sea voyage to Fremantle: in an escape movie, the focus of attention must move quickly from capture and incarceration to escape; so the director's imperative is to get the girls to Moore River so that their trek home can begin. In Pilkington's written text, however, it is only when the traveling stops that Molly begins to think about how to get home. Of course, the seriousness of the girls' predicament is far more significant than the discomfort of the homesick tourist. But what is it that makes them uncomfortable? Chains and padlocks. Bars on the windows. Loss of freedom. "Just like a gaol," thinks Molly (63). Only then does Molly acknowledge that she has "no desire to live in this strange place amongst people she didn't know" (76). The right to travel on has been taken from her. She has no choice but to try to return to where she came from. This is the terrible betrayal that deepens the tragedy of the children's removal from their community, but in the context of the film its significance is subsumed in the generic imperative of the great escape: the journey home.

Tony Hughes-d'Aeth has pointed out that Noyce's film speaks in a "universalising language of emotions" (3) choosing "one story to stand for all stories" (5). This is the way of Hollywood. How problematic does that become when a chosen story is counter-historical, or at least atypical of Stolen Generations stories? The eminent Australian Indigenous politician Lowitja O'Donoghue has spoken publicly and written about the difficulty of returning "home" (289) and the "many dilemmas" (291) involved in looking back on a "successful" career in the midst of "ongoing realities that are a result of dispossession" (293). O'Donoghue was brought up in a home for stolen or "removed" children (O'Donoghue's term). The history of that now demolished home, Colebrook Home, is a history of one-way trips. It is also a story of broken promises (Hosking 2001), typical of the lives of the Stolen Generations.

Assimilationist policies were never intended to incorporate the journey home. On the contrary, the definition of "home" under such policies was "a settled place of abode." In South Australia in 1909, the general child welfare law, the *State Children's Act 1895*, was used to remove Indigenous children from their mothers on the grounds of "destitution" or "neglect." A child could be deemed "neglected" if he or she "[slept] in the open air" (*Bringing Them Home*, 120).

Children of mixed race parentage were considered "unwanted," "unfortunate" and "miserable." They were the "drifting wreckage" of the northern country, in need of rescue "from the possibility of demoralization or premature death" (E.J. Telfer). That entailed putting distance between the children and the native camps. Repeated assertions in the *Adelaide Advertiser* in 1936 suggested that these children would be given "equal opportunities" of education and training with white children and that public money thus spent would be "well employed." But as is abundantly evident in Australia today, in retrospect, the governments responsible for enforcing policies of assimilation were not prepared to spend large sums of money on Aboriginal children and the absence of "equal opportunities" has been disastrous for the Stolen Generations. As we are shown at the end of Luhrmann's *Australia*, finally a Prime Minister has apologized to the Stolen Generations. That apology was a welcome gesture — but by no means a solution to on-going problems.

The success of Noyce's film suggests that audiences are willing to face and acknowledge the violence of removal in the face of an immediate return home, but is this a way of eclipsing what happened to the majority of children in-between the enforcement and abolition of assimilationist policies, not to mention their on-going effects? Generations of stolen or "removed" mixed race children were taken on a journey to, as Lowitja O'Donoghue says, "a different and alien culture" (293). Decades later, even when the mistakes of history are acknowledged, it is too late to provide them with a ticket "home." Where is "home"? The difficulty, as O'Donoghue insists, is that too many of the Stolen Generations remain "excluded or marginalized from [the] prevailing culture. It is not hard to understand [she says] that if you are regarded and treated as an outsider in our own land — not only as different but also as sub-human — there will be profound social and emotional consequences" (293).

Accepting that the relationship between the perspectives of films and the social and/or cultural beliefs of mass audiences is "never a seamless one" (Quart and Auster, 4), the different receptions of the Australian films *Rabbit-Proof Fence* and *Australia* nevertheless suggest profound and continuing unease in Australia with respect to the concept of reconciliation. In a recreational context, non–Indigenous audiences can weep for the Stolen Generations; we can admire the heroic efforts of those who have struggled to return to fractured families in fractured communities, somewhere, far away from us. But the idea that we might live, work, play, and dream together is, as yet, beyond our collective imagination. Luhrmann's Australia is a place of magic and a site of transformation. That audiences and critics can respond to that idea is indicated in the international recognition (CLIO Award) of the "Come Walkabout" advertisement conceived by Luhrmann, shot by Mandy Walker who also shot *Australia*, and starring Brandon Walters, *Australia*'s Nullah. But while the idealism ("Just because it is, doesn't mean it should be") of Luhrmann's *Australia* is praiseworthy, the intention of any big budget film will inevitably be compromised by the parties involved in its production and reception. This is especially so when one of those parties is a government department with single-minded nationalism and economic prosperity on the agenda.

Danny Boyle's hope for *Slumdog Millionaire* was "simply [for] people to take away from the film ... this breathtaking, breathtaking resilience of people and the joy of people despite their circumstances — that lust for life" (*The Hollywood Reporter*, January 20, 2009). Lurhmann had an artistic vision that did not wed happily with its grand theme. Reconciliation is not something that can be produced in the context of a film. If, as Nullah says at the end of the film, we tell stories "to keep the people belonging," then clearly, the majority of Australians, for aesthetic, political, or even perhaps racist reasons, are not ready to contemplate the transformative magic that *Australia* invokes. If *Australia* is not the film most Australians would have hoped for, as Conrad has asserted: "the blame needs to be shared around" (30). While "failure" (Conrad, 30) is too peremptory a judgment, the ambivalence in critical and public response to *Australia* is reflective of on-going anxiety about unresolved legacies of the past. Until we are more open to the "possibilities of a 'shared experience'" (Mishra, 3) and able to "accommodate fantasies" (4) that can be embraced by both Indigenous and non–Indigenous Australians, projects such as Luhrmann's will be limited in their appeal.

NOTES

1. For further information on Australia's "history wars" see Stuart MacIntyre and Anna Clark, *The History Wars* (Melbourne: Melbourne University Press, 2003).

2. Kate Grenville's novel *The Secret River* (Melbourne: Text, 2005) polarized critics and historians who responded differently to her representation of colonial contact and violence against Aboriginal custodians of the land. See Inga Clendinnen, "The History Question: Who Owns the Past?" *Quarterly Essay*, Issue 23 (2006), 1–72.

3. Marcia Langton, now Professor Marcia Langton, once contemplated a career as an actor. She has held the Foundation Chair of Australian Indigenous Studies at the University of Melbourne since 2000.

4. See A. O. Neville *Australia's Coloured Minority: Its Place in the Community*, introduction by A.P. Elkin. (Sydney: Currawong, 1947). A.O. Neville (1875–1954) was the Chief Protector of Aborigines in Western Australia for forty years after 1914. Neville believed that racial problems could be eradicated by encouraging trans-racial marriage. In 1947 he committed these beliefs to print, publishing *Australia's Coloured Minority*, illustrated with photographs demonstrating how "colour" could be eliminated over generations.

5. See Mattias Williams, "Is *Slumdog Millionaire* Poverty Porn?" Reuters Blogs, 28 Janu-

ary 2009, http://blogs.reuters.com/india/2009/01/28/is-slumdog-millionaire-poverty-porn/, accessed 6 November 2009; Ian Jack, "Some Say It's Poverty Porn — But Not Many," *The Guardian*, Saturday, 24 January 2009, http:/www.guardian.co.uk/commentisfree/2009/jan/24/Oscars-india-slumdon-millionaire-ian-jack, accessed 13 February 2009.

6. "Bachchan Denies Slumdog Criticism," BBC News, 16 January 2009. http://news.bbc.co.uk/2/hi/south_asia/7832705.stm, accessed 13 February 2009.

7. See contact.music.com http://www.contactmusic.com/news.nsf/story/australia-becomes-homelands-second-biggest-hit_1096363.

8. For further discussion of the difference between recreational grieving and mourning in the context of reconciliation, see Susan Hosking, "Colebrook Home and the Disappeared Past," *Westerly*, 52(2007).

Works Cited

Australian Government/Tourism Australia. "Tourism Australia Launches Luhrmann's Transformation Tourism Campaign." News Release. 8 October 2009. *http://www.tourism.australia.com/content/Australia/2008/NR%20Tourism%20Australia%20Campaign%20Launch.pdf*. Accessed 3 November 2009.

Balibah, Etienne, and Immanuel Wallerstein. *Race, Nation, Class*. London: Verso, 1991.

Birch, Tony. "'This Is a True Story': *Rabbit-Proof Fence* [Film]: 'Mr. Devil' and the Desire to Forget." *Cultural Studies Review* 8,1 (May 2002): 117–129.

Bresnan, Conor. "Around the World Roundup: 'Slumdog' Surges." *http://www.thecravecafe.net/movie-news/52-around-the-world-roundup-slumdog-surges.html*. Accessed 3 February 2009.

Bringing Them Home: The Report of the National Enquiry into the Separation of Aboriginal and Torres Strait Islander Children from Their Families. Sydney: Human Rights and Equal Opportunities Commission, 1997.

Brooks, Peter. *The Melodramatic Imagination: Balzac, Henry James, Melodrama and the Mode of Excess*. New Haven: Yale University Press, 1976.

Chakravarty, Sumita. *National Identity in Indian Popular Cinema*. Austin: University of Texas Press, 1993.

Chauvel, Charles (Director). *Jedda* [Video]. Canberra: ScreenSound Australia, National Screen and Sound Archive, 2004. Original Motion Picture Released by Charles Chauvel Productions, 1955.

Clendinnen, Inga. "The History Question: Who Owns the Past?" *Quarterly Essay* Issue 23 (2006): 1–72.

Conrad, Peter. "Gone with the Wind: An Australian Fiasco." *The Monthly* Issue 42 (February 2009): 30–36.

Contact.Music.com "Baz Luhrmann —*Australia* Becomes Homeland's Second Biggest Hit." 27 February 2009. *http://www.contactmusic.com/news.nsf/story/australia-becomes-homelands-second-biggest-hit_1096363*. Accessed 6 November 2009.

Corliss, Richard. "From Slumdog to Top Dog." *Time* 29 January 2009. *http://www.time.com/time/magazine/article/0,9171,1874832,00.html*. Accessed 25 May 2009.

"Danny Boyle Defends 'Slumdog' in Mumbai." HollywoodReporter.com. *http://login.vnewmedia.com/hr/login*. Accessed 20 October 2009.

Dixon, Robert. "Literature and Melodrama." In *The Oxford Literary History of Australia*. Eds. Bruce Bennett and Jennifer Strauss. Melbourne: Oxford University Press, 1998. 66–88.

Fleming, Victor (Director). *Gone with the Wind*. Selznick International in Association with Metro-Goldwyn Mayer, 1939.

_____. *The Wizard of Oz*. Metro Goldwyn-Mayer, 1939.

Foucault, Michel. "What Is an Author?" In *Textual Strategies*. Ed. J.V. Harari. London: Methuen, 1980. 141–160.

Gledhill, Christine. "The Melodramatic Field: An Investigation." In *Home Is Where the Heart Is: Studies in Melodrama and the Woman's Film*. Ed. Christine Gledhill. London: British Film Institute, 1987.

Gowariker, Ashutosh (Director). *Lagaan: Once Upon a Time in India*. Aamir Khan, 2001.

Greer, Germaine. "Once Upon a Time in a Land, Far, Far Away." *Guardian*, 16 December 2008. *http://www.guardian.co.uk/film/2008/dec/16/baz-luhrmann-australia*. Accessed 2 November 2009.

Grenville, Kate. *The Secret River*. Melbourne: Text, 2005.

Herbert, Xavier. *Capricornia: A Novel*. London: Rich and Cowan, [1939].

_____. *Poor Fellow My Country*. London: Collins, 1975.

Hosking, Susan. "Colebrook Home and the Disappeared Past." *Westerly* 52 (2007).

_____. "Homeless at Home: Stolen and Saved. Three Colebrook Autobiographies." *Westerly* 46 (2001).

Hughes-d'Aeth, Tony. "Which Rabbit-Proof Fence? Empathy, Assimilation, Hollywood." *Australian Humanities Review* September–December 2002. *http://www.lib.latrobe.edu.au/AHR/archive/Issue—September—2002/hughesdaeth.html*. Accessed 19 April 2009.

Jack, Ian. "Some Say It's Poverty Porn — But Not Many." *The Guardian*, 24 January 2009. *http:/www.guardian.co.uk/commentisfree/2009/jan/24/Oscars-india-slumdog-million aire-ian-jack*. Accessed 13 February 2009.

Kalina, Paul. "Chauvel's *Jedda* Led the Way." *The Age*, 15 December 2004. *http://www.theage.com.au/news/Film/Chauvels-Jedda-led-the-way/2004/12/14/1102787061956.html*. Accessed 4 November 2009.

Kelly, Veronica. "Female and Juvenile Meanings in Late Nineteenth Century Australian Popular Theatre." In *The 1890s: Australian Literature and Literary Culture*. Ed. Ken Stewart. St. Lucia: University of Queensland Press, 1996. 109–127.

Langton, Marcia. "Faraway Downs Fantasy Resonates Close to Home: Baz Luhrmann's *Australia* Offers a Frank and Fresh Take on Outback Lore." *The Age*, 23 November 2008. *http://www.theage.com/articles/11/23/1227375027931.html*. Accessed 13 February 2009.

_____. "Why Greer Is Wrong on Australia." *The Age*, 23 December 2008. *http://www.theage.com.au/opinion/why-greer-is-wrong-on-australia-20081222-73kk.html*. Accessed 13 February 2009.

Lazy Lump Revisited... "Hollywood Bollywood—*Slumdog Millionaire*." 19 January 2009. *http://lazylump.wordpress.com/2009/01/19hollywood-bollywood-slumdog-millionaire/*. Accessed 15 July 2009.

"'Lift Lives' and Controversial 'Rabbit-Proof' Posters Appear in U.S." *http://www.eniar.org/img/rabbitposter.jpg*. Accessed 20 March 2009.

MacIntyre, Stuart, and Anna Clark. *The History Wars*. Melbourne: Melbourne University Press, 2003.

McCoy, Brian. "Obama and Baz Luhrmann's *Australia*." *Eureka Street.com.au* 23 January 2009. *http://www.eurekastreet.com.au/article.aspx?aeid=11324*. Accessed 30 September 2009.

Mishra, Vijay. *Bollywood Cinema: Temples of Desire*. New York: Routledge, 2002.

Moffat, Tracey (Director). *Night Cries: A Rural Tragedy*. Chili Films, 1990.

Moreton, Romaine. "Secondary Curator's Notes." *Australian Screen: Jedda. http://australianscreen.com.au/titles/jedda/*. Accessed 6 November 2009.

National Film and Sound Archive. *http://www.nfsa.gov.au/the_collection/collection_spotlights/jedda.html*. Accessed 6 November 2009.

Neville, A.O. *Australia's Coloured Minority: Its Place in the Community*. Intro.: A.P. Elkin. Sydney: Currawong, 1947.

Noyce, Phillip (Director). *Rabbit-Proof Fence.* Hanway Films, 2002.
O'Donoghue, Lowitja. "A Journey of Healing or a Road to Nowhere." Ed. Michelle Grattan. *Essays on Australian Reconciliation.* Melbourne: Black, 2000. 288–296.
Olsen, Christine. *Rabbit-Proof Fence: The Screen Play.* Adapted from the Book *Follow the Rabbit-Proof Fence* by Doris Pilkington Garimara. Sydney: Currency, 2000.
Patterson, Christina. "Feel Good Escapism — For Those That Can Escape." *The Independent,* 17 January 2009.
Potter, Emily, and Kay Schaffer. "Rabbit-Proof Fence, Relational Ecologies and the Commodification of Indigenous Experience." *Australian Humanities Review* Issue 31–32 (April 2004). *http://www.australianhumantiesreview.org/archive/Issue-April-2004/schaffer.html.* Accessed 11 November 2004.
Quart, Leonard, and Albert Auster. *American Film and Society since 1945,* 3d ed. Westport, CT: Praeger, 2002.
Raina, M.L. "'I'm All Right Jack': Packaged Pleasures of the Middle Cinema." *Journal of Popular Culture,* 20,2 (1986): 131–141.
Ramesh, Randeep. "Bollywood Icon Amitabh Bachchan Rubbishess Slumdog Millionaire." *The Guardian,* 14 January 2009. *http://www.guardian.co.uk/film/2009/jan/14/amitabh-bachchan-rubbishes-slumdog-millionaire.* Accessed 6 August 2009.
Rose, Deborah Bird. *Nourishing Terrains: Australian Aboriginal Views of Landscape and Wilderness.* Canberra: Australian Heritage Commission, 1996.
Sheridan, Greg. "Slumdogs Shame Our Dogs." *The Australian: Weekend Australian Review,* 21–22 February 2009: 40.
Snyder, S. James. "A.R. Rahman, *Slumdog Millionaire* Maestro." *Time,* 5 February 2009. *http://www.time.com/time/arts/article/0,8599,1876545,00.html.* Accessed 8 October 2009.
Telfer, E.J. *Amongst Australian Aborigines: Forty Years of Missionary Work.* Sydney: E.J. Telfer, 1939. [Melbourne: Fraser and Morphet.]
Tourism Australia. "Tourism Australia's Campaign by Baz Luhrmann."
Williams, Mattias. "Is *Slumdog Millionaire* Poverty Porn?" Reuters Blogs, 28 January 2009. *http://blogs.reuters.com/india/2009/01/28/is-slumdog-millionaire-poverty-porn/.* Accessed 6 November 2009.

Gender, Hybridity and the Transcultural "Man Alone" in the Short Fiction of Frank Sargeson and Doris Lessing

JOEL GWYNNE

In the twenty-first century, scholars have found it necessary to resituate postcolonial theory in relation to feminism, as even though many identify as feminists, not least Adrienne Rich, Audre Lorde and bell hooks, the recognition of these voices have paled in comparison to the recognition bestowed on the male voices of Homi Bhabha, Frantz Fanon and Edward Said. Recent debates in the field of feminist postcolonial theory have aimed to recalibrate the male-dominated paradigm of postcolonial theory by focusing on overlapping concerns with gender, economics, sexuality, representation and the development of effective activism. The intent has been to racialize mainstream feminist theory and to insert feminist concerns into conceptualizations of colonialism and postcolonialism. This has often occurred in the context of revisionist criticism, through either re-assessing previously neglected work or re-evaluating popular texts in the context of gender politics. The recent interest in feminist postcolonial theory is impossible to separate from a parallel and often intersecting trend that interrogates operations of masculinity and homosexuality, evident in the context of New Zealand literature through Kai Jensen's *Whole Men: The Masculine Tradition in New Zealand Literature* (1996). Yet Jensen's text, whilst demonstrating the plurality of new approaches to masculinity in the wake of the rise of queer theory, did little to reconfigure popular perceptions of New Zealand literature as entrenched in oppositional gender constructs. To those familiar with traditional and revisionist critical appraisals of colonial New Zealand literature, one scarcely needs to provide corroborating evidence of John Reece Cole's observation of provincial New Zealand as a culture of "sly drinking with an ear cocked for a woman's reproving voice" (49).

As an autonomous signifier of colonial literature, Frank Sargeson's short stories have been read, sometimes rather reductively, as exemplifying the gender politics implied by Reece's observation. Such critical constructions of Sargeson's characters as possessing entirely polarized gender identities are often linked with their anomalous position within the literal and ideological terrains of provincial masculinity. In Sargeson's stories, the land as a context for the masculine occupations of construction, farming and sheep shearing represents not merely a world almost exclusively isolated from female contact, but by extension a world where inscriptions of masculine sensibilities are reiterated and reconstituted. Similarly, in the short fiction of Doris Lessing, where social action is also firmly rooted in the landscape, the role of women as isolated from the experience of men is also corroborated, albeit from a female perspective. Despite the obviously dissimilar national contexts of New Zealand and Southern Africa,[1] it is perhaps not surprising that Sargeson and Lessing's fiction share affinities, largely due to a shared colonial-pioneer heritage of European settlement. Similarly, it is perhaps not surprising that the work of both writers has attracted enormous attention in terms of gender representation, arguably as a consequence of the apparently substantial gender disparities between men and women in the narratives of Sargeson and Lessing. Yet, what is scarcely explored is the extent to which the short fiction of both writers represents the "Man Alone" as not merely an extremely gendered entity opposed to occupying "feminine" domestic spaces, but rather opposed to all manifestations of interior space. Indeed, Sargeson's "Man Alone," often read as both a misogynistic character-type and as evidence of Sargeson's personal misogyny, presents a rebuke of not only domestic spaces but rather any interior space that functions as central to dominant capitalist and consumerist ideologies of white bourgeois culture. Sargeson's characters are primarily hybrid constructions, and often represented as social (and sexual) deviants who are unable to successfully assimilate into any mainstream cultural space. Homi K. Bhabha's has defined hybridity as a condition in which the subject is perpetually caught in a process of identity definition, and in this essay I intend to argue that Sargeson's male characters orientate their identity through the lens of cultural hybridity, especially visible in their attraction to indigenous cultures as a means of alleviating societal alienation. This societal alienation and cultural ennui will be located, and in turn, compared to Lessing's construction of the "Man Alone" who is, I will argue, not isolated exclusively by gender, but rather by a more encompassing alienation precipitated by social and economic factors.

Yet, before evaluating the cultural hybridity of Lessing's characters in the context of gender and societal alienation, it is important to first focus on the precipitating factors of the isolation of Sargeson's characters, especially as this has been read in historical-critical terms as a gendered construction. As his characters are almost exclusively figures of victimization and difference, it is necessary to extend this critical inclination and situate them in their local provincial context, identified by Bill Pearson as a "tradition of liberal human-ism, tolerance, sympathy for the little man and an intolerance of pretension" (144). Sargeson's characters are orientated tentatively in a peculiar position between both liberal humanism and the anti-humanism of their isolated states. Indeed, on the one hand, Sargeson implies that human beings are essentially responsible for their own isolation, whilst on the other affirming the impor-tance of external, environmental factors in rendering isolation. This contrari-ness should be placed in the context of the Depression, the political and cultural instability of decolonization, and the First and Second World Wars; all, whether colonial writers explicitly acknowledge it or not, fragmented the subject within a multiplicity of discourses. Placing Sargeson's story "A Pair of Socks" (1936) in the context of Robert Chapman's seminal "Fiction and the Social Pattern" (1953) is a useful starting point. In the latter, Chapman com-ments on the condition of local fictional aesthetics:

> The concern with the isolated individual, isolated in every sense, who may or may not explode into violent gestures under the distorting weight of a pattern he does not understand, is the writers' way of examining the society they depict. The mismade character structure is not without pattern any more than the normal character structure. The forces which the social milling machine exerts to mould and trim its sound citizen coins out of the child's malleable alloy may be more accurately gauged from the bad bent pennies that result when the alloy falls under pressure. The writer cannot dismantle the whole milling machine but he can exhibit the bent pennies and help his society to draw its own conclusions about how sound coins as well as unsound coins are made, and at what cost [72].

"A Pair of Socks" is a consummate example of Chapman's "bent pennies." Its narrator is a semi-articulate working-class male, whose voice epitomizes the Sargeson vernacular, and whose dilemma is exacerbated by his limited perspective. The story is simple: the narrator's relationship with his childhood friend has disintegrated in a dispute over a pair of socks. Yet, even though our initial reaction to the opening line of "I wish I'd never gone and bought that pair of socks" is one of comic bemusement, the tragic implications of this innocuous disclosure soon become clear. Ironically, what establishes this story as so tragic is both the narrator's ignorance of the pathology of his response to the situation, and the pathology of the situation itself. Sargeson represents male friendship as man's single comfort in a stark society: as the protagonist is isolated by gender and unable to communicate, it is the unspoken myth of mateship that provides a form of inexpressible partial fulfillment. Indeed, whilst the intensity of the male bond has been understood in gay terms, it is also a response to deterministic conditions and social exclusions that seem to bind the narrator and Fred from an early age: "If the teacher would let us we'd always sit together. But it was no good sitting together in one way, because I couldn't do sums no more than Fred could. We'd want to tell each other how to get the sums out right but we couldn't" (Sargeson, 40). Isolation and dispossession remains after leaving school: "After we left school we couldn't get jobs nohow. We just used to kick around the town together" (40). This economic determinism precipitates an interdependence between characters; the narrator reflects that "if [Fred] saw anyone looking at him too much, he'd always get in close to me. He sort of depended on me that way." It is Fred's reliance on the narrator that places limitations on the behavior of both men, as the narrator reveals in admitting that any attempt to form an intimate relationship with a woman is marred by its potential implications:

> There were times I'd feel like getting off on my own for a bit but I never used to know how Fred would take it. You see I used to feel sometimes that I'd like to pick up with a sheila, so I'd tell Fred I'd be going off on my own, and he'd say O.K. And I'd ask him, wouldn't he be going off somewhere on his own too? And he'd say no, he'd be waiting for me when I came back. And sure enough he always would be. I'd feel it sort of put me in the wrong, and I'd feel a bit narked with Fred [41].

Thus, we bear witness to an irresolvable situation where two very different forms of social constraint isolate and alienate the narrator. The first is the anti-humanism of the deterministic power of the economic climate, evident in the grim reality that the only employment available to working-class men is unfulfilling and arduous, the effects of which are only alleviated through the intimacy of mateship. Yet, it is precisely the dependency of this human bond, and as the passage shows, the inequality of the power structures at the centre of it, that inhibits selfhood. If we accept for a moment Freud's conviction that human relationships thrive on the exchange of roles of submission and domination, then we can see the failure of relations in Sargeson's story: the relationship remains consistently unbalanced. It is Fred's role to place demands upon the narrator, and the narrator's role to submit to these demands. The roles remain dangerously stable in their extreme polarization, and the transgression of this code culminates in the dissolution of the relationship.

We are invited to identify Sargeson's anti-humanism in his refusal to corroborate the realist Aristotelian dictum that man is indeed a social animal. Instead, "A Pair of Socks" attests to the image of man as asocial and solitary, unable to maintain human relationships. In this instance, the narrator exercises a prohibited level of autonomy in his decision to buy his employer a pair of socks for his birthday. Fred becomes jealous and unresponsive, the working environment disintegrates and both are sacked. The response of the narrator is as disturbing as Fred's reaction:

> Of course, it's a good while ago since it happened. But I can't get it out of my mind. I never see Fred now. They say he's got a job on a scow. I couldn't get on with any other trainer. It was because of the slump. I've got a job in a grocer's shop and I'm trotting a sheila. She's a pearl of a sheila too. But when I think of the life Fred and me used to have, gee, if I don't kick myself and wish I'd never gone and bought that damn pair of socks [Sargeson, 41].

Sargeson initially pursues the realist paradigm of solitariness by isolating the narrator within a constrictive relationship and social circumstance, yet affirms a modernist solitariness through the fictional exploration of Heidegger's anti-humanist concept of existence as a throwness-into-being: humans are constitutionally unable to forge relations outside of themselves. Indeed, it is difficult to understand how a trivial dispute has degenerated into the complete dissolution of the relationship, and why the narrator regrets his behavior, instead of condemning Fred's. This is, of course, a rational analysis of the situation, yet Sargeson is concerned with the irrationality of human behavior and the subjectively conditioned solitariness that drives it.

In this discussion of "A Pair of Socks," I have aimed to illustrate how, for Sargeson, the isolated "Man Alone" is isolated among men largely due to societal factors, such as itinerancy as a consequence of unemployment, rather than due to a deliberate aversion to women. Similarly, in "I've Lost My Pal" (1938), the social and sexual deviant George, whose Sunday school teacher "had [him] for a pet!" (32) as a child, is positioned as a perverse contortion of the conventional isolated "Man Alone." His sexual abuse distinguishes him from his friends, as does their reluctance to hear of his experience, believing that George "ought to be ashamed of himself for telling things like that" (32). Tom, the principle objector, identifies transgression not in the sexual abuse itself, but its articulation, and Mark Williams has commented that "in reading Sargeson we sometimes feel that he sees New Zealanders as inarticulate, almost blank, puppets through which the powerful negations of culture speak" (22). The inarticulation that Williams alludes to is not present in the case of George, however, and the negations of culture manifest themselves through Tom's hegemonic submersion in the sexual and social conventions of white mainstream culture, demonstrated through his refusal to bear witness to George's narrative of sexual abuse. George can be seen, therefore, as signifying a counterpoint to "society," and the narrator observes: "Then George said how he hadn't much time for getting married or regular jobs or anything like that. He said you might as well be dead as work at a regular job and have to keep a nagging wife" (Sargeson, 32). While many critics would focus on the misogyny of the words "nagging wife" and conclude that George is a character who has little more than problems with women and forging human relationships, this is arguably a too simplistic reduction. Such critics would identify the itinerancy of Sargeson's characters as further evidence of the surfacing of latent misogyny, a refusal to be contained and confined by women within the domestic sphere.

This view is understandable and, similarly, in Lessing's "The Story of a Non-Marrying Man" (1972), the narrator observes a central character who has "had enough of the womenfolk, he's gone to get out of their way" (Lessing, 35). Yet, Sargeson's "The Hole that Jack Dug" (1945) and Lessing's "A Mild Attack of Locusts" (1955) demonstrate striking complexities in their delineation of the construction of male and female interaction within gendered physical space. In the former, the narrator relays his experience of visiting his fiend Jack, who has decided to dig a large hole in the garden for no apparent reason. Sargeson's construction of Jack's wife, Mrs. Parker, demarcates the garden as masculine terrain, and the house as a terrain of feminized domesticity. When inside the house, the narrator is uncomfortable with the shift into an inner space controlled by different norms and values: "one reason I stayed standing when Mrs. Parker asked me to sit down, was because I thought I'd get Jack back into the garden if I didn't sit down" (Sargeson, 246). If Sargeson's gender segregation is often criticized as biological essentialism, then it is interesting to note that similar narrative practices are easily found in Lessing's work; a writer whom it would be incredibly difficult to label as a misogynist or unconscious of patriarchal constructs. Indeed, in "A Mild Attack of Locusts," Lessing contextualizes gender within the locale of physical geography:

> The rains that year were good, they were coming nicely just as the crops needed them — or so Margaret gathered when the men said they were not too bad. She never had an opinion of her own on matters like the weather, because even to know about what seems a simple thing like the weather needs experience [115].

Lessing implies, yet more obliquely than Sargeson, that "experience," a necessarily subjective sphere, is in this instance territorialized by men: to be in possession of the experience required to judge the environmental situation is, simply, to be a man. The passage is ambiguous, however, as the terrain of masculine power is not the subject of critique, and Lessing is not concerned with Margaret's potential feelings of isolation in a fundamentally male environment. The experience required in order to evaluate weather conditions is not constructed as a fundamentally male attribute, but one that merely happens to be owned by men in this particular narrative. Indeed, an interesting counterpoint is Lessing's "Lucy Grange" (1957), in which that narrator refuses to physically and psychologically masculinize and thus conform to the behavior of other farmers' wives in relation to the impediments of the rural environment:

> the satisfactory solid women with their straight "tailored" dresses, made by the Dutchwoman at the store at seven-and-six a time, buttoned loosely across their well-used breasts, with their untidy hair permed every six months in town, with their femininity which was asserted once and for all by a clumsy scrawl of red across the mouth. One can imagine her clinching her fists and saying fiercely to the mealie fields which rippled greenly all around her, cream topped like the sea: "I won't. I simply won't. He needn't imagine that I will!" [110].

Yet, in counterpoint, "A Mild Attack of Locusts" demonstrates Lessing's construction of gender in transition, and affirms the fluid and notional nature of identities as environmentally malleable: out in the pelting storm of insects, her husband was banging on the gong, feeding the fires with leaves, the insects clinging to him all over—she shuddered. "How can you bear to let them touch you?" she asked. He looked at her, disapproving. She felt suitably humble—just as she had when he had first taken a good look at her city self, hair waved and golden, nails red and pointed. Now she was a proper farmer's wife, in sensible shoes and a solid skirt. She might even get to letting locusts settle on her—in time (110).

As the land is posited as the masculine domain of practicality and hardship, one that has little allowance for "hair waved and golden" and the pretensions of feminine gentility, the wife becomes gradually masculinized, but only in terms of outward appearance. Ideologically, she remains unchanged and fails to realize that it is necessary for the men to face the locusts at the comparatively trivial risk of their body being covered by the insects. Unlike in "Lucy Grange," where the central character is an alienated figure, Margaret has conformed to her environment in terms of gender expectations and, in doing so, has found a sacrificial coping mechanism for alienation in the form of "bad faith," a Sartrean self-denial and immersion into her assigned gender role.

Even though Lessing's characters are perhaps more diverse in their gender identity, she shares with Sargeson a strikingly similar view of the relationship between gender and physical space. Both writers complicate the issue by constructing men's separation from women's physical space as being as much a consequence of a broader societal alienation than a separation inscribed by gender differences. Indeed, returning to "The Hole that Jack Dug," the inside of the house is a sphere in which the women are "always talking about books and writers" (Sargeson, 32), a space from which men are relegated by deliberate choice rather than exclusion. The preferred menial task of digging in the garden indicates that Sargeson's construction of masculinity transcends gendered boundaries; a representation of men who are not necessarily opposed to women, but rather opposed to the confines of bourgeois middle-class culture, as represented by the narrator's isolation from the women's interest in writers he "never knows anything about" (32). Similarly, in Lessing's "The Story of a Non-Marrying Man" (1972), we are introduced to another character who is isolated from white society: "He had done all kinds of work, but 'I like to be my own master.' He had owned a store, but 'I get restless, and I must be on the move'" (Lessing, 34). It is the constrictions of a white, bourgeois monoculture, encompassing the pressure of conformity to the dominant hegemony of settler puritanism, rather than gender opposition, that both Sargeson and Lessing's characters repudiate. "The Story of a Non-Marrying Man" presents a Southern African variation of the "Man Alone," and global economic conditions of the 1930s connect the story directly with the context of Sargeson's:

> The very first sign of the Slump was in the increase in the number of people who lived by their wits, or as vagrants.... More and more often, coming through the trees up the hill, we saw walking towards us a man with a bundle of blankets over his shoulder, a rifle swinging in his hand. In the blanket-roll were always a frying pan and a can of water, sometimes a couple of tins of bully beef, or a Bible, matches, a twist of dried meat.... The presence of the maize-flour was a statement, and probably ambiguous, for the Africans ate maize-meal porridge as their staple food. It was cheap, easily obtainable, quickly cooked, nourishing, but white men did not eat it, at least, not as the basis of their diet, because they did not wish to be put on the same level as Africans. The fact that this man carried it, was why my father, discussing him later with my mother, said: "He's probably gone native" [33].

The paraphernalia of the itinerant man is clearly demarcated, and in terms of the material representation of a man without possessions, there is little to separate it from Sargeson's own characters. Yet, in Lessing's stories there is clearly a more dramatic isolation from white society. It is interesting to note that the narrator concedes that the "presence of the maize-flour was a statement," yet one that is "probably ambiguous" suggesting, rather than concluding, that this particular "Man Alone" desires an escape to a sphere of indigenous experience unattainable to most white Southern Africans, who are revealingly conveyed in extremely hostile terms:

> That was all that came out of that most typical of South African scenes, the morning tea party on the deep shady veranda, the trays covered with every kind of cake and biscuit, the gossiping young women, watching their off-spring at play under the trees, filling in a morning of their lazy lives before going back to their respective homes where they would find their meals cooked for them, the table laid, and their husbands waiting. That tea party was thirty years ago, and still that town has not grown so wide that the men can't drive home to take their midday meals with their families. I am talking of white families, of course [37].

Lessing's "Man Alone" is thus not merely a figure whose nomadic lifestyle is determined through little choice as a consequence of the economic conditions of the Depression, but rather a Sartrean figure whose lifestyle represents freedom from such bourgeois limitations. It is interesting to note that, like the character of Lessing's story, Katherine Mansfield, New Zealand's most significant short story writer, also illustrates that contact with indigenous peoples often occasions an epiphanous revelation about white society. In "How Pearl Button was Kidnapped" (1923), Pearl Button is voluntarily "kidnapped" by two Maori women; yet the detrimental experiences associated with the term "kidnapped" are the subject of a remarkably astute inversion of conventional ideology. Pearl's abduction is manifested in the form of a sojourn to the beach — a traditional location for a family day-trip. This is extremely significant, as it invites the audience to perceive the Maori as a substitute family who provide Pearl with a vibrant and creative environment in which she can emotionally develop. Prior to her abducted the narrator remarks, rather revealingly, that her mother is "in the kitchen ironing because it is Tuesday" (Mansfield, 533), signifying a monotonous and regimented lifestyle within a society that constricts the individual. The story's condemnation of white society is made clear through Pearl's retort of screaming when "rescued" by the police, who reveal the irony of the story's title by kidnapping her from her recently acquired happiness and instigating her return to the family home. It is precisely this state of existence that alienates so many of Mansfield's characters, and the freedom the Maori abductors offer Pearl is Mansfield's idealistically constructed community of comparatively immaterial happiness. Like Linda Burnell in "At the Bay" (1922), who locates security in Jonathan Trout's alienation from the masculine world of commercial materialism, Pearl cannot quite understand the relatively unconventional lifestyle of the Maori: "'Haven't you got any Houses of Boxes? Don't you all live in a row? Don't the men go to offices?'" (533). Pearl is startled when meeting Maori in the flesh, assuming that Pakeha cultural dominance extends across indigenous cultures. It is not difficult to understand why many of Mansfield's female characters, such as Kezia of "Prelude" (1918) and Laura of "The Garden Party" (1922) are metaphorically (and now Pearl, literally) positioned with the Maori. Returning to Lessing's "The Story of a Non-Marrying Man," we find a similar critique of bourgeois white society[1]:

> But the way he saw it, he had stayed for four long years in a suffocating town house surrounded by a domesticated garden. He had worked from eight to four selling groceries to lazy women. When he came homes, this money, the gold he had earned by his slavery, was spent on chocolates, magazines, dresses, hair-ribbons for his townified step-daughter. He was invited, three times a day, to sit down at a table crammed with roast beef and chickens and puddings and cakes and biscuits [Lessing, 47].

Again, even though many critics would isolate "lazy women" and "townified step-daughter" as marking the misogyny of the central character, it is perhaps more valid to identify a deeper source of resentment to the unmarried man's anger, and the passage has neo–Marxist sensibilities. Certainly, anger is focused on the fact that that narrator "worked from eight to four," and evident in his opposition to the frivolous use of the "gold he earned by his slavery." Read in this manner, his decision to flee white society to indigenous culture, to remain the unmarried man of the title becomes, then, not a statement of his relationship with women, but rather a refusal to succumb to the entrapment of consumerism of culture:

> I was free, that's the point! If you don't spend a lot of money then you don't have to earn it and you are free. Why do you have to spend money on all this rubbish? You can buy a piece of brisket for three shillings, and you can boil it with an onion and live off it for four days! You can live off mealiemeal well enough, I often did, in the bush [47].

It is a consequence on the transitional nature of Sartrean identity, the "existence precedes essence" (Sartre, 67) awareness that individuals are free to determine their own character, that ensures that Lessing's creation is a cultural hybrid: belonging to nowhere except within the sphere of his own perpetually reconstituted environment. This becomes clear when the narrator speculates/evaluates the lifestyle of the unmarried man:

> He probably bought a single sheet of paper and a lone envelope. This meant he had got them from the African part of the store, where such small retailing went on — at a vast profit, of course, to the storekeeper. He must have bought one stamp, and walked across to the post office to hand the letter over the counter. Then, due having been paid to his upbringing, he moved back to the African tribe where he lived beyond post offices, letter writing, and other impedimenta that went with being a white man [Lessing, 38].

The man's movement between two antithetical cultures, both indigenous and white communities, demonstrates the hybridity of transculturalism in the context of two post-colonial contact zones. The narrative constitutes a cross-cultural exchange, rather than a linguistic or racial amalgamation, and one has to be careful in positioning it as a hybrid concept. Bill Ashcroft has commented that reading cross-cultural interactions as hybridity often "implies negating and neglecting the imbalance and inequality of the power relations it references" (134); yet this is not the case in reading Lessing's story. Even though one could perhaps argue that the exclusion of indigenous characters from the story does not expose the whole narrative regarding the process of indigenous cultural inscription as an exchange between colonizer and colonized, the unmarried man's critique of white society ensures that neither he, nor the society of which he is a product, is situated within any particular hierarchal order. We can perhaps conclude, therefore, that like Sargeson, Lessing does not render the "Man Alone" as clearly opposed to women as sexual and social entities, nor in a process of colonizing the indigenous society to which he is intermittently aligned. Rather, I have aimed to argue how Sargeson and Lessing render the "Man Alone" as an anti-humanist and isolated figure who functions to highlight the negations of provincial culture and, in Georg Lukacs' words, "the specification of the local condition rather than the universality of the human condition" (184).

Notes

1. The national location of Lessing's stories is difficult to determine. Lessing grew up in Southern Rhodesia (now Zimbabwe), and it is often assumed that her short stories are located in a fictional space of this actual territory. For this reason, I will refer the Lessing's stories as Southern African, without the certainty of geographical specificity.

Works Cited

Ashcroft, Bill. *Post-Colonial Transformation*. London: Routledge, 2001.
Chapman, Robert. "Fiction and the Social Pattern." In *Essays on New Zealand Literature*. Eds. Curnow and Wystan. Auckland: Heinemann, 1973.
Cole, John Reece. "Rev. of *The Gorse Blooms Pale*." *Landfall* 6 (1948): 149.
Lessing, Doris. *The Sun Between Their Feet: Collected African Stories*, Vol. 2. London: Flamingo, 2003.
Lukacs, Georges. "The Ideology of Modernism." In *The Lukacs Reader*. Ed. Arpad Kadarkay. Oxford: Blackwell, 1995.
Mansfield, Katherine. *The Collected Stories of Katherine Mansfield*. London: Book Club Associates, 1973.
Pearson, Bill. *Fretful Sleepers and Other Essays*. Auckland: Heinemann, 1974.
Sargeson, Frank. *The Stories of Frank Sargeson*. Harmondsworth: Penguin, 1982.
Sartre, Jean-Paul. *Existentialism and Humanism*. London: Methuen, 2007.
Williams, Mark. *Leaving the Highway: Six Contemporary New Zealand Novelists*. Auckland: Auckland University Press, 1990.

Postmodernist Postcolonialisms and Feminisms

A Passion for Justice

Varghese Thekkevallyara

My reflections on readings such as Chandra Talpade Mohanty's "Under Western Eyes Revisited," Marina Ortiga's "New Mestizas: 'World-Travellers' and *Dasein*," Maria Lugones' "Playfulness, 'World-Travelling,' and Loving Perception," and Morny Joy's "Method and Theory in Religious Studies: Retrospect and Prognostication" take me to the topic of postcolonialism and feminism as methods, defined by postmodernism, that facilitate justice.

Hence my title for this piece: "Postmodernist Postcolonialisms and Feminisms: A Passion for Justice."[1] But the topic makes it impossible for me not to reflect in turn on the tight bond between method and theme: that is, how the theme is inherent in the methodology used.

For me, it is important to reflect on what it means to use a certain method over another. My guiding questions are: Is there a fundamental link between a certain kind of theoretical methodology and the theme that evolves when the methodology is applied? What *kind* of postcolonialism or feminism can lead to justice?

To answer these questions, I will return to the readings that I have cited in the opening of this essay as they relate to especially the following, related, methodology and postcolonial areas of social justice: postmodernism, feminism, anti-globalization, and anti-racism.

I hope that these reflections will highlight the importance of the goal of social justice for women in the postcolonial era and, further, point to the need to reflect on the ethics of the method used in getting to that goal. By the *postcolonial*, I am referring not only to the period after colonialism, as in the post-colonial, but also to the continued presence of colonial power in its varied forms, including globalization. According to Robert Young, postcolonialism "seeks to change the way people think, the way they behave, to produce a more just and equitable relation between the different peoples of the world" (Young, 7). Thus, postcolonial studies is by definition justice-oriented. It appropriately associates with feminism, anti-globalization, and anti-racism, and therefore, it does not receive a separate section here. However, it is important to dwell on the methodologies assumed in postcolonial studies. All disciplines in the humanities, the arts, and the sciences need to centralize the study of methodology as part of their study of topics and themes because, more often than not, the method as means defines the theme as ends.

Postmodernism

I use the term "postmodernism" to refer to the historical and cultural period that follows modernism. This period is intellectually defined by the theoretical method of post-structuralism. *The Penguin Dictionary of Critical Theory* describes post-structuralism as "a reluctance to ground discourse in any theory of metaphysical origins, an insistence on the inevitable plurality and instability of meaning, a distrust of systematic scientificity, and the abandoning of the old enlightenment project" (Macey, 309). Thus, post-structuralism rejects scholasticism and theistic humanism, systems of thought that involve a reliance on the metaphysical; it also challenges notions of capital and monolithic Truth, insisting that meaning is varied; it is suspicious of so-called logical systems because it views these as systems of power, and deconstructs texts that claim unity based on reason. Jacques Derrida's "Structure, Sign and Play in the Discourse of the Human Sciences" introduces deconstruction as the method of undermining texts that claim inherent unity. Both postcolonial and feminist studies depend, to a great extent, on poststructuralism and deconstruction as methods. In this section, while pointing to several of the major arguments in theorists such as Morny Joy, Chandra T. Mohanty, J.J. Clarke, and Mariana Ortega, I want to reflect on what may be the links between postmodernist theories and the justice issues of the postmodern period on which these authors focus.

Morny Joy's "Is There a Postcolonial Ethics? Towards an Ethics of Location"—as the title suggests—poses the central question: Is there a postcolonial ethics? In the essay, Joy wonders aloud if the poststructuralist method of deconstruction, especially in its emphasis on "dismantling," is sufficient to bring about—and this excellently phrased sublime idea ought to be the core of just about any pedagogy or human life—"an almost infinite concern for justice" (Joy, n.p.).

To help her on her way to what she terms "an ethics of location," by which she means the justice that is part of respectfully recognizing ("a new understanding of recognition" [Joy, 30]) the other as a woman of a different place and culture, Joy engages with selective theorists. Joy's selection of theorists suggests that there is a strong link between methodology and theme. Here the theme of activism is seen as evolving only when post-structuralism is mixed with another method that supports activism. But she continues to re-examine such mixtures also. For example, while she finds Simon Critchley's reservations on postmodernism convincing, she is suspicious of his methodology. She detects Levinasian masculinism in it that she, logically, sees as incapable of producing justice for women. Again, Joy mentions R. Radhakrishnan, who flatly states: "'The vexing issue facing postmodern epistemology is how to reconcile a radical incommensurability among multiple knowledges and knowledge games with the dire need for a politics of recognition'" (quoted in Joy, 8). Once again, Joy and Radhakrishanan proceed on the inevitable assumption that the end of justice, here "a politics of recognition," which alone acknowledges a person beyond stereotypes, has to have a suitable methodology. According to them, postmodernism by itself is simply not equipped to do this.

Insistent on moving to a feminist methodology that is beyond poststruturalist games of deconstruction, Joy considers South Asian and East Asian women writers, including Mohanty, Nivedita Menon, and Ray Chow, among several others, and concludes:

> they have constructed a highly sophisticated model of dynamic interaction, with both theoretical and applied dimensions that, to my mind, constitutes a mode of exacting personal awareness and interpersonal respect that establishes the basis for both an ethics and politics of recognition — based on what I term an ethics of location [Joy, 9].

This is not the place to refer to the specifics of the theories of these feminist scholars, but what I want to point out is that Joy, in choosing these feminists and in not choosing others clarifies my thesis that there is an inherent link between theory and theme, that "a highly sophisticated model of dynamic interaction, *with both theoretical and applied dimensions*" (emphasis added) alone can lead to an ethics of location.

Briefly, it is not possible for Joy to arrive at the theme of activism through a methodology that is engrossed in basically pointless undermining, pure deconstructing. So, Joy rightly adopts the productive elements of deconstruction and yet insists on recognizing the importance of the universal (Joy, 26) in order to move "beyond naming only differences to seeking out similarities" to form "strategic coalitions" (Joy, 31).

Similarly, Mohanty, in "Under Western Eyes Revisited," requires "a materialist and 'realist'" perspective that is "antithetical to that of postmodernist relativism" (Mohanty, 511) in order to arrive at a productive model of pedagogy of women's studies, namely of "the feminist solidarity or comparative feminist studies model" (Mohanty, 521). And to produce his somewhat exoticized version of "new Orientalism," J.J. Clarke, in "Orientalism and Postmodernism," relies entirely on the deconstructivist technique even as it is seen as being derived from Oriental religious sources. In conclusion, the theme that evolves in each case depends to a great extent on the theory that guides it: pure postmodernist/ poststructuralist theories produce dubious visions of justice for women of the two-thirds world.

Feminism

Feminism assumes that there is unfair inequality between women and men. I use the apparently redundant term — unfair inequality — to distinguish sexism from instances of "fair inequality" as in the case of the under-aged not being permitted to vote or drive. So, the goal of feminist theories is to work out a method of removing unfair inequality and bringing about justice. There are also different kinds of feminism, not just liberal and radical versions, but also feminisms that evolve from the experience and scholarship of women and men of the two-thirds world, both native and diasporic.

The works of Mohanty, Joy, Musa Dube, and Daniel Boyarin point to the role of different kinds of feminist studies and their place in a search for justice. In "Under Western Eyes Revisited," Mohanty describes three models of feminist pedagogies: the feminist as tourist model in which the Eurocentric view remains even as this model arbitrarily draws in evidence of otherness and difference in the two-thirds worlds; the feminist as explorer model in which the two-thirds worlds alone fall under "area studies," whereas the metropolitan center (Women's Studies in the U.S.) remains an aloof observer; and the feminist solidarity model. This last model, which she advocates, is based on a recognition of the inherent worth of human beings (which cannot simply be deconstructed and left at that). Hence she looks for "common differences" (Mohanty, 503), differences that do not necessarily alienate but rather bond relationships between the two-thirds world and the one-thirds world.

It is interesting to note that Mohanty's perspective is feminist but not exactly poststructuralist. She argues: "if the dominant discourse is the discourse of cultural relativism, questions of power, agency, justice, and common criteria for critique and evaluation are silenced" (Mohanty, 520). Like Joy, she recognizes the importance of location and also of going across locations, in a comparative analysis. Her method is more Marxist; she is influenced by Marx and Lukac. As I note earlier, she says: "My view is thus a materialist and 'realist' one and is antithetical to that of postmodernist relativism" (Mohanty, 511). It is, however, ironic that as a Marxist, she uses the word "realist" to describe institutional and ideological situations. As I understand it, Marxists think that false consciousness and ideologies make us assume that such situations are "real."

I rather see a link between Mohanty's third and preferred method of feminist pedagogy — "the feminist solidarity model or the comparative feminist studies model" and that of liberation theology. Liberation Theology's *praxis* is also Marxist and committed to helping the subaltern but without rejecting the metaphysical. This observation leads me to the next area of social justice: how anti-globalization is linked to postcolonial and feminist studies.

Anti-Globalization

Anti-globalization defines globalization in terms of colonialism, capitalist exploitation, and economic, political, and cultural invasion. It refuses to buy into the "global village" theory, which assumes that globalization is fundamentally a good thing resulting in benevolent proximity and increased neighborhood with even the remotest parts of the earth. Instead it sees through this rhetoric of benevolence and exposes the unfairness within the movement of globalization.

A postcolonial theory that sees colonialism as a thing of the past — as a matter of eighteenth or nineteenth century studies, for example — but with only certain leftovers such as the influence of colonial language and colonial culture is capable of neither understanding nor solving the imperialistic aspects in globalization. That is why Mohanty insists on Women's Studies being a pedagogy of anti-globalization, an anti-capitalist pedagogy. In Mohanty's preferred pedagogical model (of feminist solidarity or comparative feminist studies), it is also important to consider how globalization as the new *avatar* of colonialism influenced Women's Studies. Thus, the model considers anti-globalization from a feminist perspective, too. Mohanty's thesis is Gandhian in spirit. One of the last notes left by Gandhi, what is famously known as Gandhi's talisman, runs as follows:

> I will give you a talisman. Whenever you are in doubt, or when the self becomes too much with you, apply the following test. Recall the face of the poorest and the weakest man [woman] whom you may have seen, and ask yourself, if the step you contemplate is going to be of any use to him [her].

> Will he [she] gain anything by it? Will it restore him [her] to a control over his [her] own life and destiny? In other words, will it lead to swaraj [freedom] for the hungry and spiritually starving millions? Then you will find your doubts and your self melt away [Gandhi, 65].

As in Gandhi's talisman, in which Gandhi asks that we check to see if the poorest of the poor benefit from something we set out to do, Mohanty asks that we look at globalization from the perspective of "poor indigenous [native/ tribal/dalit] and Third World/South women" (Mohanty, 505). This methodological perspective will yield the best thematic results. But to achieve this, Mohanty says, "we need an anti-imperialist, anticapitalist, and contextualized feminist project to expose and make visible the various, overlapping forms of subjugation of women's lives" (Mohanty, 515).

Once Mohanty adopts this methodology — of anti-capitalist pedagogy — the themes of injustice are clearer to her. She is able to reflect on an important problem not covered in her earlier essay, "Under Western Eyes": "the question of native or indigenous struggles" (Mohanty, 506). Thus, she can join hands with ecologists such as Vandana Siva, scholars and activists who point to the extent to which globalization invades the environment and thus the lives of the least privileged in the two-thirds world. Mohanty further unravels the multi-layered venom of globalization: "capital as it functions now depends on and exacerbates racist, patriarchal, and heterosexist relations of rule" (Mohanty, 510). These sophisticated and redemptive insights are unlikely to evolve if Mohanty's methodology was endless deconstruction. Rather, these insights depend largely on a nuanced postcolonial methodology which is defined by feminism, marxism, and anti-racism.

Anti-Racism

> A mode of classification of human beings which distinguishes between them on the basis of physical properties (e.g., skin colour, facial features) which purportedly derive from genetic inheritance. The key problem with this mode of classification is that the processes of selection regarding what ought to count as "racial" and therefore "natural" (i.e., non-cultural) differences are themselves inextricably linked to the existence of cultural norms concerning what defines a "difference" as peculiarly "racial" [Edgar and Sedgwick, 323].

As Edgar and Sedgwick point out, physical differences that are race based become an issue of racist discrimination because the process of selecting for classification what counts as racial-and-natural is itself a product of (Eurocentric) norms on what is difference and what is racial. Thus, anti-racism recognizes that racial values are defined and enlisted by colonially motivated powers and discourses. Anti-racist methodology aims to expose and dismantle these powers and discourses in an attempt to realize the equality of all races. Anti-racism combined with feminism perceives the female of the two-thirds world as doubly colonized, by race and gender. A postcolonial or feminist methodology that ignores issues of race will likely have limited or unhelpful themes as its concern and thus cannot be said to contribute to justice.

In "Playfulness, 'World-Travelling,' and Loving Perception," Maria Lugones asks us not to be too much at ease in our own cultural world but to proceed with "loving perception" to the world of others, much as Joy advocates an ethics of location. Lugones terms this "world travelling." Where Michel Foucault rules postmodern studies with his double pronged Power/Knowledge, Lugones's simple diction, "love," comes as an uneasy surprise. Yet, that is how a racialized person would like to be perceived—with loving, not arrogant, perception. It then makes sense and should make good anti-racist theory.

Youssef Yacaoubi's "Thinking a Critical Theory of Postcolonial Islam" was itself an invitation for me to travel worlds. While I had read introductions to and themes on Islam, this is the first work of Islamic critical theory that I have read. The fact that Yacaoubi not only posits Islamic theory as a portion of postcolonial studies but also takes to task Islamic scholars for ignoring the marginal voices—the minor myths and rituals—in Islam has been for me highly thought-provoking. I am now motivated to read more—to know more of other worlds.

According to Lugones, travel is not a "touristy" experience; more fundamentally, it is marked by a core transformation: "the shift from being one person to being a different person" (11). As she emphasizes, this is not a make-believe act. The transformation is genuine at its core. Yet, "one does not *experience* any underlying 'I'" (Lugones, 12). Ortega's Heideggerian analysis resists the remote possibility of personhood in Lugones's theory. I think that Ortega is right to suspect that Lugones believes in the existence of a core person through all the various phases of world traveling. It is important that Lugones assumes this personhood, for only then can she insist on the unconditional dignity of this person as a human being, requiring or demanding the loving perception. This human being can be the racialized woman who deserves loving perception even as she has to learn to perceive with love.

Lugones further modifies this loving perception and world-traveling with the concept of "playfulness." On initially seeing this term, I wondered if she was going to talk about postmodern game theories that, for example, deconstruct and celebrate uncertainty, irresponsibly. Lugones, too, links playfulness and uncertainty. But the uncertainty is of a different kind: "the uncertainty is an *openness to surprise*." This is termed a "metaphysical attitude" (Lugones, 16). By distancing herself from Georg Gadamer's "agonistic sense of play," in which play is in the mode of win-lose, Lugones encourages a win-win situation. As she infers, the agonistic sense of play is racist and can sadly explain the European games of colonialism and globalization, and their pathetic consequences for the two-thirds world. Lugones' choice of methodology as feminist, anti-racist, postcolonial, critical, yet to some extent humanist, supports her thematic vision of not only justice but also of love.

Conclusion

The preceding analysis of the various readings repeatedly points to the fact that postcolonial feminist scholars in search of justice believe it is important to consider issues of globalization and racism as these impact on the place of women in the two-third worlds. Their goal of justice, which includes anti-globalization and anti-racism, also requires that they reflect on their methodology.

Postcolonial studies by inception and growth, through theorists such as Edward Said, Gayatri Spivak, and Homi K. Bhabha who were products of Western postmodernism, has been founded on poststructuralist methods. The self-reflection of postcolonial feminist scholars such as Joy, Mohanty, Dube, Lugones, and Ortega reveals the close link between their methodology and their degree of success in their attempts to bring about justice. Their arguments in general suggest that pure forms of postmodern methods fail to expedite justice. For example, mindless deconstruction and game theories are not the right means to the right ends of justice. On the other hand, a healthy mix of deconstruction and Marxism that is also anti-racist, as Mohanty points out, can take one to a more justice-oriented Woman's Studies. And, as Joy recommends, "perhaps a healthy dose of postmodern suspicion, supplemented by cultural critique, could be therapeutic" (Joy, 218).

These reflections and related readings have provided me with a lesson in methodology and especially on how method is not a thing apart from the content. As the age-old saying goes, the style is the man (old sayings are indeed patriarchal!); then it is possible to say that the method is the theme and the theme the method.

NOTES

1. I am grateful to Morny Joy for her comments on an earlier version of this essay.

WORKS CITED

Bhabha, Homi K. *The Location of Culture*. London: Routledge, 1994.
Boyarin, Daniel. "Gender." *Critical Terms for Religious Studies*. Ed. M. C. Taylor. Chicago: University of Chicago Press, 1998. 117–135.

Chidester, David. "Primitive Texts, Savage Contents." *Method and Theory* 15 (2003): 272–283.

Clarke, J. J. "Orientalism and Postmodernism." *Oriental Enlightenment: The Encounter Between Asian and Western Thought*. London: Routledge, 1997.

Derrida, Jacques. "Structure, Sign and Play in the Discourse of the Human Sciences." *Writing and Difference*. Chicago: University of Chicago Press, 1978. 278–294.

Dube, Musa. "Postcoloniality, Feminist Spaces and Religion." *Postcolonialism, Feminism and Religious Discourse*. Eds. Laura E. Donaldson and Kwok Pui-lan. New York: Routledge, 2002. 100–121.

Edgar, Andrew, and Peter Sedgwick. *Cultural Theory: The Key Concepts*. London: Routledge, 2002.

Gandhi, Mahatma. *Mahatma Gandhi: the Last Phase*, Vol. II. Ed. Pyarelal. Ahmedabad: Navajivan, 1958.

Joy, Morny. "Is There a Postcolonial Ethics? Towards an Ethics of Location." *Hindu Ethics*, Vol. 2. Ed. Purushottama Bilimoria. Dordrecht: Springer. (Forthcoming.)

___. "Method and Theory in Religious Studies: Retrospect and Prognostication." *Temenos* 43,2 (2007): 65–88.

Lugones, Maria. "Playfulness, 'World-Travelling,' and Loving Perception." *Hypatia* 2,2 (1987): 3–19.

Macey, David. *The Penguin Dictionary of Critical Theory*. London: Penguin, 2000.

Mohanty, Chandra Talpade. "Under Western Eyes Revisited." *Signs* 28,2 (2003): 499–535.

Ortega, Marina. "New Mestizas. 'World-Travelers' and *Dasein*." *Hypatia* 16,3 (2001): 1–29.

Said, Edward. *Orientalism*. New York: Random, 1978.

Spivak, Gayatri. *In Other Worlds: Essays in Cultural Politics*. New York: Methuen, 1987.

Young, Robert. *Postcolonialism: A Very Short Introduction*. Oxford: Oxford University Press, 2003.

Yacoubi, Youssef. "Thinking Critical Theory of Postcolonial Islam." *Difference in Philosophy of Religion*. Ed. Philip Goodchild. Aldershot: Ashgate, 2003. 135–154.

Postcolonialisms, Globalization and Iconic Architecture

LESLIE SKLAIR

Despite the fact that architecture and the built environment confront all of us in our daily lives they have received relatively little attention in discussions of globalization, capitalism or postcolonialism. Therefore, I begin by examining the general idea that certain types of architecture can be hegemonic in a class sense, that is just like other art forms (notably literatures and the plastic arts) certain buildings and spaces can serve specific class interests alongside their recognized aesthetic qualities. This is argued convincingly by Bentmann and Muller (1992) in their book on the villa as hegemonic architecture, a brilliant study of how the villa, largely associated with the great architect Palladio, faithfully reproduced the class structures and divisions of northern Italy in the sixteenth century. The construction of Hilton hotels in what would be known as the Third World after 1945 provides a more recent example. As Conrad Hilton himself said, his hotels were literally "a little America" for upper-middle class travelers, a "space of modern luxury and technological desire [signifying the] new and powerful presence of the United States" or, more accurately, its dominant class, in the post-war world (Wharton, 2). Between 1949 and 1966, Hilton hotels were built in San Juan, Istanbul, Mexico City, Havana, Port of Spain, Tehran, Hong Kong, Athens, Tunis, Tel Aviv, Cairo, Barbados, and Bridgetown. The Istanbul Hilton, a typical example, was built in the International Style (notably transparent glass revealing a mini-mall in the spacious atrium) on one of the city's best sites. Illustrating a classic postcolonial theme that will reappear in this narrative, it was claimed that in fitting out the hotel, ancient Turkish tile-making was reinvented. Wharton comments: "Whether these tiles were modified or reinvented, they were deployed as a sign of the Other within a dominant aesthetic of American Modernity" (Wharton, 26).

Coterminous with the public relations industry that disseminates them, city symbols (like the Sydney Opera House) and national symbols (like government buildings in Chandigarh and Brasilia, the Three Gorges Dam in China, and skyscrapers in many postcolonial cities), reinforce processes of global image-creation that can be mobilized in the interests of the powerful. As we shall see below, Petronas Towers in Kuala Lumpur, Beautiful Indonesia in Miniature in Jakarta, and República de los Niños in Buenos Aires, all use architecture to reconstruct history, to create new national identities, to boost tourism and to consolidate the power of local and transnational elites. In the era of globalization, these processes have evolved in surprising ways.

Globalization, at least as a sociological concept, has always been too frail to sustain the theoretical and substantive burdens loaded on to it. It needs to be deconstructed. In order to do this I distinguish three modes of globalization in theory and practice — namely generic, capitalist, and alternative globalizations. Globalization in a generic sense is too often confused with its dominant actually existing type, namely capitalist globalization. In previous work (specifically in *The Transnational Capitalist Class* and *Globalization: Capitalism and Its Alternatives*), I have argued that capitalist globalization is driven by a transnational capitalist class (TCC), comprising four main fractions: those who own and/or control the major transnational corporations and their local affiliates (the corporate fraction); globalizing politicians and bureaucrats (the state fraction); globalizing professionals (the technical fraction); and elites of merchants, media, and advertising (the consumerist fraction). Architecture and urban design provide plenty of examples.

Generic Globalization and Capitalist Globalization

My basic premise is straightforward: generic globalization offers almost unlimited emancipatory potential for life on earth, while capitalist globalization subverts this potential for the selfish interests of the transnational capitalist class. I define generic globalization in terms of four phenomena of increasing significance since the middle of the twentieth century:

1. the electronic revolution, notably transformations in the technological base and global scope of the electronic mass media and to most of the material infrastructure of the world today;
2. new forms of cosmopolitanism;
3. postcolonialisms[1];
4. the creation of transnational social spaces.

These four phenomena are the defining characteristics of globalization in a generic sense. Each clearly offers in principle tremendous emancipatory potential over a wide range of economic, political and social issues. However, as capitalism began to globalize in the second half of the twentieth century, the emancipatory potential of generic globalization has been systematically undermined (see "The Emancipatory Potential of Generic Globalization"). While the impact of the electronic revolution and new forms of cosmopolitanism are discussed briefly below, the main focus here is on iconic architecture in the context of postcolonialisms and transnational social spaces. Historically, iconic architecture was generally driven by state and/or religious elites, while in the age of capitalist globalization originating in the electronic revolution, those in control of capitalist globalization, the TCC, have become increasingly implicated in the production of iconic architecture serving their own class interests.[2] Vale argues in his study of power and identity embedded in the design of parliament buildings in the Third World in the second half of the twentieth century that "grand symbolic state buildings need to be understood in terms of the political and cultural contexts that helped to bring them into being" (1992, 3), and he goes on to demonstrate that, despite the stated aim of postcolonial state architecture to create national identity, what really happens is the reinforcement of existing hierarchies. These existing hierarchies — led by (in my terms) emerging state and corporate fractions of the TCC — become more connected with the multifarious world of capitalist globalization, and old and new iconic architecture tends to become more consumerist.

Architecture operates hegemonically in terms of the four defining characteristics of generic globalization in the abstract, and capitalist globalization in the concrete with significance for the study of postcolonialisms. First, there is no doubt that the electronic revolution has transformed the practice and the reception of architecture in the era of capitalist globalization. A very clear statement of the former is to be found in the research of Tombesi ("A True South for Design? The New International Division of Labour in Architecture"), in which overwhelming evidence of the creation of a new international division of labor in architecture is presented. While architects have always worked "abroad," since the 1990s digital technology has facilitated qualitatively new relationships between design offices in the First World and low cost local architectural labor occupying low cost office space in the Third World, both in terms of the design process and the operation of architectural markets. In the U.S., the percentage of architecture firms transferring drawings electronically rose from 35 percent in 1996 to 83 percent in 1999 (173). Not only does digital technology make it possible to build previously unbuildable designs, but these designs can be transmitted across the globe almost instantaneously.

In a case study of how this has impacted on Indian architecture, Tombesi et al. ("Routine Production or Symbolic Analysis? India and The Globalization of Architectural Services") show that (as predicted by my class polarization thesis) this has benefited the globalizing-commercial as opposed to the domestic-traditional segments of the industry. With the rise of consumerism and demand for luxury homes, office blocks and five star hotels, in the 1990s "fully computerised new firms rose to industry leadership as exclusive purveyors in India of the latest in fashionable architectural imagery worldwide" (83).[3] Thus, as generic globalization opens up architectural and developmental possibilities, capitalist globalization provides the framework for the TCC to exploit these in its own class interests in new markets.

The new technology has had a somewhat different impact in China, effecting an unprecedented transformation of the cities as well as the nature of architectural labor. The number of architects in the late 1990s was ten percent of the number in the U.S. but, according to one estimate, they designed five times the volume of projects (in millions of square meters) while earning one tenth of the design fee per job. In Shenzhen Special Economic Zone, extraordinary records have been set, such as five designers working for one night with two computers designing a 300-unit single family housing development and one architect working for seven days producing a 30-story concrete residential high rise. Most of these high rises are off the shelf with distinctive hats or facade variations, based on "architectural recipes" often lifted from foreign publications, and domestic competition entries. The system is highly dependent on foreign architectural firms, through government requirements for foreign firms to have domestic joint venture partners in Chinese projects (Lin, in Chung et al.). Where Shenzhen has led, the rest of China has followed, and over the last twenty years, this model has transformed the skylines of many cities in China (see Cartier, Ren).

New forms of cosmopolitanism can also be easily identified in the field of architecture in the person of globally iconic architects (starchitects). The majority of contemporary architectural icons in the Third World have been designed by starchitects from the First World, many of whom are in great demand to build a spectacular building to put some city "on the map," especially in China, the Gulf states, and some former Soviet Republics. Few iconic architects from the Third World have completed projects in the First World, though there are many whose work is universally admired, for example Luis Barragan from Mexico, Oscar Niemeyer and Paolo Mendes da Rocha from Brazil, and Baghdad-born Zaha Hadid — all winners of the Pritzker prize (the equivalent of the Nobel for architects) — and others, notably Carlos Villanueva from Venezuela, Charles Correa from India, Hassan Fathy from Egypt, and Ken Yeang from Malaysia. Their work is generally considered more "local" (regional) than "global" (modernist), to which contentious distinction I now turn.

Postcolonial Understandings of Architecture and Transnational Social Spaces

My argument assumes that there has been a gradual tendency shift in capitalist hegemony between the pre-global era (roughly, in my view, up to the 1960s with the advent of the electronic revolution) and the era of capitalist globalization. In the pre-global era, capitalist hegemony legitimated itself on claims to cultural superiority by colonialists/imperialists, producing a form of racist Orientalism. For architecture, this is expressed in many ways — for example, in the idea of the tropical vernacular, poorly and/or quaintly designed buildings for threatening tropical climates. In the present era of capitalist globalization, ideological hegemony is based more on the claims to cultural superiority of a transnational capitalist class, producing a form of consumer-ist postcolonialism, expressed in terms of hybridity as a marketing tool in architecture. As we shall see below, this hybridity favors particular materials and design forms and is almost always in the direction of capitalist consumerism. As Vale observes in his study of postcolonial parliament buildings: "part of the national identity of some developing countries has come to be defined according to the dictates and tastes of Western consumers" (54).

The literature on postcolonialisms and architecture since around the 1920s can be seen as the most important branch of one of the most fundamental debates in the history of architecture — namely the contrast between what we can call international modernism (IM) and architectural regionalism (AR) — though these are not the only terms in which it is portrayed.[4] Briefly put, IM refers to buildings characterized by thin or curtain walls as opposed to massive load-bearing walls, regularity as opposed to symmetry, new materials (glass, steel, reinforced concrete) as opposed to stone and earth, and minimal decoration. Despite the original radical intentions of most of its founders, IM resulted in the monotonous tower blocks and glass and steel skyscrapers that dominate the skylines of most cities on earth. AR, on the other hand, is based on the idea that the vernacular — namely buildings using local methods and materials for small scale site-specific projects — should be the guiding principle for architecture.[5] The history and theory of postcolonial understandings of architecture, before and after the end of formal colonial rule, revolve around these idealized tropes of IM and AR, the dominant metaphor being the imposition of First World versions of IM on Third World communities whose needs would be better served by versions of AR. The reality is, unsurprisingly, somewhat different.

In the decades before and after the end of formal colonial rule in Asia and Africa, there is ample evidence to suggest that reactions to IM and AR of indigenous and colonist architects in the actual and nominal colonies and in the imperial powers spanned a wide spectrum (see Crinson). In Latin America, of course, formal colonial rule ended in the nineteenth century, but the same holds true for architects there. In the first half of the twentieth century, many European architects fled persecution taking IM with them: for example, the Russian émigré, Gregori Warchavchik, who built the first modernist house in South America, the Casa Modernista (Sao Paulo, 1928), and the German Eric Mendelsohn, who arrived in Palestine in 1934 and helped create the image of Tel Aviv as a modernist city. The two greatest architects of the period, Le Corbusier and Frank Lloyd Wright, both traveled. Outside their home countries, Wright's influence mainly bore fruit in Mexico[6] and Japan, Le Corbusier's more widely in Europe, Latin America and, in the 1950s, as part of the team that developed Chandigarh, the capital of the Punjab, in newly independent India. Those they influenced are to be found all over the world, building international modernist buildings with regional vernacular characteristics and/or regional vernacular buildings with international modernist characteristics.[7]

Brazil, often considered to be the first country to create a national style of modernist architecture, appears to be something of a special case — though in Turkey (see Bozdogan) and Indonesia (see Kusno) there were also strong early state-sponsored modernist movements that came into creative contact with traditional regionalist forces. However, only in Brazil was a whole new national capital city built along modernist lines (though Canberra is a partial exception). The story of Brasilia revolves around President Kubitschek, who provided the political will; the eminent Brazilian architects Lúcio Costa (actually born in France), who created the masterplan and the communist Oscar Niemeyer, who designed most of the buildings; and Le Corbusier and the Soviet Constructivists, who provided the inspiration. The president promoted Brasilia, located deep in the interior of this vast country, as a motor of regional economic development, as a hub of a new communications revolution for national integration; and, with the architects, as a material embodiment of the blueprint for the socialist utopia. In the middle of the twentieth century, Brasilia's planners were calling it "the capital of the twenty-first century" (cited in Holston, 85; see also Vale, Chapter 4, and Fraser, Chapter 3). As Holston convincingly argues, the intentions of each of these parties were not always realized. The architectural context in which all this was taking place was a vibrant modernist movement that began in the 1940s and took the so-called

"Brazilian Style" to international prominence, with a wildly successful exhibition and book under the same title — "Brazil Built" — at the Museum of Modern Art in New York in 1943. Deckker, in her definitive history of the movement, *Brazil Built: The Architecture of the Modern Movement in Brazil*, shows that the "Brazilian Style" had as much political as aesthetic significance, being seen by some in Brazil as a symbol of American imperialism, but by others as Brazil's true path to modernization and development. Holton, in his book on Brasilia, expresses this in the following terms: "an architectural sign [the appearance of a building, for example] may remain constant while its denoted meanings shift dramatically with changes in use, context, and intention" (97). The main lessons of this case for the postcolonial understandings of architecture and urban planning are first, that the end results of such a project (and probably even single buildings) are highly unpredictable over time with respect to aesthetics, politics, use, and reception; and second, that the categories of IM and AR pose as many questions as they answer.

What is clear is that whether we see international modernist buildings with regional vernacular characteristics or regional vernacular buildings with international modernist characteristics, the identity of the architect still matters and, no less important, the identity of the architect (indeed any artist) is a social construct. This raises the key question of representation, an issue con-

Congress buildings, Brasilia.

Brasilia Cathedral, by communist architect Oscar Niemeyer.

structively problematized but not resolved by the subaltern studies project[8]—
a project that has particular resonance for the architecture and postcolonialism
debate. In a devastating critique of what he labels "postcolonial celebrities,"
in particular those occupying comfortable university chairs in the First World,
Araeen argues that continuing western cultural domination "does not necessarily manifest in suppressing other cultures, or artistic forms of other cultures,
but denying other cultures, or peoples from other cultures, their subject positions in modernism" (4). Those postcolonials who are used in an essentialist
Orientalist manner to represent the Other in architecture — Barragan for Mex-
icaness, Niemayer for Brazilianess, Correa for Indianess, Fathy for Arabness,
and so on — are denied their subject status in modernism as they are celebrated
for their bogus regional exoticism. In a convincing critique of Critical Regionalism and its Western theorists, Eggener (2007, 399) points out: "it is ironic
that writers discussing the places where these [regionalist] designs appeared
so often emphasized one architect's interpretation of the region over all others:
Tadao Ando for Japan, Oscar Niemeyer for Brazil, Charles Correa for India,
Luis Barragon for Mexico. In other words, a single correct regional style was
implied or imposed, sometimes from inside, more often from outside." Prakash
speaks of "Identity Production in Postcolonial Indian Architecture: Re-Cov-
ering What We Never Had":

> When one talks of an Indian architect, or of an architect from the "non-Western" world, it seems necessary to deal with the question of identity. While discussing Western architects one can get away with dealing with supposedly universal architectural issues like aesthetics and technology, but it seems necessary that in discussing the work of an architect from India the issue of identity be specifically raised in addition to, or in dialogue with, issues more directly aesthetic or architectural. Architects of the West do not specifically make Western buildings. Architects of the non–West are expected to. Even architects of the West working in the non–West in one way or another find themselves obliged to deal with the issue of non–Western identity [Prakash in Nalbantoğlu and Wong, 39; see also Kalia].

The construction of the Petronas Twin Towers (PTT) in Kuala Lumpur, Malaysia (a "moderate" Islamic state) is a good if convoluted example of how such issues are typically addressed under conditions of capitalist globalization. The architect, Cesar Pelli, was born in Argentina in 1926 and moved to the United States in 1964. Pelli had attracted international attention with his enormous towers in the World Financial Center in New York (1981) and in Canary Wharf in London (1986); so it was no great surprise that he won the international competition for PTT in 1991. The project was the centerpiece of then–President Mahathir's *Wawasan* (Vision) 2020, based on two 88-story towers 451.9 meters high, with a skybridge between the 41st and 42nd floors. PTT is owned and largely tenanted by the consortium led by Petronas, the state petroleum company, as part of the Kuala Lumpur City Center plan. The architect reported that "it was never specified that the towers should become the tallest buildings in the world, just that they be beautiful" (Pelli et al., 1997, 66), though the fact that the tallest building in the world would be located (for a short time, at least) in Kuala Lumpur was certainly appealing to the Malaysian client.[9] Pelli & Associates won, apparently, not only because their "proposal met the desire for a uniquely Malaysian design" but because meeting this desire also solved a problem in IM skyscraper design. In Pelli's own words: "Linking the Petronas Towers to Kuala Lumpur and Malaysia required rethinking the character of the traditional skyscraper to unburden it of American or European connotations. ... [the] shape of the towers has its origin in Islamic tradition, in which geometric patterns assume greater symbolic importance than in Western culture" (68).

Where, then, does this "uniquely Malaysian design" come from? At one level, as noted above, it comes from the Islamic geometry of the floorplan, but at another, deeper level it comes from the break with modernist tradition embodied in the symmetrical arrangement of the towers and what this means for the space between them. Pelli explains: "Through Frank Lloyd Wright, many architects have been influenced by Lao Tzu's teaching that the reality of a hollow object is in the void and not the walls that define it. ... This

Petronas Twin Towers, Kuala Lumpur.

quality of the building is not derived from Malaysian tradition. But because it appears for the first time in Kuala Lumpur, it will be forever identified with its place" (70). Just as the Eiffel Tower, whose structure and form were not French in origin, became synonymous with Paris, PTT will become synonymous with Kuala Lumpur. This is clearly a rationale that is open to many types and layers of interpretation. Suffice it to say here that, at one level and for some professionals and ideologues, it painlessly reconciles IM and AR in a conciliatory postcolonial direction. It is also worth noting that the ground floor of PTT has become one of the most iconic shopping malls in Asia and that, as Pelli predicted, the Petronas Towers complex has become a first class marketing symbol for Kuala Lumpur and Malaysia as a whole, despite its purported "break with modernism."

The (sometimes literally) concrete representation of generic globalization is found in the creation of what has been termed transnational social spaces — notably, skyscrapers, globally-branded shopping malls, theme parks, waterfront developments and transportation nodes — spaces that, despite their regional characteristics — could be almost anywhere in the world (see, for example, Abaza, Marshall, King). They are routinely referred to as "icons of

Above: PTT Mall. *Left:* The T-shirt confirms that Petronas Twin Towers have become synonymous with Kuala Lumpur.

modernity" and, as we have seen, the ways in which dominant classes in postcolonial societies appropriate symbols of modernity (and tradition) is fundamental to understanding the role of architecture in class society. A study of how the Chinese state enters the global market through the heritage industry describes how preservation is presented locally through a clean new Shanghai Museum still surrounded by dirty streets. "And suddenly you realize that the museum does not think of itself as being part of a local space at all, but as a part of a virtual global cultural network" (Abbas, 782)—excluding, we might add, the subaltern local Other. This is not uncommon, as Edensor (in Chapter 5) shows for the Taj Mahal, and Wharton (in Chapter 4) for the "forceful Modernity" of the Hilton hotel in Tel Aviv diverting attention from the Arab slums to the east as its prime site looks out to the west and the sea.

Abbas argues that it is not in transnational states but in re-imagined cities that we find transnational social spaces. This is happening all over the world. In the late 1990s, 13 of the 30 largest architect-developer firms working in Asia were based in the United States, Australia, or the United Kingdom. This circumstance "leads inevitably to a collection of architectural projects that are remarkably the same in cities such as Tokyo, Shanghai, Singapore and Jakarta" (Marshall, 2). However, all of these megaprojects will have partners on the ground, not just architects, but engineers, real estate agents, bankers, lawyers, and support staff, out of which new local affiliates of the TCC will emerge as part of transnational urban growth coalitions. Once again Kuala Lumpur and what has been dubbed Malaysia's Multimedia Super Corridor (MSC) provide a potent example. The MSC (Bill Gates was on the International Advisory Panel) is an extension of Kuala Lumpur, spanning Petronas as the (former) tallest building in the world, Cyberjaya as the world's first fully smart city, and Putrajaya as the first multimedia paperless seat of government, to KL International Airport as the biggest airport in the region. This "carefully articulated 'hybrid' MSC landscape ... embraces not only the economic magnetism of modern global-city architecture but also the repackaged symbolisms of tradition and culture that reifies the national integrity of the country," complete with strategic placement of new mosques (Boey, 207).

While this immense project has stalled somewhat in recent years, the rhetoric and some spectacular architecture remain. Nevertheless, frequently hidden from the tourist gaze, as indicated for Shanghai and Tel Aviv above, the iconic buildings of the MSC obscure the lives and living conditions of the poor (see also Bunnell). Kusno forcefully makes the same point for Jakarta, and, indeed, this appears to be true for most if not all globalizing cities, and not just those in the Third World—it is a condition of existence of transnational social spaces from above. On the surface, this appears to turn the earlier critique of capitalism—private affluence and public squalor—on its head. Through the culture-ideology of consumerism, promising the fruits of capitalist globalization to all (fortified by platitudes like "the rising tide lifts all boats"), transnational social spaces from above create apparent public affluence through iconic architecture. This is achieved through an appropriation of modernist iconicity with regionalist characteristics which prevailing postcolonial modes of representation translate into a language that sits comfortably

A new mosque in Putrajaya, by the lake: a tourist attraction?

with the culture-ideology of consumerism of capitalist globalization. Three main audiences are targeted by those who run such globalizing cities. First and most directly, these spaces and buildings seek to attract the national and international tourist trade, an important component of which is business-tourism (trade shows, conferences, sports events, etc.); second the local urban upper middle class, whose numbers have increased rapidly over the last few decades in most cities; and third, indirectly, the local working class who are encouraged to participate by looking at and taking occasional outings in their new, gleaming, city centers, public buildings and suburban shopping malls, promoted as sources of civic and national pride even in the poorest countries (see Abaza, as well as my own essay "Iconic Architecture and the Culture-Ideology of Consumerism").

Perhaps the most extraordinary example of this phenomenon is taking place in Shanghai under the banner of "One City, Nine Towns." To provide appropriate accommodation for its newly prosperous upper middle class and expatriates, numbering around half a million, the Urban Planning Institute in Shanghai has begun to create a series of satellite communities, "each inspired by a country that played a pivotal role in the colonial and commercial history of the city ... China is slowly coming to terms with its colonial past and has been inviting foreign investment back into Shanghai. Now, a scheme is underway to mark the impact of colonialism — not in the city centre but out in the suburbs."[10] As of summer 2009, this vast project envisages a Spanish town modeled on Barcelona, a British Thames Town (complete with Tudor cottages, a castle and a maze and with plans to attract a Scottish whiskey retailer and shops selling English Premier League souvenirs, and various fast food outlets and restaurants, hoping to bring in weddings), a German town designed by Albert Speer (son of Hitler's architect), a Scandinavian town, and sundry others. However ridiculous this might seem, in comparison with the haphazard highrise development of Pudong in Shanghai City, some Chinese architects take a more benign view of the nine towns (see Lu and Li, in Herrie and Weggerhoff).

Not all transnational social spaces have been created anew in the era of capitalist globalization. Indeed, one of the most prominent types of transnational social space is the postcolonial rebranding of ancient monuments as prime tourist and consumerist sites (Vale). Tourism at ancient monuments has existed for centuries, boosted by the invention of photography in 1839 and accelerated spectacularly since the growth of the internet. The Taj Mahal is a paradigm case. As Pal demonstrates: "The best-known symbol of Indian civilization is essentially a creation of Western enthusiasm" though its contemporary significance for internal tourism in India also is growing rapidly (194). This and the consumerist significance of the Taj, as well as the prime importance of commission in the local tourist economy, is brought out by the ethnographic study of Edensor, showing that tourist paths around the Taj focused on "realizing anticipated consumption ... the next stop is invariably a craft emporium" (109). It comes as little surprise to learn that the Indian Department of Tourism called in the U.S. National Parks Service for help with its development plans for the site in the 1990s.

Let me bring this necessarily incomplete discussion to a close with reference to one of the most successfully iconic transnational social spaces of the global age — with the public and urban boosters if not with architects — namely the Disneyland phenomenon. Feierstein (in Herrie and Weggerhoff) tells the fascinating story of the Peronist building projects in Argentina (1945–55). Evita's unique contribution was República de los Niños, a city scaled to the height of ten year olds, with copies of the British Houses of Parliament, gothic Palace of Justice, Venetian Ducal Palace-style bank, and Palace of Culture (modeled on the Taj Mahal exterior, and the Alhambra interior).[11] Legend and current websites tell that this inspired Walt Disney! The first Disneyland opened in California in 1955. In 1966, a military coup brought General Suharto to power in Indonesia, proclaiming a New Order for the nation, whose most famous architectural expression became the Beautiful Indonesia in Miniature Park (Mini) which opened outside Jakarta in 1980 (Kusno, 74–79). Apparently, Mrs. Suharto was inspired by a visit to Disneyland and took it upon herself to create this more complete and more perfect version of it in Indonesia. The centerpiece of Mini was a large lake with islands to represent the whole country, surrounded by replicas of ancient monuments and religious buildings, a 1,000 room hotel and shopping malls. Each of Indonesia's 26 provinces is represented by displays of "genuine customary architectural styles." For example, Borobudur, the most famous ancient monument in Indonesia is, according to the locals, best seen

Cuba - Crumbling colonial splendour

12 days from £1399pp
Departs various dates from October 2009 to March 2010
Existing in a time warp since the 1950's, Cuba is on the verge of change, and now is the perfect time to visit before its distinctive character is altered forever. This tour, designed to offer a flavour of the authentic Cuba, takes in some of the main architectural and scenic highlights including the faded colonial grandeur of Havana, Cienfuegos, Trinidad, and the Vinales Valley tobacco-growing region.

Istanbul, Ephesus & Troy

Architecture in the service of tourism.

at Mini rather than at the actual confusing and inconvenient ruins (Pemberton). "What has been crucial in this process are the replica of tradition and not the tradition itself" (Kusno, 79). This is true for all three cases — in Buenos Aires, Disneylands and Jakarta — and for many more, in the era of capitalist globalization the transnational capitalist class, led either by corporations or by the globalizing state fraction and usually both, appropriates existing iconic monuments or builds new ones in the interests of the culture-ideology of consumerism. Postcolonial understandings of iconic architecture help to explain why the struggle between modernism and traditional culture is almost always resolved in the interests of capitalist consumerism (see my essay "Iconic Architecture and the Culture-Ideology of Consumerism").[12]

NOTES

1. I am using this concept in its widest interpretation as in, for example, the varied contributions to Nalbantoğlu and Wong eds. While acknowledging its complexities (and those of the closely related concept of Orientalism) I try to avoid becoming embroiled in abstract debates around them, for which see the scholarly, albeit inconclusive, analysis in King (2004, especially chap. 3).

2. I define iconic architecture in terms of the fame of buildings and spaces and their distinctive aesthetic and symbolic significance. Buildings and architects can be iconic locally, nationally, regionally and globally (see Sklair "Transnational Capitalist," "Ionic Architecture").

3. And not just in India. See also, among many others, the case of the World Trade Centre in Cairo, constructed by the wealthy Sawiras family "a success story, symbolizing the triumph of the new class of tycoons in Egypt" (Abaza, 111).

4. See, for example, two wide-ranging collections, Nalbantoğlu and Wong, eds., and Herrie and Wegerhoff, eds.

5. These are very rough summaries of very large literatures. For authoritative statements of IM see Hitchcock and Johnson and of AR see Canizaro. For a textbook overview of both IM and AR, see Curtis. Also of note is Eggener's "Placing Resistance: A Critique of Critical Regionalism," one of the first attempts to connect Critical Regionalism and postcolonialism.

6. Luis Barragan's El Pedregal upper-class gated housing estate in Mexico City, "a major revision of the International Style, an icon of Mexican cultural identity yet still intensely personal, poetic, and mysterious" (Eggener, 179) was marketed in Mexico with reference to Wright's Fallingwater.

7. For these and many other examples see, on Mozambique (Sidaway and Power), Ghana (Intsiful, in Herrie and Wegerhoff), Uganda (Olweny and Wadulo, in Herrie and Wegerhoff); Turkey (Nalbantoğlu, in Nalbantoğlu and Wong, and Bozdogan), Israel (Levin, Weizman); Argentina (Feierstein in Herrie and Wegerhoff), Brazil (Holston, Deckker, Philippou and Lehmann, both in Herrie and Wegerhoff), Mexico (Eggener, Herzog); Latin America in general (Fraser); China (Chung et al., Rowe and Kuan, Broudehoux, Lu and Li, in Herrie and Wegerhoff, and Ren), India (Prakash, in Nalbantoğlu and Wong, Tombesi et al., and Kalia), Indonesia (Cairns in Nalbantoğlu and Wong, and Kusno); Australia (Lovanovska, in Nalbantoğlu and Wong, and Baker in Herrie and Wegerhoff).

8. Citing literature for this is fraught with difficulty. The overview that I have found most useful is Chapter 5 of Currie's *Beyond Orientalism: An Exploration of Some Recent Themes in Indian History and Society.*

9. See King (*Spaces*, chapter 1). There is a picture of PTT on the cover of the paperback edition of this book.

10. From the website of Gregotti Associati, who won the contract to design Pujiang,

modeled on a classical Italian town plan, although the chief architect, Augusto Cagnardi, claims to have identified the same model in ancient Chinese cities.

11. After the Peronista period, it gradually decayed. In 2001 (the fiftieth anniversary of the death of Evita), its commercial and ideological potential was realized and renovations began to rebrand it as a tourist attraction in Buenos Aires.

12. Transnational social spaces from below, such as those that migrant communities create in globalizing cities (for example Filipino community meeting places around Statue Square in Hong Kong, some "Chinatowns") and virtual communities of migrants all over the world, are also important, but outside the scope of this paper.

WORKS CITED

Abaza, M. "Shopping Malls, Consumer Culture and the Reshaping of Public Space in Egypt." *Theory, Culture and Society* 18,5 (2001): 97–122.

Abbas, A. "Cosmopolitan De-Scriptions: Shanghai and Hong Kong." *Public Culture* 12,3 (2000): 769–786.

Araeen, R. "A New Beginning: Beyond Postcolonial Theory and Identity Politics." *Third Text* 50 (2000): 3–20.

Bentmann, R., and M. Muller. *The Villa as Hegemonic Architecture.* Trans T. Spence and D. Craven. Atlantic Highlands, NJ: Humanities, 1992.

Boey, M. "(Trans)national Realities and Imaginations: The Business and Politics of Malaysia's Multimedia Super Corridor." In *Critical Reflections on Cities in Southeast Asia.* Eds. T. Bunnell, L. Drummond, and K.C. Ho. Singapore: Times Academic, 2002. 185–214.

Bozdogan, S. *Modernism and Nation Building: Turkish Architectural Culture in the Early Republic.* Seattle: University of Washington Press, 2001.

Broudehoux, A.-M. *The Making and Selling of Post-Mao Beijing.* London: Routledge, 2002.

Bunnell, T. *Malaysia, Modernity and the Multimedia Super Corridor: A Critical Geography of Intelligent Landscapes.* London: Routledge, 2004.

Canizaro, V.B., ed. *Architectural Regionalism. Collected Writings on Place, Identity, Modernity, and Tradition.* New York: Princeton Architectural, 2007.

Cartier, C. "Transnational Urbanism in the Reform-era Chinese City: Landscapes from Shenzhen." *Urban Studies.* 39,9 (2002): 1513–32.

Chung, C.J., J. Inaba, R. Koolhaas, and S.T. Leong. *Great Leap Forward.* Cambridge: Harvard Design School, 2001.

Crinson, M. *Modern Architecture and the End of Empire.* Aldershot: Ashgate, 2003.

Currie, K. *Beyond Orientalism: An Exploration of Some Recent Themes in Indian History and Society.* Calcutta: K.P. Bagchi, 1996.

Curtis, W. *Modern Architecture Since 1900.* London: Phaidon, 1996.

Deckker, Z.Q. *Brazil Built: The Architecture of the Modern Movement in Brazil.* London: Spon, 2001.

Edensor, T. *Tourists at the Taj: Performance and Meaning at a Symbolic Site.* London: Routledge, 2001.

Eggener, K.L. "Placing Resistance: A Critique of Critical Regionalism." In Canizaro. 395–407.

_____. "Towards an Organic Architecture in Mexico." *Frank Lloyd Wright: Europe and Beyond.* Ed. A. Alofsin. Berkeley: University of California Press, 1999. 166–183.

Fraser, V. *Building the New World: Studies in the Modern Architecture of Latin America, 1930–1960.* London: Verso, 2000.

Herrie, P., and E. Wegerhoff, eds. *Architecture and Identity.* Berlin: Lit Velag and Habitat-International, 2008.

Herzog, L. *From Aztec to High Tech: Architecture and Landscape across the Mexico-United States Border.* Baltimore: Johns Hopkins University Press, 1999.
Hitchcock, H.-R., and P. Johnson. *The International Style.* 1932. New York: Norton, 1996.
Holston, J. *The Modernist City: An Anthropological Critique of Brasilia.* Chicago: University of Chicago Press, 1989.
Kalia, R. "Modernism, Modernization, and Postcolonial India: A Reflective Essay." *Planning Perspectives* 21 (2006): 133–156.
King, A. *Spaces of Global Culture.* London: Routledge, 2004.
Kusno, A. *Behind the Postcolonial: Architecture, Urban Space, and Political Cultures in Indonesia.* New York: Routledge, 2000.
Levin, M. "Regional Aspects of the International Style in Tel Aviv and Jerusalem." In *Critical Regionalism.* Ed. S. Amourgis. Pomona: California State Polytechnic University, 1991. 240–257.
Marshall, R. *Emerging Urbanity: Global Urban Projects in the Asia Pacific Rim.* London: Spon, 2003.
Nalbantoğlu, Gülsüm Baydar and Chong Thai Wong, eds. *Postcolonial Space(s).* New York: Princeton Architectural, 1997.
Pal, P., ed. *Romance of the Taj Mahal.* Los Angeles and London: Los Angeles County Museum of Art and Thames and Hudson, 1989.
Pelli, C., C. Thornton, and L. Joseph. "The World's Tallest Buildings." *Scientific American* 277,6 (1997): 64–72.
Pemberton, J. "Recollections from 'Beautiful Indonesia' (Somewhere Beyond the Postmodern)." *Public Culture* 6 (1994): 241–262.
Ren Xuefei. *Building Globalization.* Chicago: University of Chicago Press, 2010.
Rowe, P., and S. Kuan. *Architectural Encounters with Essence and Form in Modern China.* Cambridge: MIT Press, 2002.
Sidaway, J., and M. Power, "Sociospatial Transformations in the 'Postsocialist' Periphery: The Case of Maputo, Mozambique." *Environment and Planning A* 27 (1995): 1463–1491.
Sklair, L. "The Emancipatory Potential of Generic Globalization." *Globalizations* 6 (December 2009): 523–537.
_____. *Globalization: Capitalism and Its Alternatives.* Oxford: Oxford University Press, 2012.
_____. "Iconic Architecture and Capitalist Globalization." *City* 10,1 (2006): 21–47.
_____. "Iconic Architecture and the Culture-Ideology of Consumerism." *Theory, Culture, and Society* 27,5 (2010): 135–159.
_____. *The Transnational Capitalist Class.* Oxford: Blackwell, 2001.
_____. "The Transnational Capitalist Class and Contemporary Architecture in Globalizing Cities." *International Journal of Urban and Regional Research* 29,3 (2005): 485–500.
Tombesi, P. "A True South for Design? The New International Division of Labor in Architecture." *Architectural Research Quarterly* 5,2 (2001): 171–179.
Tombesi, P., B. Dave, and P. Scriver. "Routine Production or Symbolic Analysis? India and the Globalization of Architectural Services." *Journal of Architecture* 8 (2003): 63–94.
Vale, L. *Architecture, Power, and National Identity.* New Haven: Yale University Press, 1992.
_____. "Mediated Monuments and National Identity." *Journal of Architecture* 4 (1999): 391–408.
Weizman, E. *Hollow Land: Israel's Architecture of Occupation.* London: Verso, 2007.
Wharton, A. J. *Building the Cold War: Hilton International Hotels and Modern Architecture.* Chicago: University of Chicago Press, 2001.

Radical Homelessness
David Malouf Writing in the "Blut" of Martin Heidegger
GRANT FARRED

"Only if we are capable of dwelling, only then can we build." Martin Heidegger, "Building Dwelling Thinking"

The salient feature of Martin Heidegger's work is that he consistently thinks how we are in the world; Heidegger thinks how to live in the world. That is, Heidegger is concerned not only with what it means to live in the world — to be, the project of *Sein und Zeit*. It is for this reason that phrases such as "ready to hand" (the physical tools — the hammer being a favorite example for Heidegger — with which we make our place in the world as well as the thinking with which we make our way to Being) and "to care" (for the Self, for the Other; our stewardship of the planet, which enjoys understated attention in *Was Heisst Denken?*), reverberate so loudly in *Sein und Zeit*. In many ways, these two issues, Being and inclining toward Being (thinking), preoccupy Heidegger in his essay "*Bauen Wohnen Denken*" — "Building Dwelling Thinking." In "*Bauen Wohnen Denken*," however, Heidegger goes further. Here he thinks not only what it means to live but what is required to live, *Wohnen*, where we do. This is thinking, to recast Heidegger's argument from "The Origin of the Work of Art," toward — in the direction of — the Open:

the Open is won within which everything stands and from which everything withholds itself that shows itself and withdraws itself as a being. Whenever and however this conflict breaks out and happens, the opponents, lighting or clearing and concealing, move apart because of it. Thus the Open of the place of conflict is won. The openness of this Open, that is, truth, can be what is, namely, *this* openness only if and as long as it establishes itself within its Open [Heidegger, "The Origin of the Work of Art," 60].

The Open is, in the first instance, the site that makes — encourages — "conflict," drawing difference itself out into the "clearing"; the Open allows difference to come fully into itself— it facilitates, and charts, the process by which "opponents" "move apart." The Open is made for conflict so that "truth" might emerge into "openness," the "openness within its Open." Truth means nothing less than a "setting up in the unconcealed"— to live with the prospect of uncovering, revealing; it establishes the ground for everything to be shown to itself, as itself (Heidegger, "Origin," 61).

Key, in the second instance, is to understand the Open in its relation to Being — that "from which everything withholds itself ... and withdraws itself as a being." "Being," Heidegger goes on to say, "by way of its own nature, lets the place of openness (the lighting-clearing of the There) happen, and introduces it as a place of the sort in which each being emerges or arises in its own way" ("Origin," 61). To be is, in this regard, akin to the thinking of dwelling: it is a "place of the sort in which each being emerges or arises in its own way": the place in which each being finds its place, the place which makes Being possible. It is the place in which each being is, as much as anything, in its own place. In this place, each being is unto itself, in its Being. In this place, each being knows how it came to its being because it grasps the Open as the "place of conflict that has been won." "The Open is won within which everything stands and from which" we must think for the Open because from there, following the "lighting-clearing of the There," it becomes possible to discern Being, what Being might be. Or, from where our inclining toward Being might begin.

To dwell is, following this line of argument, an act that is characterized by a gathering. To gather is to bring our thoughts together and to, at once, recognize the convergences in our thinking and the inclining toward that which is visible but not (yet) be drawn into our thinking. To gather depends on our ability to make things visible — to see, as it were, because of the "lighting-clearing of the There," what is and is not yet there; to work for the "There" is to strive for that place where Being might arise, might be possible (because of what lies beyond the being's immediate purview). In this delineation of dwelling, Heidegger establishes the governing premise of "*Bauen Wohnen Denken.*" Building and dwelling must, in the same project, be thought together (gathered into each other) and apart — they must be brought into conflict so that it is "lighting" and "clearing" that predominate, and every act of "concealing" is tantamount to an invitation to think; to think building and dwelling in their gathering and their divergence. Strictly speaking, we must begin from the premise that it is only possible to build if we know — "if we are capable of" — how to dwell: "genuine buildings give form to dwelling in its presencing and house this presence" (Heidegger, "Building Dwelling Thinking," 159). Dwelling precedes building: "the nature of building is letting dwell" (Heidegger, "Building," 160). A building can be "genuine" only if it seeks to be, to make itself in advance, a dwelling, if building *a priori* proceeds from dwelling itself so that the building, in and by its construction, intends itself to do nothing other than house dwelling — to make the house fit for dwelling. In order to build, the physical structure must *a priori* be instructed in, prepared for, the art of "presencing" — the house that is built, the land that is inhabited, or settled, must be fit to "house presence."

In his discussion of happiness, David Malouf's delineation is replete with Heideggerian overtones,[1] not the least of which is "presencing": "Well-being, contentment, gladness, quiet satisfaction, delight — all conditions that belong the inner world of feeling; a sense of being at home in our own skin, at home with the world, at one with ourselves. It is a state that can be settled and continuous, but that can also be a matter of surprise, when we might think of it as joy" (Malouf, "The Happy Life," 11). As a writer whose Heideggerianness has long since been established, there is little surprise in finding Malouf's happiness to be, in truth, a contemplation on Being, which Malouf suggests we know as the desire to be "at home in our own skin," to find "contentment" in our "inner world," to live in the unity of the fourfold ("at home in the world") and to be open to "surprise," which is nothing but the purest form of "joy" — to be in the world contingently, fully expectant of what is not anticipated. Following the ancients (Aristotle, Epicurus, the Stoics), dwelling is our inner life, exposed fully by Heidgger and Malouf to the life forces that surround us.

In this regard, Heidegger's thought presents a challenge to how we conceive of living in a house, or a home, for that matter. A house is only, in the discourse of domestication, a home if it is, before itself (before its being built or inhabited) a dwelling — if it is Open to its own openness. In the terms proposed by this essay, Heidegger must be taken up as the proponent of a radical homelessness. If the building in which one lives, no matter how grand, modest, or even makeshift, is not a dwelling — that is, it is not possible to identify the building as a "location," that which gives "life" to "space," gives the "in-ness" to space without which we cannot conceive of location — then one is, if we attribute an extremity to Heidegger's thought, homeless. To live in a house that does not permit dwelling is to be homeless, in a philosophical sense. (The structure where building is not gathered into, gathered up by, dwelling remains precisely that, the structure of homelessness.) Or, more properly, given the centrality Heidegger assigns to the "fourfold" — "earth and sky, divinities and mortals"—one is homeless in a spiritual sense: "To preserve the fourfold, to save the earth, to receive the sky, to await the divinities, to escort mortals—this fourfold preserving is the simple nature, the presencing, of dwelling" (Heidegger, "Building," 158). "The location," Heidegger insists, "*admits* the fourfold and it *installs* the fourfold" (Heidegger, "Building," 158; original emphasis). Without the fourfold, which is the spirit, which gives spirit (spirituality, a sense of that which is sacrosanct, possibly even sacred), there can be no location; without the location, that which at once "admits" (welcomes) and "installs" (inaugurates, is at the basis of) the fourfold, dwelling is not possible, cannot be thought. Only a dwelling can be a home. Without dwelling, there is nothing but homelessness, and only those who dwell are not homeless: "Dwelling ... is the *basic character* of Being in keeping with which mortals exist" (Heidegger, "Building," 160; original emphasis). Our Being is toward dwelling, that place in which "each being emerges or arises in its own way." Dwelling is nothing less than, is before all else, the "basic character" of who we are; dwelling is, in the Heideggerian vernacular, *volkstümlich*, those traditions that are critical to who we are and traditions that are, it is necessary to recognize, steeped in *blut*; steeped in the blood of sharing, in a blood that shares tradition; dwelling is that mode of being in the world that we share, are capable of sharing. More emphatically phrased, dwelling is, in Heidegger's terms, our very *raison d'être*—it is why "mortals exist." No wonder then his injunction to how we must live, no wonder then that for him the absolute condition for building is that it must be fit for dwelling: "Only if we are capable of dwelling, only then can we build." The physical structure that has not been gathered into dwelling demands that we think, again, about how we build, and what our building is designed to do. Only a shared building, that building constructed in the spirit of *volkstümlich*, permits of dwelling. It is only a shared building that can mitigate against homelessness.

How are we to know those who dwell? Simply, of course, by their capacity to dwell, so that Heidegger demands a thinking of homelessness entirely incommensurate with our contemporary understanding of, say, the "plight of the homeless," where homelessness designates, most commonly, only those who have no building in which to live. The homeless, in our sense, are those who are more readily identifiable as the poor, the indigent, or the mentally ill, those who seek survival in their makeshift refuges—cardboard boxes, plastic containers, salvaged bits of wood and tarpaulin, scrap metal on the streets of major cities (or small towns) the world over. (This phenomenon is obvious from, say, the critiques of a Mike Davis—*Planet of the Slums* to movies such as *Slumdog Millionaire*.) In Heidegger's terms, whatever the plight of those who have no buildings to call home, we might be said to have thought very little about the particular homelessness that derives from not making a dwelling for the fourfold, however much we have attended (or, not, as is too often the case) to the matter of building—that is, safeguarding vulnerable "mortals"—for the poor or the indigent.

If it is only dwelling that can "locate" mortals in the landscape, then this might be said to be, in distinct ways, of course, the very stuff of Malouf's fiction. Thinking the difficulty of dwelling is everywhere in the Australian Malouf's writing. It is there in *An Imaginary Life*, the most Heideggerian of Malouf's work, as it is in his autobiography, *12 Edmonstone Street*—"It is always in a state of becoming," he says of his childhood body, a text that embodies the architecture of *volkstümlich*, resonating as it does with the entanglement of *blut*; the ties that bind Malouf, sometimes more uncomfortably than others, to his father's Lebanese traditions and his mother's English ones (Malouf, *12 Edmonstone Street*, 61). Dwelling is addressed in every Maloufian writing, from *Remembering Babylon* to *The Conversations at Curlow Creek* to, from *Johnno* to his short fiction, prominent among them stories such as those on which this essay focuses, "The Valley of Lagoons" and "Blacksoil Country." Malouf's writing of dwelling is marked by his insistence that the desire to be "located," as Heidegger might have it, is to be found not only in the colonized (in whom we would, rightly, expect the writing of dwelling to be concentrated, considering the effects of dispossession)—the Australian Aboriginals who have been dispossessed of their land, their dwelling—but also in the erstwhile colonizer. Malouf's fiction repeatedly reveals the homelessness of white Australians and their desire, on the part of some of the colonizers, to overcome it. This is a constituency, politically dominant, where people do not know how to dwell in this land; they do not know how to dwell in a land to which they have title but cannot, may never, own. In Malouf's fiction, white Australians are in possession of the deed of sale, have had their title since the time of colonization; and yet, the land is not theirs; dwelling on this land is beyond them, is denied them.

Malouf's writing is an address to an Aboriginal and a settler-colonial homeless that is unequally shared or asymmetrical. In all his work, Malouf attends fully to the origins and the disproportionate effects of colonial dispossession. Malouf's work critiques, with a poetic insistence, the particular violence of colonialism in Australian that sought to deny, or, in its worst instantiation, destroy dwelling, never forgetting the damage done to the earth.

When Angus, a white teenage boy from the Queensland hinterland (Malouf's home state) lost in the woods on his first hunting trip (in truth, it is Angus' best friend Braden's coming of age trip), looks around, the ecological devastation is obvious: "and little smooth-crowned hills that had once been wooded and dark with aerial roots and vines, till the loggers and land-clearers moved in and opened all this country to the sky, letting the light in; creating a landscape lush and green, with only, in the gully breaks between, a remnant of the old darkness and mystery" (Malouf, "The Valley of Lagoons," 49). Safeguarding the fourfold begins with the relationship between human beings and the earth (intensified in this instance by a relationship to the sky, "opened all this country to the sky," the consequence of violence done to "all this country" by non-dwellers), what Heidegger names "care" in *Being and Time* (caring for what is readily to hand, for what is first to hand, nearest to hand, the earth, making of Heidegger's Being a radical environmentalist). The trust that enables the fourfold to come into its own, maintain itself, has been violated here by the "loggers and land-clearers" — those who do not know how to dwell. Those who build, "creating a landscape lush and green," do not know how to care for the indigenous vegetation, so full of mystery ("wooded and dark with aerial roots"), which once thrived in the "smooth-crowned hills." It is only in the "gulley breaks between" acts of clearing, we imagine, where dwelling is still possible — where a "lighting-clearing" offers a glimpse of the "There."

It is not that Heidegger opposes building because, as he says, "to build is in itself already to dwell" ("Building," 146). Or that he is against working the land and reaping the benefits of that labor: "this word *bauen* however *also* means at the same time to cherish and protect, to preserve and care for, specifically to till the soil, to cultivate the vine" ("Building," 147). Heidegger, ever the descendant of peasant stock, the guardian of the soil and its fruits: to "preserve and care for," that is of primary importance in undertaking the act of building — "*bauen*." Once caring has been forsworn, dwelling is rendered impossible. It matters not, then, that "man" "will be a designer and builder of shelters, a maker of clothes and tools; the fashioner of the weapons he will need to keep him safe" (Malouf, "The Happy Life," 18). There is, as always, the condition of gathering into the fourfold: "But to do all this [Man's building] he will need to develop in himself such 'interior' and godlike qualities as the power of imagination, of invention" (Malouf, "The Happy Life," 18). Dwelling, as both Heidegger and Malouf understand it, is that mode of being that comes from, that takes its cue from, what Malouf names the gods (Prometheus foremost among them) and Heidegger divinities.

In both Heidegger and Malouf's sense, this essay will argue, the postcolonial is, *in toto*, *in extremis*, for all those involved, the perpetrators (colonizers) and the native populace (Aboriginals), the condition of a radical (because it is and remains unthought) homelessness; for, even when Malouf's writing so animates the condition of radical homelessness, even when his work is so unrelenting in its thinking of the lack of dwelling, in the sense that dwelling is both *verstümlich* and *Wohnen*, it is the condition of postcoloniality that remains unremarked upon.

It is in his ability to "surprise," to posit the desire for dwelling as asymmetrically shared, that Malouf issues an injunction: we must think dwelling from the ground — that crucial term in Heidegger's project. Dwelling comes not with, because or from the postcolonial. The first condition of dwelling is that dwelling is. And, because it is, dwelling is *a priori*: it comes before the postcolonial, it comes — as it were — into the postcolonial as itself. It knows itself before the postcolonial. The postcolonial, if there is to be Maloufian "joy," must be gathered into dwelling. When will, the Heideggerian-Maloufian question might be, postcoloniality care for dwelling?

The Time of Dwelling

> Man the Maker, whose peculiar gift is craft or *techne*, the capacity to forge, shape, fashion; to take a world that had no place for him and make it his own. To turn wilderness into a fruitful landscape and lay down roads to move on [David Malouf, "The Happy Life," 18].

The primary effect of the violence done to the Aboriginal community in Australia, all too often in the name of "forging a fruitful landscape," has been to render them radically homeless. Malouf's work thinks, to run the risk of an etymological redundancy, the Aboriginal community as autochthonous, as indigenous to the soil of the continent. Colonialism disrupted this relationship because it denied them full access to their land — to their dwelling; as a consequence, the fourfold was disrupted in its entirety, the relationship between the earth and the sky, the mortals and the divinities violated, making both the admission and the installation of the fourfold impossible.

If the Aboriginal is denied access to anywhere, that is, to any one place, that is, everywhere, on the land, then they are — in those locations where they once dwelled and where they are now forbidden to enter — homeless in their own homes; to be without a dwelling, a proper, full dwelling, is to be homeless; removed from their dwellings by the "roads" that were "laid down." As the young posthumous narrator of "Blacksoil Country," Jordan McGivern, remarks, for his father the Aboriginal who perpetrates violence against them, the Aboriginals have no rights, because theirs was a code of being that had no standing in his world. The Aboriginal's was an inscrutable mode of being in and for the land, their "rules and laws hidden away" in what was for Mr. McGivern mere "makeshift savagery:" "Given they had not place of settlement nor roof over their heads to keep the sun off, nor walls to keep out the wind and the black dust that made another duller blackness where they were already blacker than the most starless night" (Malouf, "Blacksoil Country," 121). Dwelling in the land is everything — or, anywhere, everywhere — for the Aboriginal. That is because the land is itself dwelling. The Aboriginal Self stands in relation to the land itself through, as McGivern's violence makes tragically evident, *blut*, a *blut* that has itself become a (colonial) tradition undoing the fourfold. Understood in this way, it is the land that instantiates, in Malouf's figuring of dwelling, the decisive break with any notion of building in a structural sense: dwelling is the land; dwelling is being for the land; dwelling is unthinkable except in an autochthonous relation to the land. Dwelling is indivisible from the land, even in *blut*.

McGivern's violence notwithstanding, for the Aboriginal dwelling is inconceivable without (unfettered access to) the everywhere (the "There" that has been gathered into the Here). Without dwelling as the *Wohnen* of *verstümlich*, the location of tradition and blood (or, tradition through blood), the Aboriginals are radically homeless because they have been made unprotected strangers in their (own) land. There is, for this reason, something instructive about Mr. McGivern's (fundamentalist) colonialist grasp of dwelling — his adherence to the notion that ownership can only be deduced from title and deed. Because the Aboriginal cannot produce the documents of colonialism, theirs has become — when confronted by the likes of a Mr. McGivern — a precarious mode of being. Without a "place of settlement," they are exposed to the full force of the elements — sun, wind, and an especially harsh "black dust," so fierce that it threatens to return the Aboriginal to an inkish invisibility — "blacker than the most starless night." Malouf's sense of Aboriginal precariousness begins, as all thinking on the issue should, with the Other's life itself. Dwelling is, before all else, only possible if there is life; it is only possible if life itself is immunized against the McGivernian desire for the Other's invisibility.

Malouf's oeuvre, however, always resists the binary thinking of Self and Other. For Malouf, to agitate for dwelling is to work for the protection of life itself, not simply the life of the Other or the Self. "Blacksoil Country" is, after all, an account of the Other's retribution — the killing of a young white boy (Jordan) — because of the father's unjustifiable murder of Aboriginals. "Blacksoil Country" is the voice of a sundered colonial life (Jordan's) that, in its fatal, final, precariousness, finds in (its) posthumousness the language to properly express its desire for dwelling in the land of the Other, in the land, and this, as we shall see, is crucial, with the Other — possibly even as the Other. In Malouf's terms, precariousness must be approached as plenitude and not a (mere) dialectic. Jordan's death is not the "simple," invariably asymmetrical, exchange of one colonial life for several Aboriginal lives.

There is historical sharpness to Malouf's metaphor of invisibility because it reveals the extent of dispossession. The Aboriginal has been faded into an indiscernible blackness, indistinct in this land that was once — and still, in the sense of the fourfold, remains — theirs. It is this ownership of the land that is not ownership so that it is, finally, nothing but the aptitude for dwelling, that Jordan McGivern's father — a bitter man who has moved his family from one no-prospect job to another in search of self-respect — fails, fatally, to recognize. A newcomer to the territory, Mr. McGivern is employed by "Mr. McIvor" to "manage and work a run of a thousand acres, unfenced and not marked save on a map" (Malouf, "Blacksoil Country," 127). Jordan's father refuses to uphold the "easy" relations (what we might construe as a "tolerant" if not tolerable racism) between settlers and the Aboriginals ("'Oh, the blacks are all right is you treat 'em right,' Mick Jolley would say") (Malouf, "Blacksoil," 116).

Because of Mr. McGivern's belligerence, he shoots an Aboriginal "messenger" who is crossing the McIvor land he is managing. Jordan, the young narrator (who, like Angus, is in love with the land: "I loved it. This is my sort of country"), immediately knows the extent of his father's transgression (Malouf, "Blacksoil," 121). It was local custom that Aboriginal messengers were permitted free reign to all land, including that "belonging" to the settlers. McGivern does not know the land, so he cannot know its laws, especially those that are not written in colonial invective. Jordan is attuned to the Other's desire to dwell: "it was true. They were messengers. Given a part of play like any sergeant or magistrate, and recognized as such even by strangers. Though not by us. Which made us, in some ways, the most strangers of all" (Malouf, "Blacksoil," 127). Jordan, lover of the land, goes to the heart of the matter: his father, not him (so his is an improper invocation of the plural "us" — the dweller's first loyalty is to the land, not the father), is the true outsider, the truly non-autochthonous manager, because the only status he can be afforded is to the grammatically awkward "most strangers of all." McGivern must properly be known as the strangest: he for whom Heideggerian "location," the place that knows itself as a place, the place that has been built for dwelling, is impossible. The strangest are outside of the fourfold. McGivern is the strangest because he, who is utterly incapable of dwelling (the stranger who is also doomed to the life of itinerant laborer, wandering as he does from hardscrabble job to hardscrabble job, his beleaguered family in tow), fails to uphold the pact between colonizer and colonized that is respected by "even by strangers." To be confronted by the strangest, a McGivern who is not in love with the land, is fatal for the Aboriginal.

To be denied dwelling is one thing, one violent thing. To be denied passage through where dwelling was once possible (the effect of disenfranchisement), that is, to be prohibited mere transience (that is agreed by all but the strangest), is the nadir of colonialist violence. McGivern's contempt is, in this way, instructive. It is aimed, primarily, at "local custom," itself the odd byproduct of colonialist expansion moderated by an uncomfortable accommodation with — or, maybe, just a certain fear (a recurrent theme in Malouf's work, though nowhere quite as hauntingly as in *Remembering Babylon*) — of the indigenous way of being. According to this custom, the messengers must be permitted the right of all ways by all and yet it is only, of course, the messengers (diviners of a sort, if they are not divinities) who must be allowed this privilege, this unhindered relationship to the land. Of all the Aboriginals, it is only they who can, in the business of performing their traditional tasks, dwell fully.

What Jordan senses in his father, as we shall see momentarily, is that those who do not seek dwelling — let alone know of its existence — are ignorant of what it is they do. The only place for a McGivern is outside the fourfold. This much is evident even to the preadolescent Jordan: "I don't believe he knew what he had done" (Malouf, "Blacksoil," 127). What McGivern had done was set in motion a series of fatalities because Jordan, our posthumous narrator is, after his father's act, found with his "skull caved in" (Malouf, "Blacksoil," 129). It is paradoxical, if biblical (since it is the child who pays for the sins of the father), that it is not McGivern who is punished for his actions. Instead it is Jordan, the white colonizer who understands the land, who pays the price for his father's violent disregard for the pact between colonizer and colonized. After all, it is Jordan who grasps that the "country," after the murder of the messengers, now "had a new light over it. I had to look at it in a new way"(Malouf, "Blacksoil," 128).

The effect of death, for Jordan, is nothing less than dwelling. While the "blacks in every direction are being hunted and go to ground" in response to his killing, Jordan achieves dwelling: "me all that while lying quiet in the heart of the country, slowly sinking into the ancientness of it, making it mine, grain by grain, blending my white grains with its many black ones" (Malouf, "Blacksoil," 130). In death, according to Malouf, there is the entwinement of dwelling as the political complication of gathering. Dwelling is Time, Time as an ancient divinity — Time is where all things, earth, sky, mortals (colonizer and Aboriginal), divinity — come together. Time is the divine regard for the earth and mortals. In this regard, it is Angus who best articulates Malouf's Heideggerian tendencies. Lost in the land, Angus grasps — and in so doing, animates — the philosophical force of *Sein und Zeit*: "It was time, not space, I was moving into" (Malouf, "Valley," 42). Dwelling is only possible in Time. Space, Angus learns, does not, cannot, make dwelling possible. To dwell is to be in Time, to dwell is to "move into" Time.

Most importantly, for Malouf, who writes Jordan into the postcolonial through writing him into Time, Time is dwelling: it is offered to all who observe the fourfold. To dwell is to give the Self up to Being (being "There," in the land itself), to the "ancientness" of the country, to take cognizance of Time at work, Time making dwelling possible: "making it mine, grain by grain, blending my white grains with its many black ones." To dwell in death, to dwell not because of death but because the (colonizing) Self knew itself as in search of a oneness with the land (dwelling) before death, is to recognize the peculiarity of the post/colonial (white) Self as a recent arrival to this land. Dwelling, Jordan's death makes clear, must be learned, in life as well as in death. Dwelling is, for Malouf, nothing less than Time itself.

Malouf, however, never forgets the cost of the colonizer's achievement of dwelling. The colonizer's death has fatal implications for the colonized, as Jordan himself knows well. After all, in death Jordan understands himself as the catalyst for violence against those with whom he shares dwelling: "Jordan McGivern. A name to whip up fear and justified rage and the unbridled savagery of slaughter. For a season" (Malouf, "Blacksoil," 130). In dwelling, Malouf's colonizing Self sees itself— sees McGivern and his ilk, those who observe the local compact with "the blacks" as well as those who do not — for what the colonial project is: the rationalization —"justified rage"— of the "savage slaughter" of the dwellers, those who are radically homeless and yet closer to dwelling than those who hold the title to the land they can never own. The colonizer who has achieved dwelling must live, as it were, in death, with the violence committed in its name: "Jordan McGivern. A name to whip up." While Jordan moves toward dwelling, "lying quiet in the heart of the country," the "blacks in every direction are hunted and go to ground." What kind of dwelling, radical or not, is that?

Dwelling, in Malouf's fiction, reveals itself as a bloody, violent, undertaking, full of turbulent questions that arise out of the "white grains" seeking to commingle with the "black ones," the ones who were there before, the ones who dwelled the earth as mortals before they became the earth's dwellers. Is it possible, in the light of the "unbridled savagery of slaughter," for "white grains" and the "black ones" to dwell together? Or, does all dwelling belong to Time, that time where the ancientness of the "black ones" struggles with itself to accommodate Jordan's "Ma ... raising her eyes to the land and gazing off into the brimming heart of it?" (Malouf, "Blacksoil," 130). And what is the "brimming heart of it" but, of course, the love of Time, Time itself?

Or, is there in Malouf's work yet another thinking of dwelling? Those who achieve dwelling, regardless of who they are, will never be homeless? They are guaranteed the status of "grains" in the "ancientness?" Those who seek dwelling, who "move into" Time, will find it? Find it because their Being is inclined to it? Because they have been gathered up into the (Other's) grains that is everywhere around them? (Here it is useful to adhere strictly to Heidegger's explication of gathering as "express[ing] something that does not belong to it" (Heidegger, "Building," 153). The "white grains" seek out the grains of the Other. Is that what makes it possible for Jordan and the messengers (we can safely presume) to dwell together, adding the latest layer to ages ("ancientness") of sedimentation of grains? Is this dwelling itself, this dwelling that is Time, this dwelling in and because of death that is denied to non-dwellers such as McGivern?

Is "colonialist," the Self's perpetration of violence against those who dwell or seek dwelling, the proper designation for the non-dweller? For he or she who works, actively or not, consciously or not, against dwelling? Or, is it settler, surely McGivern's preferred term? We would, in Malouf's oeuvre, be hard pressed to come up with a title more fitting than colonialist or settler because "builder," we know, is not available. After all, he or she who builds retains, unfailingly, the potentiality for dwelling. Even in death, as "Blacksoil Country" makes abundantly clear. To build, in Jordan's posthumous sense, is to imagine — to create, to gather, to be gathered into — a lasting bond with other mortals, with the earth, with the sky and all the divinities. It is, as an act of (fatal) subalterneity, to build a dwelling (from) below; to build up the fourfold, we might even say, from the earth to the sky in praise of mortals and the divinities.

The Being of Dwelling

Without dwelling, there is no possibility of Being. The land, as Angus recognizes as he wanders lost in the land, is Time giving Being to being. A Maloufian Being that might be gathered into dwelling:

> I moved deeper into the solitude of the land, its expansive stillness — which was not stillness in fact but an interweaving of close but distant voices so dense that they became one, and then mere background, then scarcely there at all — I began to forget my own disruptive presence, receding as naturally into what hummed and shimmered all around me as into a dimension of my own being that it had taken my coming out here, alone, in the slumberous hour after midday, to uncover, I felt drawn, drawn on [Malouf, "The Valley of Lagoons," 41].

Enunciated here is the most profound desire of the colonizer who seeks dwelling: "I began to forget my own disruptive presence." In order to dwell, the colonizer must overcome his history of "disruption": the colonial violence done to dwelling. It is the act of making the Aboriginal homeless that is drawn into question here by the settler's violence against the land, a violence that, as we know, deprives the Other of shelter while not understanding the land itself as the only (and ultimate) protection against nature. When the colonial

Self forgets itself and gives itself up to the earth by "receding as naturally into what hummed and shimmered all around me as into a dimension of my own being," it not only finds itself moving toward dwelling, as if inexorably, but its being is almost seduced by the nature of dwelling. In tending to "what hummed and shimmered all around," Angus opens himself up to, Heidegger would say, nothing less than the existence of Being: Being opened up to itself. Being is, in this way, what is both expected — it is what has been thought toward — and what reveals itself, as Malouf explains, as a surprise.

This, for Angus, is the "joy" moving toward Being. And yet, Being is not what Angus expects to encounter when he wanders off from the camp. It is Being that Angus confronts in this "dimension of [his] own being." What Malouf offers in Angus is dwelling as that encounter with the Self, with Being, that makes presencing possible: the Self becomes visible when it understands itself as "disruptive" and determines to leave that behind. Dwelling is the presence of presence as Being. Angus, almost literally, gives himself up to the earth into which he is passing, "moving deeper into the solitude of the land, its expansive stillness," to find as yet unformed (forming because of the encounter) "dimension" of being in the time of repose ("the slumberous hour after midday"). Angus's encounter with the possibility of being, because of what it brings to consciousness, to language, into existence, raises dwelling as the possibility of being as peace. Dwelling, then, is that made of being, not to put too fine a point on it, that is at peace with the Self in the world — that is, it can sight the "There," it understands how to achieve dwelling in its purest form. To sight the "There" is to know that it must be approached with care, in the spirit of caring for the earth, in order to learn how to care for the Self in the cause of peace. Dwelling is being at peace, to be free and at peace — with mortals, earth, sky and the divinities.

As deliberate (and sympathetic) as Malouf is in his depiction of Angus' movement toward Being, "The Valley of Lagoons" retains the force of asymmetry — memory for the future — through the presence of the dweller, Matt Riley, the Aboriginal who leads the expedition to the Lagoons. It is not, however, simply a matter of Riley returning to the land (the adolescent Angus refers to him, after his initial introduction, as "Matt"; the other adults are all accorded full formalities —"Mr."; such is the persistence of colonialist language. The Other, even as dweller, cannot be afforded the form of address proper to his standing). Instead, "The Valley of Lagoons" offers dwelling in its precariousness: dwelling can be disrupted by absence. It can, as Riley's experience makes evident, be recovered, and quickly, but it is affected by the lack of continuous dwelling. When the dweller leaves the place of *blut*, so too the essence of dwelling leaves him — abandons him, it might be suggested, to non-dwelling; or, to a precarious dwelling:

> From the moment we climbed down out of the trucks and the light of its broken waters enter us, and breathed in its sweetish water-smelling air, and took its dampness on our skins — from that moment something was added to Matt Riley, or given back; and he took it, with no sign of change in the quietness with which he went about things, or in his understated way of offering his own opinion or disagreeing with another's. He had re-entered a part of himself that was continuous with the place, and with a history the rest of us had never known [Malouf, "Valley," 34].

Tellingly, it takes very little to dwell again, to dwell as if there had been no interruption: all it requires is for the "broken waters to enter" Matt Riley and, "from that moment something was added to Matt Riley, or given back; and he took it." Dwelling is a form not only of re-entry, but of acquisition: the mortal gains "something" from the "broken waters" or is "given back" what is, as is his right as dweller, to him. Dwelling is, literally, in this instance, the "something" the mortal gathers from that location between the earth and the sky. Dwelling transforms utterly, in that moment of descent to the earth — "From the moment we climbed down out of the trucks," and yet it reveals no palpable alteration in the re-entered, reconnected, dweller — "no sign of change in the quietness with which he went about things." To be reconnected to dwelling is to be gathered back into the Self—"He had re-entered a part of himself that was continuous with the place"—through an intense sense of being properly located: to dwell is not only to be in the right place, it is to be known by the place.

It is for this reason that, as Angus correctly intuits, dwelling is not a place that can be taken with you. Dwelling demands its proper ground. Dwelling is its own essential place. Dwelling demands fidelity: the Other must be true to the place of dwelling because that is the only place where dwelling is possible. (Dwelling depends on, in Heidegger's terms, a physical "in-ness.") The disconnected (albeit temporarily) dweller can dwell only in the place of dwelling. It is the dwelling that lends the dweller his particularity: "The land out there was Matt's grandmother's country, and the moment he entered it he had a different status: that was the accepted but unspoken ground of his authority. That and the knowledge of the place and all its workings that came with the land itself" (Malouf, "Valley," 33). In this geographical delineation, dwelling is located in the act of return — the resumption of the interrupted continuity (it would be incorrect to think as dis-continuity), the reactivation of that "part of himself that was continuous with the place." Dwelling can be, a priori, articulated as autochthony: the dweller must be of the land in order to know dwelling, the dweller must be of the land in order to be gathered into dwelling. The land gathers the dweller to itself when the dweller returns to the only place where dwelling is possible.

The sense of particularity, in Malouf's asymmetrically figured dwelling, is, like Matt Riley, quietly unrelenting. Dwelling in the Valley of Lagoons reconnects Matt Riley to a "history the rest of us had never known" so that his "different status" locates him not only — hierarchically speaking — above the non-dwellers (dwelling is only possible for Braden; all the others, with Angus precariously perched in between, are outside of dwelling), but emphatically unto himself as dweller. That is what it means to have exclusive access to the "history" of the location of dwelling; that is what it means to have an "authority" grounded in his "knowledge of the place," to know "all the workings" of the dwelling "that came with the land itself."

A relationship to the land that is, above all, strictly matrilineal: "'His grandmother's country' was a phrase that referred, without raising too precisely the question of blood, to the relationship a man might stand in to a particular tract of land, that went deeper and further back than legal possession. When used in town, it had 'implications,' easy to pick up but not to be articulated. A nod to the knowing" (Malouf, "Valley," 34). It is the grandmother alone who is capable of returning Matt Riley to this "particular tract of land;" it is the grandmother alone who instantiates the *blut* of Heidegger's *verstümlich*: Matt Riley can only dwell because of his grandmother's *blut*, seeped into the soil; it is *blut* that grounds him Here. What could ground the dweller more than blood of a dead relative? The Other's "authority," the Other's place in this land, is grounded in that "something" — the colonizer's violence, genocide, the particular precariousness of women — that has "worked" its way autochthonously into the land. It is, of course, not what Angus means (how could he know it?) when he declares himself and his fellow white travelers to be outside of that "history the rest of us had never known." Angus could not know it, and, yet, how could he not, he who is so attuned to the loud unspoken resonances of those "nods to the knowing?" And, yet, how could he know it? The *blut* of the grandmother is too precious to be known to those who can, at best, hope to come to dwelling. To dwell, then, is to come to the *verstümlich* of *blut* in full memory of the "land itself." It is to come into the *blut* of the *Wohnen*. To dwell is, in Malouf's rendering, to be in blood — the bloodiness of Being. What those knowing nods means, as Angus is well aware, is that the Self knows that "legal possession" cannot stand in the face of *blut*; that is why the grandmother's blood, which so saturates the ground of dwelling, goes "back deeper and further than legal possession." The Valley of Lagoons, the location of Braden's *bildungsroman*, is the time of a powerfully reinforced asymmetry between dweller and seeker of/for dwelling, between dweller and non-dweller; it is what makes the commingling of "grains" the task of a bloody gathering. It is not the rejection of the Self that inclines toward dwelling, but it registers as the fierce, persistent expression of a struggle with — not against —

that something that does not yet "belong to it." Appropriate, then, that Jordan most easily approaches dwelling in death. Death is a very important part of life. To be it is necessary, as Heidegger insists, to be toward death.

The There and the Their

Against the background of colonial violence, of the asymmetrical violence done to dwelling in the cause of colonialism, Malouf's delineation of dwelling offers itself as a matter for postcolonial thinking. The first line of thinking is, of course, can there be a postcolonial that is fit for dwelling? Where peace and freedom obtain? Or, Malouf's dwelling stands as a violent caution, marked, we might say, by the *blut* of Heidegger's *verstümlich*: saturated by the absence of a tradition of peace and freedom, and utterly, un-thinkingly — which is to say that it has constructed itself, the postcolonial nation-state, as a solid edifice, with no room for dwelling — against dwelling. Only a Maloufian dwelling, we might deduce, can stand against so undwellable — we must retain the integrity of dwelling; it will not suffice to name it "uninhabitable" — a structure. The matter that deserves the most direct address, however, is the recognition that in order to build the postcolonial in a land a priori given to dwelling, the lack of the presence of dwelling must be brought into full view of the "lighting-clearing."

The lack of dwelling is constitutive of Malouf's work. It exists at the very core of his thinking, which we now know, again, in a very particular regard, to be Heideggerian. The force of Malouf's work is that dwelling is there, in the "There." Dwelling, in its most articulate asymmetry that is also, in the same act, a gathering of the Their (Malouf's fourfold, we might venture), colonizer, the colonizer, the dead in their grain-ular form (the dweller Jordan) and the dead who are not arrived (Angus), stands there before the postcolonial as the challenge of the There. How does the postcolonial build a dwelling capable of addressing, and, of course, finally, overcoming radical homelessness? What will it mean, what will it take, to build a dwelling There where *blut* is everywhere, is everything? A building where the Their can be gathered, for the first time or after re-entry, each marked by their own *blut*, into a dwelling, into a *verstümlich*, a *Wohen* in Time?

I would like to thank David Ellison for his reading of the essay. Also, I am grateful to John Niederbuhl and Derica Shields for their assistance.

Notes

1. See, in this regard, Michael Ackland, "Triumphant Word: Malouf's Heideggerian Vision in *An Imaginary Life,*" *Hungarian Journal of English and American Studies* 12.1–2 (2006): 239–

244; Paul Kavanagh, "Elegies of Presence: Malouf, Heidegger and Language," *Provisional Maps: Critical Essays on David Malouf*, ed. Amanda Nettlebeck (Nedlands, Western Australia: Center for Studies in Australian Literature, 1994), 149–62.

WORKS CITED

Ackland, Michael. "Triumphant Word: Malouf's Heideggerian Vision in *An Imaginary Life*." *Hungarian Journal of English and American Studies* 12,1–2 (2006): 239–244.
Heidegger, Martin. "Building Dwelling Thinking." *Poetry, Language, Thought*. Trans. Albert Hofstadter. New York: Harper and Row, 1971. 143–162.
_____."The Origin of the Work of Art." *Poetry, Language, Thought*. Trans. Albert Hofstadter. New York: Harper and Row, 1971. 15–87.
Kavanagh, Paul. "Elegies of Presence: Malouf, Heidegger and Language." *Provisional Maps: Critical Essays on David Malouf*. Ed. Amanda Nettlebeck. Nedlands, Western Australia: Center for Studies in Australian Literature, 1994. 149–162.
Malouf, David. "Blacksoil Country." *Dream Stuff: Stories*. Toronto: Vintage Canada, 2001. 116–130.
_____."The Happy Life: The Search for Contentment in the Modern World." *Quarterly Essay* 41 (2011): 1–55.
_____. *12 Edmonstone Street*. London: Random, 1999.
_____. "The Valley of Lagoons." *The Complete Stories*. New York: Vintage International, 2008. 3–50.

Global Victorians

Is Colonial Decadence to Blame
for Postcolonial Deconstruction?

Clara A.B. Joseph

There are causal similarities between literary criticism in the Victorian age and our own just as there are between Victorian colonialism and Postmodern (American) "neo-colonialism." Certain systems (literary studies, included) are necessary to maintain certain other systems (colonialism). An instance of Victorian colonialism is Prime Minister Disraeli's procurement for Queen Victoria of the coveted title "the Empress of India" in 1877. This announcement was only, of course, the fireworks to the actual manipulation of power — from the East India Company (a company that saw many eminent Victorians, such as J.S. Mill and did not see other eminent Victorians, such as Arthur Symons, because the latter jumped ship), and the naked coercion applied (without pretense of civility) on Indian rulers, the mid-noon theft of livelihood and life, while the Queen painstakingly took to Hindi lessons. An instance of Postmodern colonialism is the experience of hundreds of thousands of peoples who have been robbed of their oil resources and dignity by the United States and its Allies. When people are being amputated and destroyed, it is extremely humbling to ask: Excuse me, is there a link here to literary theory? But that is exactly what I am asking. As an earning member of the faculty of humanities, an institution that makes its living by selling academic thinking to eager students, it is in fact my responsibility to ask precisely this question. In asking this question if I am searching for similarities and differences between the two periods, I also hope to be forewarned of similar consequences triggered not just by politicians and administrators (and these are by default not assumed to exist in the humanities) but by lovers of literature and critics of literature (and these we say we can find in the humanities).

Overall, I assume that the study of literature and also the faculty of humanities and the social sciences contribute immensely to the attitude of people towards what passes before their eyes (books, newspapers, the TV screen, films, cartoons, paintings, advertisements, social situations, etc.) and their understanding of such spectacle.

The creative writers and critics of Victorian England, in turn shaped by and shaping various American, Asian, and European writers — we have all heard of the high esteem that Edgar Allan Poe and his symbolist poetry was held in by the Aesthetics and Decadents and we also are aware of the extent to which Arthur Symons' *Symbolist Movement in Literature* (1899) influenced the works of W.B. Yeats and T.S. Eliot, the latter presenting to modern Western literature the only instance of a Godless Peace in the almost Vedic incantation "shanti, shanti, shanti" at the end of a poem unsurprisingly called "The Wasteland" — either engaged or did not engage with colonialism, the single most politically and socially determining event of its time. The Aesthetic movement, that is said to have obtained its philosophical grounding from Immanuel Kant's discovery of the "pure" aesthetic experience as consisting of a "disinterested" contemplation of an object which "pleases for its own sake," sought to free art from all influences. Its dictum was Art for Art's sake. Of the Poem *per se*. This was art that would stay "disinterested" in the face of rabid industrialization and colonization. Such art would be autonomous: it would attain a freedom, without responsibility. Its extreme version, manifested in the Decadent movement, would stand disinterested in the face of even nature. Down the ages, many scholars would point to this worldview and accompanying lifestyle as the cause behind the ultimate depravity, even the early death of writers such as Charles Baudelaire.

All this does not mean that the writers of the Aesthetic or Decadent movements did not mention colonialism in their oeuvre. They did. In fact, a rather thought-provoking poem by Baudelaire called "To a Girl of Malabar" refers to the unsettling influence of colonialism on the colonized (and possibly on the colonizer). Gayatri Spivak in her article, "Imperialism and Sexual Difference" accuses Baudelaire of homogenizing the colonized in failing to preserve the cultural and geographical specificities of the subject of the poem. The Malabar Girl from South West India (the Malabar region) is unlikely to be in the Mauritius and Réunion, places that Baudelaire visited in lieu of India, she argues. Spivak also takes to task Baudelaire's carelessness in naming the subject and his romanticizing of the colonial subject. Thus mention is indeed made, even in the genre of "disinterestedness" to important political and cultural events of the time. As the premier scholar to translate Derrida's *Of Grammatology* into English from the French Gayatri Spivak is also well known as an adept practitioner of deconstructionist techniques. As a post-structuralist, then, Spivak too testifies to her and her theories' engagement with the politics of the times.

Postmodern literary theories, theories that have variously responded to the Modern Times, the link between the Victorian and our times, carry several ominous similarities with the aforementioned movements — the Aesthetic and the Decadent — similarities that also are not without consequences or, for that matter, relevance to major political and social events of our time. Derrida's insistence that "there is nothing outside the text," a phrase that has been variously but ultimately interpreted as the textualizing of everything rather than a claim that "that which is outside of the text is nothing," is for me strongly suggestive of the "art for art's sake" lesson of the Victorians and, if I may add, the New Criticism of the Modern times. Despite the fact that post-structuralists, the philosophical and theoretical category of the postmodernists, would grimly distance themselves from Romanticism, Aestheticism, New Criticism, and Structuralism, the fact remains that their engagement with thought and life remains at the level of discourse; like adept Latin dancers they have learnt the "linguistic turn." In other words, post-structuralists, despite their mutual dis/agreements, cannot escape the bind of language. They replace Descartes' world of sensations with the world of language. Only two absolutes emanate from the linguistic level: the absolutism of relativism and the absolutism of constructivism. Structures of class, gender, caste, race, and you name it are intelligently recognized as such by these theorists: structures that can theoretically be de-structured to facilitate a shifting of power relationships. The findings and assumptions are highly useful in studies: New Historicism, Neo-Marxist studies, Gender studies, Postcolonial studies, etc. Post-structuralist techniques of dismantling, undermining, the word is — deconstructing — structures of power are disarmingly encouraging in a world gone awry. Yet post-structuralists, like the Decadents, promote something like disinterestedness — indifference. Swimming in the sea of textual structures of relativism the post-structuralist mode of survival is dependent heavily on an amoral, non-committal (neither right nor wrong) attitude — an indifference — that goes hand and gloves with a profitarian capitalist system. That is, just as Aestheticism's and Decadence's disinterestedness was precisely what was needed in the face of brutal government policies (and I am referring here to the British government's "civilizing" colonial policies worldwide [including Ireland] and their disregard for the victims of industrialization on home territory even), today post-structuralist indifference, which is sheerly the other side of ubiquitous relativism, is very convenient in the context of death and despair visited upon millions of peoples because of the so-called "democratic" policies of the Bush/Blair governments and their Allies, and the indifference of these governments to ever-increasing unemployment and poverty on home territory.

Further, like Victorian Decadence, post-structuralist deconstruction has turned into an ideology that questions the certainties of theists and moralists; the link between the two periods is also the link between "The Death of God" and the "Death of the Author." So, if someone speaks of justice the retort is: whose justice? Both politics and redemption supposedly rest in this questioning, while it is generally acknowledged that universal justice, the notion that giving the other what is due to the other in the spirit of love and truth — and one is not speaking of "generosity" here, is a myth that should by no means survive the terrible Enlightenment. If this is the case, how can postcolonial studies, an area committed to political and social justice in the face of colonialism, succeed on the foundation of post-structuralist theories and the linguistic turn?

That reality and knowledge are social constructions, that it is necessary to reject all dichotomous thinking — even right and wrong), that one's stance has to be anti-foundationalism, that it is necessary to deny universals, that one has to reject essentialism, that there are no metanarratives, that the writing of post-structuralists if convoluted merely encourages readerly, if not authorial, meaning, these tenets of post-structuralism (except for the last) have been part and parcel of Decadence as of Structuralism. In "The Decadent Movement in Literature," Symons writes of the signifying characteristics of the Decadent Movement and of its poet, Paul Verlaine:

> It is the poetry of sensation, of evocation; poetry which paints as well as sings, and which paints as Whistler paints, seeming to think the colours and outlines upon the canvas, to think them only, and they are there... To fix the last fine shade, the quintessence of things; to fix it fleetingly; to be disembodied voice, and yet the voice of a human soul: that is the ideal of Decadence, and it is what Paul Verlaine has achieved.

This is the "poem *per se*"—"seeming to think the colours and outlines upon the canvas, to think them only." It is also that which denies the transcendent in the "disembodied voice, and yet the voice of a human soul." Notably the emphasis is not on the human soul but on the voice of a human soul — the poem *per se*. (Derrida would say, the "voice" here is the signifier of "absence," and thus the denial of a spirituality he had a hard time recognizing.) Can the above-mentioned shared premises and assumptions equip a post-structuralist postcolonial studies in its purpose of not just understanding the oppressive discourses but also in, hopefully, righting wrongs?

And this is where a famous post-structuralist postcolonialist such as Homi K. Bhabha comes under scrutiny. Bhabha's essay in *The Location of Culture*, "Signs taken for wonders: Questions of ambivalence and authority under a tree outside Delhi, May 1817" is famous for his conceptualization of a key concept, "hybridity," formulated against the backdrop of a Victorian

India. Hybridity, according to Bhabha who is notorious for spawning key terms in the very process of defining one, manifests itself in "the Third Space" of post-structuralist constructionism. Hybridity is not the creation of a third identity through the combination of two pure and separate identities, as one might assume in an allusion to horticulture. It is rather a process (which Bhabha calls the Third Space — the location of a process, "the location of culture") already in existence, the pre-condition of an identity, what I have referred to elsewhere as "hybridentity," that reveals in fits and starts its own "impurity," its unpopularized and marginalized discourses that tend to catch the (Imperial) Other off guard. In Bhabha's own words:

> For me the importance of hybridity is not to be able to trace two original moments from which the third emerges, rather hybridity to me is the "third space" which enables other positions to emerge. This third space displaces the histories that constitute it, and sets up new structures of authority, new political initiatives, which are inadequately understood through received wisdom [Bhabha, "Third Space" 211].

Within Lacanian psychoanalysis, a complex study and practice that marries psychology and linguistics — Freud and Saussure, such determinism of an already engaging process-space makes sense as also in a Derridean insistence on the perpetual deferral of difference (the *différance*). Bhabha, after all, builds his theories on Lacan and Derrida. But for a theory that hopes for change and a better world such bedfellows are deeply suspect.

Scholars and critics such as Aijaz Ahmad, Benita Parry, Chandra Talpade Mohanty, and John Krianiauskas have variously challenged the worth of a linguistic model for the analysis of issues of economic and cultural oppression. Krianiauskas argues that Bhabha presents an "asocial agency," one unmediated, unconscious (Brah and Coombes, 244). My own conclusion, however, is that while Bhabha might want to see agency in the non-human, in the determined and determining discourse, his extensive use of passive sentences (that won him a prize for bad writing — the prize was awarded in 1998 by the journal *Philosophy and Literature*) merely reflects the absence of a human agent and, therefore, of agency. An agent [ad. L. *agens, agentem*, acting, pr. pple. of ag-^{e}re to act, do], to go by its etymology, is someone who does something, acts. Such an agent is not the subject of determination/constructionism, but a human person with dignity, rights, and responsibilities. Post-structuralist performance theorists have defined even performance (see the early Barthes or the present Culler for example) as initially and ultimately constructed, neither granting choice nor recognizing consequences for the act. A post-structuralist postcolonial analysis of the terrible performance of colonialism cannot produce results any different. Like the Aesthetics and Decadents then, Bhabha too, by virtue of the theories he picks rejects the vital privilege of human responsibility and thus forgoes the one chance to change the post-colonial or rather the "neo-colonial."

The non-agential aspect of Bhabha's "hybridity" is, I argue, a child of Baudelaire's Aestheticism, a movement taken to extremes in the Decadent works of Swinburne, Rossetti, Wilde, and Symons. In his essay, "The Decadent Movement in Literature" (1893) Arthur Symons describes Decadence as "an interesting disease" of a luxurious (colonial) civilization, marked by "an intense self-consciousness, a restless curiosity in research, an over-subtilizing refinement upon refinement, a spiritual and moral perversity." This period and its poets labeled by Edward Said as "Orientalist" is closely linked to the political and economic colonization of millions of peoples. Yet, this link has hardly been recognized as significant for the study of literary theory. A close analysis of the several assumptions in Symons' literary criticism parallels rather shockingly those in the essay by Bhabha. And in a larger project I may undertake this comparison. But to conclude, let me comment on a presentation by the poet and scholar George Elliott Clarke at the University of Calgary. It was a presentation of his most recent collection of poems, *Illuminated Verses* (2005). This is a chapbook illustrated with photos of black female nudes, mostly young ones who still preserve their curves and look good against mostly water — the sea, the ocean, the beach. There are also a few pictures of some firm-bodied older women as also backgrounds of greenery — suggestive of woods, a forest perhaps. A verse begins mixing the "surf" and the "negrita," and ends declaring that the woman subject is Philosophy and that "her voice surges, apocalyptic, *The Fire Next Time*" (Clarke and Scipio, 6). The last phrase, alluding to James Baldwin's book of non-fiction prose, but in the present context barely communicating any warning against injustice or emphasizing the inherent dignity of a human person, whether black or female.

Meanwhile a young black woman presents the spectacle of her nudity. Her face is turned away and so one is left gazing at the head of wet hair, the neck, the arms, the breasts, the stomach, the vagina, and the thighs, all against the deep blue of an unnamed ocean. This unidentified woman can make sense only as a text — the poet tells us "she embodies *Philosophy*." "Her voice surges," claims the poet in the next line. I listened hard. I heard nothing other than the wild beating of my own heart as it asked in anger: How two black men, photographed with clothes on, named, and introduced — George Elliott Clarke and Ricardo Scipio — could bury some women's colonial pasts so neatly in that absent black face, an unidentified *negritude*. But it is precisely this absence, what Derrida defines in "Tympan" as the absence of the letter writer and the letter reader that, like Bhabha's theories, triggers meaning that links this postmodern work with the poetics of the Decadence. I quote from Baudelaire's *Flowers of Evil*, from his poem "To a Girl of Malabar": "Your feet, fine as your hands, ... Your velvet eyes are darker than your flesh" (Baudelaire, 319). In juxtaposing these similar verses (one rhymed, the other "free,"; one Victorian, the other "Canadian," or is it "American"?) I am suggesting that perhaps postmodern art, as evident in its post-colonial avatar may already have acquired ingredients that once became the Decadence and, further, that the indiscriminate canonization of post-structuralist theorists, even within postcolonial studies, points to the fact that such a postcolonialism can indeed sustain such literature, such indifference.

WORKS CITED

Ahmad, Aijaz. *In Theory: Classes, Nations, Literatures.* London: Verso, 1992.

Baldwin, James. *The Fire Next Time.* New York: Dial, 1963.

Barthes, Roland. "The Death of the Author." In *Image-Music-Text.* Trans. Stephen Heath. New York: Hill and Wang, 1977. 142–148.

Baudelaire, Charles. *Flowers of Evil: And All Other Authenticated Poems.* Trans. Philip Willoughby-Higson and Elliot R. Ashe. Chester: Cestrian, 1975.

Bhabha, Homi K. "Signs Taken for Wonders: Questions of Ambivalence and Authority Under a Tree Outside Delhi, May 1817." *The Location of Culture.* London: Routledge, 1994. 102–122.

_____. "The Third Space. Interview with Homi Bhabha." In *Identity, Community, Difference.* Ed. Jonathan Rutherford. London: Lawrence and Wishart, 1990. 207 – 21.

Brah, Avtar, and Annie Coombes. *Hybridity and Its Discontents: Politics, Science, Culture.* New York: Routledge, 2000.

Clarke, George Elliott, and Ricardo Scipio. *Illuminated Verses.* Toronto: Kellom, 2005.

Culler, Jonathan. *The Literary in Theory.* Stanford: Stanford University Press, 2007.

Derrida, Jacques. *Of Grammatology.* Trans. Gayatri Chakravorty Spivak. Corrected ed. Baltimore: Johns Hopkins University Press, 1997.

_____. "Tympan." In *Margins of Philosophy.* Chicago: University of Chicago Press, 1982.

Eliot, Thomas Stearns. *The Wasteland and Other Poems.* New Rochelle, NY: Spoken Arts, 1956.

Parry, Benita. "Problems in Current Theories of Colonial Discourse." *Oxford Literary Review* 9.1–2 (1987): 27-58.

Rutherford, Jonathan, ed. "The Third Space: Interview with Homi K. Bhabha." *Identity: Community, Culture Difference.* London: Lawrence & Wishart, 1990. 207–221.

Said, Edward. *Orientalism.* New York: Vintage Books, 1979.

Spivak, Gayatri. "Imperialism and Sexual Difference." *Oxford Literary Review.* 7.1–2 (1986): 225–240.

Symons, Arthur. *Symbolist Movement in Literature.* sl: sn, 1958 (1899).

About the Contributors

Bill **Ashcroft** is a founding exponent of post-colonial theory and co-author of *The Empire Writes Back* (1989), the first text to examine systematically the field of post-colonial studies. He is also the author or co-author of 12 other books including *Post-colonial Transformation* (2006) and *On Post-Colonial Futures* (2001). He teaches in the English Department of the University of New South Wales.

Om Prakash **Dwivedi** is an assistant professor of English at MITS India. Recent publications include *Changing Nations/Changing Worlds: The Concept of Nation in the Transnational Era* (2012), *The Other India: Narratives of Terror, Communalism and Violence* (2012) and *Literature of the Indian Diaspora* (2011).

Grant **Farred** holds a joint appointment in Africana studies and English at Duke University. He has published widely in the fields of postcolonial theory, cultural studies, the formation of intellectuals, literary theory, and sport and contemporary politics. Recent books include *Long Distance Love: A Passion for Football* (2008), *Phantom Calls: Race and the Globalization of the NBA* (2006) and *What's My Name? Black Vernacular Intellectuals* (2003). He is general editor of *South Atlantic Quarterly*.

Alistair **Fox** holds a personal chair in the Department of English and is director of the Centre for Research on National Identity at the University of Otago. His past publications include *The English Renaissance: Identity and Representation in Elizabethan England* (1997), *Reassessing the Henrician Age: Politics and Reform 1500–1550* (1986) and *Thomas More: History and Providence* (1983).

Joel **Gwynne** is an assistant professor of English at the National Institute of Education, Nanyang Technological University, Singapore. He has published articles in *Journal of Postcolonial Writing*, *Kunapipi: A Journal of Postcolonial Writing*, *Commonwealth: Essays and Studies*, *Journal of Gender Studies*, and *Journal of Contemporary Asia*. Recent publications include *Sexuality and Contemporary Literature* (2012) and *The Secular Visionaries: Aestheticism and New Zealand Short Fiction in the Twentieth Century* (2010).

Susan **Hosking** lectures in the English Department at the University of Adelaide. Her research interests include Australian fiction, film and cultural studies, in the context of postcolonialism. She has published on Katharine Susannah Prichard, Mudrooroo (Colin Johnson) and Archie Weller, among other topics. She has co-edited two books of essays: *Something Rich and Strange: Sea Changes, Beaches and the Littoral in The Antipodes* (2009) and *Reading the Malay World* (2009).

David **Huddart** is an associate professor in the Department of English at the Chinese University of Hong Kong. He is the author of *Homi K. Bhabha* (2005) and *Postcolonial Theory and Autobiography* (2008). His interests cover postcolonial literature, literary theory, and the history of English languages.

Clara A.B. **Joseph** is an associate professor of English at the University of Calgary with a research specialization in postcolonial studies. She is a co-editor of *Global Fissures: Postcolonial Fusions* (2006) and *Theology and Literature: Rethinking Reader Responsibility* (2006), is on the editorial boards of *ARIEL* and the *Journal of Postcolonial Writing*, and is the author of *The Agent in the Margin: Nayantara Sahgal's Gandhian Fiction* (2008).

Martin **Kich** is a professor of English at Wright State University. In 2000, he received the university's Trustee's Award, recognizing sustained excellence in teaching, scholarship, and service. His publications include *Western American Novelists* (2000), contributions to essay collections, articles and shorter contributions to reference works on literary and cultural topics.

Roderick **McGillis** is a professor emeritus of English at the University of Calgary. His publications include *Voices of the Other: Postcolonialism and Children's Literature* (2000), *Les Pieds Devant* (2007), *He Was Some Kind of a Man: Masculinities in the B Western* (2009) and *Voices of the Other Children's Literature and the Postcolonial Context* (2012).

David **Punter** is a professor of English and research dean, Faculty of Arts, at the University of Bristol. He has published extensively on Gothic and Romantic literature, contemporary writing and culture, and on literary theory and the postcolonial. His latest publications include *Rapture: Literature, Addiction, Secrecy* (2009), *The Influence of Postmodernism on Contemporary Writing: An Interdisciplinary Study* (2005), *Metaphor* (2005), and *Modernity* (2007).

Leslie **Sklair** is a professor emeritus in the Department of Sociology at the London School of Economics and Political Science. He is the author of *Globalization: Capitalism and Its Alternatives* (2002), *The Transnational Capitalist Class* (2001), *Sociology of the Global System* (1995), and *Capitalism and Development* (1994).

Varghese **Thekkevallyara** has an MA in philosophy from the University of Kerala, India, and a master of divinity from the University of St. Michael's College in Toronto. He is an independent researcher.

Janet **Wilson** is a professor of English and postcolonial studies at the University of Northampton and is editor of the *Journal of Postcolonial Writing*. Recent publications include *Katherine Mansfield and Literary Modernism* (2011) and *Rerouting the Postcolonial: New Directions for the New Millennium* (2010).

Shaobo **Xie** is an associate professor in the Department of English at the University of Calgary. He is book review editor of *ARIEL*. His works include *Alternative Positions: Cultural Critique and Critical Culture*, *New Directions in Postcolonial Studies* (*ARIEL* 40th anniversary special issue co-edited with Wang Ning), and *Cultural Politics of Resistance* (1999).

Index

203

www.ingramcontent.com/pod-product-compliance
Lightning Source LLC
Chambersburg PA
CBHW031133270326
41929CB00011B/1602